THE
EDWARDIAN
TEMPERAMENT

§1895–1919§

The Edwardian Temperament

§1895–1919§

Jonathan Rose

OHIO UNIVERSITY PRESS
ATHENS, OHIO
LONDON

Library of Congress Cataloging-in-Publication Data

Rose, Jonathan.
  The Edwardian temperament, 1895–1919.

  Rev. and expanded version of the author's thesis
(doctoral—University of Pennsylvania).
  Bibliography: p.
  Includes index.
  1. English literature—20th century—History and
criticism.   2. English literature—19th century—
History and criticism.   3. Great Britain—Intellectual
life—19th century.   4. Great Britain—Intellectual
life—20th century.   5. Great Britain—History—
Edward VII, 1901–1910.   I. Title.
PR471.R67   1986   820′.9′00912   85-21574
ISBN 0-8214-0821-6
ISBN 0-8214-0842-9 pbk.

To my parents,
who were patient

Contents

Acknowledgments

I am very grateful to all the individuals and institutions that allowed me to study and, in some cases, to quote from unpublished manuscripts in their possession. These include the British Library, for the George Bernard Shaw, James Joyce, A. J. Balfour, Henry Campbell-Bannerman, Harley Granville Barker, A. E. Housman, J. M. Barrie, Macmillan family, H. W. Nevinson, Ernest Rhys, C. P. Scott, Maurice Hewlett, and Henry Harben papers; the British Library of Political and Economic Science, for the Passfield and Charles Booth papers and the George Bernard Shaw diaries; J. S. M. Booth and the Director of the University of London Library, for the Charles and Mary Booth papers; the University College London Library, for the Oliver Lodge and Arnold Bennett correspondence; the Victoria and Albert Museum Library, for the C. R. Ashbee, J. M. Barrie, Sydney Cockerell, and Philip Webb papers; the British Theatre Museum, for the Henry Arthur Jones, John Masefield, and Arthur Wing Pinero correspondence; the Richmond Library, for the Douglas Sladen papers; the University of Sussex Library, for the Monk House and Rudyard Kipling papers; the Cambridge University Library, for the Benjamin Kidd and Ernest Rutherford papers; the Masters and Fellows of Trinity College Cambridge, for the Clive Bell, F. W. H. Myers, and Henry Sidgwick papers; Michael Halls and the King's College Library, Cambridge University, for the E. M. Forster, Goldsworthy Lowes Dickinson, Roger Fry, John Maynard Keynes, and John Sheppard papers; the Bodleian Library, Oxford University, for the Gilbert Murray, Kenneth Grahame, J. L. and Barbara Hammond, John Masefield, H. W. Nevinson, and Evelyn Sharp papers; the Nuffield College Library, Oxford University, for the Fabian Society and G. D. H. Cole papers; the Rhodes House Library, Oxford University, for the Sydney Olivier papers; the University of Birmingham Library, for the John Galsworthy and Joseph Chamberlain papers; the Edinburgh University Library, for the Charles Sarolea papers; and the National Library of Scotland, for the J. M. Barrie, John Buchan, Rosebery, R. B.

Cunninghame-Graham, and R. B. Haldane papers. I also owe a debt of thanks to the late Dorothy Masterman, for the C. F. G. Masterman papers; M. H. Penty, for the A. J. Penty papers; Felicity Ashbee, for the C. R. Ashbee memoirs; Eleanor O'Keeffe, John Beloff, and the Society for Psychical Research, for the Oliver Lodge correspondence; Pamela Diamand, for the Roger Fry papers; the Society of Authors, for the George Bernard Shaw and E. M. Forster papers; the Harry Ransom Humanities Research Center, the University of Texas at Austin, and Dan H. Laurence, for the George Bernard Shaw correspondence; the trustees of the John Galsworthy estate, for the John Galsworthy correspondence; and Alexander Murray, for the Gilbert Murray correspondence.

This book is a revised and expanded version of my doctoral dissertation, which was written with fellowship support from the University of Pennsylvania. I also received generous assistance from the English-Speaking Union—a travel-study grant from the Philadelphia chapter and charming hospitality from members when I was studying in London, Brighton, Birmingham, and Edinburgh.

My dissertation committee—headed by Lynn Lees and including David DeLaura, Bruce Kuklick, and Daniel Hirschberg—patiently helped me hammer this book into shape. Invaluable advice and criticism was also provided by Robert Wohl, Neville Masterman, Alfred F. Havighurst, Richard Ellmann, Norman MacKenzie, Alan Kors, Peter F. Clarke, Bentley B. Gilbert, Sue Lonoff, Mary Davis, James Obelkevich, and John Cerullo. And I am specially indebted to Joan Simmonds, Catherine and Brenda Masterman, and Paul Diamond, who acquired merit by feeding an impoverished student.

Introduction

Intellectual historians do not know quite what to make of Edwardian Britain. They generalize easily about "Victorianism" and "modernism," but it has proved far more difficult to define a peculiarly "Edwardian turn of mind." Some scholars have concluded that there was no such thing, only a mix of contradictory movements and ideas that, according to Samuel Hynes, "did not add up to a coherent system of beliefs or define a large common goal." The Edwardian period, in fact, is not usually treated as a period in its own right. More often it is attached to histories of nineteenth-century or postwar Britain, or else it is classified as a "transitional" phase, still very Victorian but gradually becoming modern, interesting mainly as a field of cultural "conflict of old and new."[1]

Actually, much Edwardian thought was neither old nor new but particularly Edwardian, and there were a number of large goals widely shared among Edwardian artists and writers. The broad common denominators of Edwardian cultural life become apparent when one resorts to a method of analysis used by Walter Houghton in *The Victorian Frame of Mind*—when one approaches ideas "at the fundamental level below that of formal doctrine and schools of thought."[2] As Arthur Lovejoy noted in *The Great Chain of Being*, the most sophisticated philosophies and works of art are inevitably grounded on "implicit or incompletely explicit *assumptions*, or more or less *unconscious mental habits* . . . often of so general and so vague a sort that it is possible for them to influence the course of a man's reflections on almost any subject."

Lovejoy wrote those words over a half century ago, and intellectual history has advanced a long way since then. The methodologies used by Lovejoy and Houghton would today be considered inadequate for a number of reasons. In tracing the development of ideas, they failed to consider the influence of the literary marketplace, economic conditions, party politics, and popular culture, among other things. This book tries to take account of all these factors, but it still shares one basic premise with Lovejoy and Houghton—that complex systems of belief are based on very simple habits of mind. In Edwardian Britain, one can discern several underlying mental habits that were followed by a variety of political sects, by intellectuals working independently in different genres and disciplines, and by philosophical opponents who would have been mutually appalled to hear that they were thinking along similar lines.

This book, then, deals not so much with developed ideas as with attitudes, assumptions, tastes, and temperaments. It describes six broad intellectual movements that together undergirt a large and important body of British art and thought. Two of these movements took the form of simple catchwords—*Life* and *Efficiency*—each having distinctly Edwardian meanings and implications, each profoundly affecting the cultural climate of the period. A generation can reveal itself in the clichés it uses, and (to cite Lovejoy again) one of the most valuable investigative methods at the disposal of the intellectual historian is "philosophical semantics—a study of the sacred words and phrases of a period or a movement, with a view to a clearing up of their ambiguities, a listing of their various shades of meaning, and an examination of the way in which confused associations of ideas arising from these ambiguities have influenced the development of doctrines or accelerated the insensible transformation of one fashion of thought into another, perhaps its very opposite."[3]

In addition to the above, this study employs other methods wherever they can be usefully applied to a given problem. Thus, the national efficiency movement is subjected to a class and professional analysis, a psychological approach is taken to the Edwardian cult of childhood and games, and statistics are brought into play throughout the book. Overall, this is an interdisciplinary study that points out the connections and parallels among developments in literature, the arts, philosophy, science, social thought, and theology. It is a general overview designed for the student and the layman as well as for the specialist who wants to explore areas outside his specialty. It incorporates (and sometimes questions) the conclusions of secondary works, but it is based chiefly on research into published and unpublished primary sources.

The reader should be warned of the limits of this study. It does not pretend to be a representative sampling of mass public opinion. Rather, it concentrates on those Edwardians who produced innovative and lasting creative work, who continue to interest us today as artists, writers, and thinkers. The individuals discussed here were selected for the quality and influence of their work, not because they were necessarily typical of British society as a whole. When historians speak of, say, the Enlightenment, they mean the distinctive intellectual legacy of that era; they are not implying that everyone who lived during the eighteenth century was enlightened. In that restricted sense only, this book deals with what I have called the Edwardian temperament; and even within those bounds, it does not attempt an exhaustive survey of British culture. It focuses on a few selected ideas, which, though they were certainly influential, were not the sum total of Edwardian thought. Another historian could have quite legitimately chosen to write on other topics. I decided to concentrate on these themes because they are essential to an understanding of the best minds (and many of the second-rate minds) of the period.

Finally, this book treats only Britain proper. Ireland was another country with other preoccupations; it should be (and has been) treated separately. I do, however, discuss Irish authors who were working in England or were connected with English literary circles.

Edward VII reigned from 1901 to 1910, but I have had to define the "Edwardian" era as extending from 1895 to 1919, for the trends explored here really flourished throughout those twenty-four years. Of course, these dates are only rough boundaries, beyond which I stray whenever necessary. Intellectual "periods" are always difficult to date exactly because attitudes and movements are things that fade in and out very gradually. Nevertheless, 1895 was a watershed in several important respects. It was the year of the Oscar Wilde trials, which triggered a sharp public reaction against Decadence. Thereafter, fin de siècle pessimism began to give way to hopeful anticipation of the new century. There was a turning away from the fatalism of Thomas Hardy, who published his last novel in 1895—the year in which George Bernard Shaw and H. G. Wells began to achieve literary success, each registering a determined protest against fatalism. On or very close to this date, Henry James, Rudyard Kipling, Kenneth Grahame, and Edith Nesbit all embarked on the literary experiment of exploring the world through the eyes of children. Eighteen ninety-five also saw the launching of the Jameson Raid and the London School of Economics, both of which focused public debate on the issue of "imperial efficiency." And in 1895 the Liberal Party suffered its first crushing electoral defeat under manhood suffrage: the age of Gladstone was decisively ended, and Liberals began to develop a program of social welfare to meet the demands of twentieth-century voters.

As for a closing date, most historians end the Edwardian age in August 1914, but in fact, the lamps did not go out all that abruptly. Each of the intellectual trends dealt with here continued well into the First World War, some of them reaching their highest pitch of development. That is why the story has to be carried through to 1919. By then, certainly, those attitudes had been radically transformed by the Great War and the peace that followed it.

1. Secular Religion

Of all the philosophical problems that troubled the Edwardians, none disturbed so many people as deeply as the decline of Victorian religion. This was a question that engaged nearly every important thinker of the period, as well as the millions of ordinary British men and women who were, at this time, drifting away from their churches. Of course, the Edwardians were also concerned with social reform, art, literature, and science, but the innovative work they did in each of these fields was very largely a product of and a substitute for disintegrating religious beliefs. To an extraordinary extent, intellectual activity in Edwardian Britain was fueled by the diversion of frustrated religious energies into other areas of thought.

Assaulted first by the geological theories of Sir Charles Lyell, then by biblical criticism, then by Darwinism, and finally by the comparative anthropology of religions popularized by Sir James Frazer in *The Golden Bough* (1890), orthodox Christianity was losing credibility among educated people. It had also lost its grip on the uneducated masses: surveys conducted in the London metropolitan area in 1851, 1886, and 1903 revealed a steady decline in churchgoing, especially among industrial workers. The Victorians had produced more books on religion than on any other topic, 18.6 percent of all titles published in 1879, but the proportion fell to less than half that by 1893.[1] After 1851 the expansion of the Protestant clergy generally failed to keep pace with the growth of population.[2] By 1883 there was an estimated shortage of 2500 Anglican priests, and the deficit continued to grow. As a profession, theology was no longer attracting the best students: Balliol, to take one of the most luminary of the Oxford colleges, sent half of its graduates into the ministry at the beginning of Victoria's reign but only 4 percent in the 1890s.[3]

Victorian politics, morality, art, literature, charity, and education had been saturated with religious principles and controversies, and the decline of religion left an enormous intellectual vacuum behind it. Without God, the universe lost all coherence and purpose in the minds of many late Victorians. Rationalist materialism, carried to its furthest extreme, led to the conclusion that all things, including man himself, were mere temporary collections of free atoms, with no guiding spirit giving them direction, unity, and permanence. Gone also was a God-given standard of morality, belief in an immortal human soul, and the prospect of reward or punishment after death. Many religious doubters (like Henry Sidgwick and Beatrice Webb) feared that, without these spiritual sanctions, social morality would break down and mankind would lapse into unrestrained hedonism.

Then, in the 1890s, as if to confirm all these awful predictions, the Decadent movement blossomed. Oscar Wilde and Aubrey Beardsley provided a public object lesson in the horrifying consequences of un-bridled skepticism. Samuel Hynes has shown that *decadence* was a popular Edwardian scare word, though it connoted more than just the *Yellow Book* coterie. Social commentators saw signs of national decadence in the incipient decline of British commercial and imperial supremacy, in the stunted and sickly inhabitants of city slums, in the rise of socialism and class conflict, and in the sterility of contemporary art.[4]

Above all, decadence meant the loss of old faiths. Long before Wilde and Beardsley, thinkers like Thomas Carlyle, John Stuart Mill, Mat-thew Arnold, Henry Sidgwick, and T. H. Green had described the Vic-torian age as a decadent age—decadent because religion and reason were no longer compatible, because Christianity had been undermined and no new consensus of belief was ready to take its place. Arnold de-fined the entire period since the French Revolution as an "epoch of concentration," in which doubt and unbelief had stifled creative art and permitted only criticism to flourish. Each of these men, however, saw history moving in cycles of decay and renewal, and they were convinced that if religious faith and secular reason could somehow be reunited, a renaissance would follow—an "epoch of expansion," as Arnold called it, a creative age "of synthesis and exposition, not of analysis and discovery."[5]

The Edwardian age was that epoch of expansion. It was a period in which artists, writers, philosophers, scientists, and sociologists re-sponded to the decline of religion by reconciling faith and reason, merg-ing the two in a higher and broader synthesis. Different individuals worked out this reconciliation in different ways, but they generally ap-proached the problem simply by abolishing the distinction between the spiritual and the mundane. They invented substitute religions, or substitutes for religion, that were firmly grounded on secular fact, and they infused spirituality into worldly things. If they no longer attended church, they remained intensely religious, for they had taken religion out of the churches and dispersed it into areas heretofore considered profane, if not sacrilegious. Among Edwardian intellectuals, a recurring pattern can be traced: they commonly passed through a phase of doubt or disbelief, ultimately discovered that they could not do without one or another of the comforts provided by religion, and went on to construct some form of secular faith. This is not a universal model, but it does fit most of those Edwardian artists and thinkers whose work has proved to be of enduring interest.

This effort to reunite the world and the spirit had one particularly important byproduct. In reconciling their theological difficulties, a great many Edwardians developed a reconciling turn of mind. They fell into the general habit of eliminating conflicts—conflicts between ideas, individuals, and social classes—through neat syntheses of opposites. This period produced a remarkable crop of omnibus philosophies harmonizing different points of view and conceiving all things as one thing. When we read Edwardian literature for its clichés, we discover that *divided, divorced, split, shattered, disintegration, dissolution,* and *in separate compartments* are the overworked pejoratives. *Unity, oneness, wholeness, bonds, synthesis, relation,* and *connection* are the cardinal virtues. The attitudes of an entire generation cannot be reduced to a slogan, but E. M. Forster's commandment "Only connect" was a dominating theme in Edwardian thought. Once, Christianity had provided a sense of universal connectedness: all things were created, related, and rendered coherent by God. Without God the Edwardians were forced to reknit the fabric of the cosmos on their own, uniting worldly realities and otherworldly aspirations to form a harmonious system of belief.

Some Victorians had made a principle of *compromise,* but *connection* is a very different thing. A compromise is a halfway house between two alternatives, and truth, as E. M. Forster saw it, is "not halfway between anything." What Forster and so many of his contemporaries were looking for was a complete fusion of the mystical and the real, "only to be found by continuous excursions into either realm."[6] The decline of conventional religion, John Galsworthy wrote in 1911, had incited a vigorous "cross-breeding of philosophies," and "Orthodoxy fertilised by Science" had spawned a new faith: "The Western world has dimly been rediscovering . . . that the Universe is all of a piece, Equipoise su-

preme; and all things equally wonderful, and mysterious, and valuable."
Galsworthy could "not help thinking that historians, looking back from
the far future, will record this age as the Third Renaissance," as vital as
fourteenth-century Italy and classical Greece.[7]

From the vantage point of the near future, the Age of Galsworthy
looks less than Periclean. Edwardian secular religion was an unstable
mixture, and it separated out again after the First World War. For as
long as it lasted, however, it did generate an extraordinary ferment of
art and ideas. In its various forms, secular religion inspired a legion of
novelists, ranging from James Joyce and Virginia Woolf to Maurice
Hewlett and Arthur Conan Doyle. It was the guiding faith of several
important intellectual coteries, including the Fabian Society and the
Bloomsbury Group. It stimulated innovative work in literature, social
welfare, philosophy, biology, sexual psychology, mathematics, and any
number of other fields. The quest for secular religion forced the Edwardians to think along unconventional lines, and it gave the age its
distinctive mental character: synthesizing, inventive, idiosyncratic, and
sometimes sharply entertaining.

The Psychical Researchers

Perhaps the most audacious of these attempts to find a secular basis
for religion was undertaken by that remarkable scientific organization,
the Society for Psychical Research. Founded in 1882, the SPR was devoted to the investigation of mental telepathy, extrasensory perception,
and survival after death. It sought to confirm, explain, predict, and re-
produce these phenomena, to bring the supernatural within the domain
of natural science. The SPR was a serious and rigorous enterprise that
devoted much of its energies to the exposure of fraudulent mediums.
Members were not required to believe in the existence of psychic forces,
and many of them remained skeptics all their lives; the SPR only demanded an open mind and a willingness to investigate. The ultimate goal
of the psychical researchers, however, was to reconcile science and religion. By controlled experiment, they sought a psychological explanation for mystical visions and tried to prove the existence of an immortal
human soul.

The popularity of psychical research among the Edwardians can and
has been exaggerated.[8] Some writers, like Henry James, Joseph Conrad,
and E. W. Benson (the archbishop of Canterbury), disliked what James

called the "certified ghosts" of the SPR—predictable spirits that took all the mystery out of mysticism.[9] For E. M. Forster in "The Purple Envelope" and Saki in "The Hedgehog," the psychical researcher was a plodding figure of fun, left utterly baffled by an encounter with a genuine ghost. For the sake of public relations, the SPR often pressed honorary memberships on celebrities like W. E. Gladstone, but he at least was hardly a true psychical researcher. One should also bear in mind that there were many prominent debunkers of psychical research, like the zoologist Ray Lankester.

Still, after making all the necessary qualifications, the fact remains that psychical research attracted the interest of a large and thoroughly respectable segment of the Edwardian intellectual community. The SPR membership included several eminent scientists: Sir Oliver Lodge, Sir William Crookes, Lord Rayleigh, J. J. Thomson, the biologist William Bateson, and the psychologist William McDougall. There were also a number of clergymen—among them the bishops of Carlisle and Ripon—as well as the philosophers Henry Sidgwick, F. H. Bradley, G. F. Stout, F. C. S. Schiller, and J. H. Muirhead. The SPR could boast an impressive list of literary figures: J. A. Symonds, Arthur Conan Doyle, W. B. Yeats, F. W. H. Myers, Walter Raleigh, Andrew Lang, May Sinclair, Alfred Sutro, and A. C. Benson. It included such prominent academics as Gilbert Murray, Goldsworthy Lowes Dickinson, and A. C. Bradley, and also some leading editors: W. H. Hutton and John St. Loe Strachey of the *Spectator*, W. T. Stead of the *Review of Reviews*, and Edward Marsh of *Georgian Poetry*. There were SPR members in the highest reaches of British society: Lord Curzon, James Bryce, and Prime Minister A. J. Balfour, who had been president of the organization. Among the Fabian socialists, Frank Podmore was one founder of the SPR: his psychical investigations afforded him "some kind of inarticulate assurance that there is a unity and a purpose in the Cosmos." Other Fabian members included Edward Pease, Sydney Olivier, H. G. Wells, the Reverend R. J. Campbell, and Mrs. Bernard Shaw;[10] while Mr. Shaw, Beatrice Webb, and Edith Nesbit dabbled in the occult outside the SPR.[11] Arnold Bennett briefly toyed with spiritualism in his 1909 novel *The Glimpse*, and in 1913 Rupert Brooke wrote a sonnet inspired by the *Proceedings of the Society for Psychical Research*.[12]

Arthur Balfour was driven to psychical research by the specter of "decadence," which he saw everywhere—in modern literature and art, in socialism, in the decline of Britain as an imperial power, in the exhaustion of the world's natural resources, and particularly in the decay of religion. Balfour's skepticism went far beyond questions of theology. In his 1879 volume *A Defence of Philosophic Doubt*, he insisted that science is as "irrational" as religion, a futile attempt to comprehend an unimaginably complex universe, founded on unprovable axioms, fallible observations, partial knowledge, and the systematic suppression of data that contradict accepted theories. In *The Foundations of Belief* (1895), however, Balfour turned away from "destructive criticism" and embarked on a "work of construction." He still distrusted scientific reasoning as "a force most apt to divide and disintegrate," but now he affirmed the possibility of "the unification of all belief into an ordered whole, compacted into one coherent structure under the stress of reason." If religion and science were both based on unproven assumptions, perhaps it was the same assumption—that is, God. Science and theology, Balfour argued, might be reconciled insofar as both presumed a dogmatic, unverifiable faith in God in order to make sense.[13]

Shortly after publishing *The Foundations of Belief*, Balfour, together with Wilfrid Ward (the Catholic writer), Dr. Edward Talbot (later bishop of Rochester), and Charles Gore (canon of Westminster), organized a discussion club named the Synthetic Society. It was modeled on the old Metaphysical Society of 1869–1880, but whereas the earlier group had encouraged criticism of all accepted belief, its Edwardian successor undertook the "construction" of a new foundation for religious faith, and it barred atheists from membership. It included psychical researchers like Sidgwick, Lord Rayleigh, F. W. H. Myers, Oliver Lodge, and Lowes Dickinson; three notable Idealist philosophers, R. B. Haldane, James Ward, A. S. Pringle-Pattison; as well as G. K. Chesterton, Lord Hugh Cecil, William Temple (later archbishop of Canterbury), W. H. Hutton, James Bryce, and George Wyndham.[14]

The example of Balfour illustrates that psychical research acquired momentum from a loss of faith not only in orthodox Christianity but in orthodox materialist science as well. The discovery of radio waves (1888), X rays (1895), and radioactivity (1896) confronted scientists with phenomena they could not explain in conventional terms, phenomena so radically new as to appear almost occult. These discoveries were bound to open minds to unconventional fields of inquiry like psychical research. To Balfour, Lodge, and William Crookes, the existence of radio waves suggested that mental telepathy, extrasensory perception, and clairvoyance were at least worthy of investigation.[15] It is no coincidence that many pioneering researchers in radio, X rays, and radioactivity were also SPR members. J. J. Thomson discovered the electron in 1897, discrediting the materialist axiom that atoms are indivisible. In 1888 Oliver Lodge had proved the existence of radio waves in the laboratory, only a few months after H. R. Hertz (who later became a corresponding member of the SPR) did the same in Germany; and in 1894 Lodge conducted the world's first public demonstration of wireless telegraphy. Sir William Crookes was the inventor of the cathode ray tube, used by Wilhelm Roentgen to generate X rays, and Oliver Lodge did much to publicize that discovery.[16] Until 1896, Oliver Heaviside, an unconventional researcher in electromagnetic theory, warned Lodge away from investigating mental telepathy because it contradicted a dogma of materialist science: that bodies cannot act on each other at a distance. But Roentgen's discovery of rays that could pass through solid matter impressed Heaviside as "a physical example of the possibility of the direct action of one brain upon another at a short distance." He soon began to speculate wildly about all kinds of occult phenomena, wondering whether levitation and saints' halos might be produced by high-frequency waves.[17]

To some Edwardians, the discovery of radio waves suggested a vision of universal oneness. "For the first time Light was linked to Electricity" along the electromagnetic spectrum, declared Oliver Lodge. "They are no longer distinct sciences." Arthur Balfour concluded that "a very large stride has been made towards establishing the unity of the great physical powers of nature."[18] The guild socialist A. J. Penty proclaimed that radiation science and psychical research pointed to "the existence of a universal consciousness interpenetrating all matter as the explanation of the contradictory results of investigations conducted by the chemist and the physicist, the astronomer, and the geologist."[19] The same phenomena convinced the homosexual crusader Edward Carpenter that "the subtlest forces and energies, totally unmeasurable by our instruments, and saturated or at least suffused with intelligence, are at work all around us."[20]

Oliver Lodge also discovered something like God in electromagnetic radiation. He merged physics, psychics, and theology in a sort of unified field theory based on a hypothetical universal fluid known as the ether. Materialist scientists since Descartes and Newton, having assumed that energy could not be transmitted across a vacuum, had explained the passage of light and gravity through the apparent emptiness of space by postulating the existence of an all-pervasive ether. It was supposed to be invisible, infinitely dense, yet without mass or weight, allowing planets to slip through it without the slightest friction.[21] Einstein's Relativity Theory, advanced in 1905, explained action across a vacuum without resorting to a contrived ethereal hypothesis. Nevertheless, Lodge continued to put forward the ether as a transmitting medium not only of certain types of radiant energy but also "of all manner of force, from gravitation down to cohesion and chemical affinity."

Lodge entertained a powerful Edwardian prejudice in favor of connectedness. He did not care to live in an atomistic universe of free molecules having no "continuity" among them. He even disliked Max Planck's Quantum Theory because it packaged radiant energy in discrete, indivisible particles. Lodge preferred to think of all things as continuous, and he ventured to suggest that the ether might be "the universal connecting medium which binds the universe together, and makes it a coherent whole instead of a chaotic collection of independent isolated fragments." He saw in the ether an elemental substance that variously took the form of matter, energy, life, and mind. This all-encompassing theory, he claimed, demonstrated "how the materialistic side of things is to be reconciled and unified with the more spiritual side." In fact, Lodge's ether was practically the equivalent of God, an "Immanent Grandeur" manifest everywhere "in the woven fabric of existence."[22]

Thomas Kuhn notes that aesthetic factors can influence the acceptance or rejection of scientific theories.[23] This was clearly the case with Lodge, who took up psychical research largely to satisfy a taste for oneness. In the early 1880s he had tried to find a materialist explanation for the findings of the SPR, but he had been forced to marshal a great variety of theories (chance, fraud, misperception, coincidence) to account for everything, and this inconsistency made him uncomfortable: "When in science one has to try so many different explanations, sometimes one and sometimes another, it is an indication that we are off the track, and have not really got an explanation at all. The complete theory is always a unifying one, and is satisfying to the mind when properly grasped."[24]

In 1902 L. P. Jacks, a friend of Lodge's, launched a periodical devoted to the construction of a unified system of spiritual and secular belief. The *Hibbert Journal* was founded as a theological quarterly open to contributions from every conceivable school of religious thought, with the aim of finding some common ground that might ultimately serve as the basis of a "Church Universal." "The Goal of thought is One," the editors proclaimed in their first issue.

> Truth is to be found not in the conclusions to which any single line of thought may lead but in the totality of conclusions to which all lines have led, and are still leading, the instructed Reason of man. Though separate members of this Totality may appear discordant as between themselves, we imagine that in the vast combination they become elements of some final harmony. . . . Amid all varieties of religious *opinion*, the goal of religious *aspiration* is One. The thoughts of men, though separated at the beginning, and on their own level, by every degree of intellectual difference, have yet a common End, raised by infinity above all human levels, to which, as to a focal point, they inevitably converge. Thus in the last analysis we reach a principle which gives an inner unity to reverent minds.[25]

Jacks, a Unitarian minister, was convinced that religion had been led into a dead end by professional theologians. "The present crisis of thought," he told Oliver Lodge, required a new secular approach to religious issues. Accordingly, the *Hibbert Journal* would be written by

> the non-professional theologian—i.e., . . . every man with a heart & brain. . . . I want to get men of brain & earnestness in the typical walks of life to tell us what they are thinking about religion. . . . I want an artist, a doctor, a lawyer, a soldier, a merchant, a statesman yes & even a woman (!) to speak. Why not also Pierpont Morgan? Assuming that he doesn't care a damn about Religion let him write an article to tell us why. . . . Do you catch on to the general idea & see its importance? No parson need apply.[26]

In fact, the *Hibbert Journal* did accept contributions from professional churchmen, but it also published a variety of philosophers (Bertrand Russell, James Ward, John Dewey, Bernard Bosanquet, C. S. Peirce, J. H. Muirhead, A. S. Pringle-Pattison, Josiah Royce, F. C. S. Schiller, Edward Caird, G. F. Stout, J. M. E. McTaggart, Henri Bergson), literary personalities (Andrew Lang, W. H. Mallock, G. K. Chesterton, Leo Tolstoy, Max Nordau, John Galsworthy, Rabindranath Tagore, Ernest Rhys), politicians (A. J. Balfour, Ramsay MacDonald, R. B. Haldane, Theodore Roosevelt, James Bryce), scholars (Gilbert Murray, G. M. Trevelyan, Arthur Lovejoy), soldiers (Lord Roberts—the Boer War hero), and several ordinary men and women from "typical walks of life."

Jacks joined the Society for Psychical Research in 1909 and later served as its president. He prodded Oliver Lodge into writing articles on psychical research and the reconciliation of science and religion, which were among the most popular features of the *Hibbert Journal*.[27] Another contributor was G. Lowes Dickinson, the Cambridge don who served as mentor to E. M. Forster and several members of the Bloomsbury Group. Dickinson's religious beliefs had come apart while he was studying at Cambridge in the early 1880s. He immediately set about searching for a new unifying philosophy in the work of Plato, Plotinus, Hegel, Shelley, Goethe, and the SPR. Once he deeply impressed his fellow undergraduates with a paper that compared a variety of religions and ended by declaring them all correct and consistent with one another.[28]

A similar unifying vision may be detected even in the Sherlock Holmes stories of Arthur Conan Doyle. Born a Roman Catholic, Doyle had been transformed into a pure materialist by his medical training and his reading of Darwin. Then the occult investigations of scientists like Sir William Crookes stimulated his interest in the Society for Psychical Research, which he joined in 1893. Holmes made his debut in *A Study in Scarlet* (1887), in which he based his methods of detection on the principle of universal connectedness: "All life is a great chain, the nature of which is known whenever we are shown a single link of it." Thus, given an isolated scrap of evidence, Holmes is able to deduce his way along the great chain of being until he has pieced together a solution to the crime. Critics have described Moriarity and Doyle's other master criminals as representing all the destructive, disintegrating tendencies of the "decadent" nineties. If this is the case, then Holmes, by constructing "an entirely connected case" through a "logical synthesis" of all the facts, restores law and order in the cosmos as well as on the streets of London.[29] Granted, Holmes consistently refuses to consider supernatural explanations of crimes ("No ghosts need apply").[30] But he cannot accept that "our universe is ruled by chance," and in "The Naval Treaty" he bluntly asserts that "there is nothing in which deduction is so necessary as in religion. . . . It can be built up as an exact science by the reasoner."[31]

Doyle undertook psychical research in that scientific spirit. He hailed Oliver Lodge for attempting to discover "spiritual truths which do not depend upon that two-edged business Faith, but upon direct reason."[32] The priest-detective Father Brown, introduced by G. K. Chesterton in 1910, founded his criminology on an equally rational religion. Brown insists that Roman Catholic theology is entirely consistent with worldly reason and can therefore be used to "connect" clues in logical sequence. Thus he uncovers "the real explanation of the [crime] and the universe," solving a mystery that "has but one solution."[33]

A distinction should be drawn between serious psychical researchers and spiritualists, who also flourished during the Edwardian period. Spiritualists were believers rather than objective investigators, more credulous and far less rigorous than the scientists of the SPR. Nevertheless, they believed they had reconciled faith and science in a religion that could be verified by empirical observation. Although table rapping had been a popular drawing-room diversion in England since the 1850s, it was not until the turn of the century that spiritualism acquired all the trappings of an organized movement—a successful national organization (founded in 1891) and regional subgroups (15 by 1912), permanent and well-appointed churches (complete with choirs, Sunday schools, and Gothic architecture), and even professional unions for mediums (organized in 1900 and 1906). There were about 150 local spiritualist societies in Britain in 1895, increasing to 240 in 1902 and 390 by 1908.[34]

Rebelling against his father's agnosticism, William Butler Yeats used spiritualism to construct a new faith and a private mythology that became the inspirational basis for his poetry. In 1885 with George Russell ("A. E.") he organized the Dublin Hermetic Society, devoted to the exploration of the occult and Eastern theologies. He also became involved with Theosophy, a new cult that promised to effect a "synthesis of science, religion, and philosophy." Madame H. P. Blavatsky, the founder and prophet of the movement, drew on recent work in anthropology to point out myths and motifs shared by many religions. This, she concluded, proved that all faiths were derived from a common source, which she identified as Theosophy, supposedly an ancient primal cult that incorporated all truths contained in other religions. Theosophy attracted a small but passionate following among bohemians, suffragettes, and the men of the Irish Renaissance. Yeats's enthusiasm for the new religion was, however, dampened by the Society for Psychical Research, which exposed Madame Blavatsky as a fraud in June 1885. Yeats always insisted on subjecting spiritualism to scientific tests. He conducted numerous experiments to verify Theosophy, all of them embarrassing failures, until he was eased out of the movement in 1890. He continued his spiritual researches with the Hermetic Students of the

Golden Dawn, a cabalistic group that included many eminent scientists, among them the astronomer-royal of Scotland.[35] By 1913 Yeats had joined the Society for Psychical Research.

The motivating idea behind Yeats's mystical investigations was an obsessive quest for oneness. In a 1919 essay he recalled the very day in the late 1880s when of a sudden

> this sentence seemed to form in my head, without my willing it, much as sentences form when we are half-asleep: "Hammer your thoughts into unity." For days I could think of nothing else, and for years I tested all I did by that sentence. I had three interests: interest in a form of literature, in a form of philosophy, and a belief in nationality. None of these seemed to have anything to do with the other, but gradually my love of literature and my belief in nationality came together. Then for years I said to myself that these two had nothing to do with my form of philosophy, but that I had only to be sincere and to keep from constraining one by the other and they would become one interest. Now all three are, I think, one, or rather all three are a discrete expression of a single conviction.[36]

By 1899 Yeats had synthesized Christianity, Celtic and classical myths, spiritualism, Theosophy, Druidism, Rosicrucianism, Hinduism, William Blake, Dionysius worship, cabalism, magic, the anthropology of Sir James Frazer, and an esoteric symbolism of his own invention. The result was a substitute religion that supplied the raw material of legends, themes, and symbols that Yeats used to create poetry. He was now convinced that poetry and religion were one, that "whatever of philosophy has been made poetry is alone permanent, and that one should begin to arrange it in some regular order, rejecting nothing as the make-believe of poets." Art would become the rites of a new religion, which would "re-unite the perception of the spirit, of the dream, with natural beauty." Yeats's mythic art tried to generate "rich fusions" by reconciling all opposites, reestablishing the connections between the individual and society, the artist and his audience, and the Apollonian and Dionysian traditions of Western culture.[37]

Epiphanies

Yeats was only one of several Edwardian authors who made literature into a unifying surrogate theology. Richard Ellmann has pointed out the same tendency in James Joyce, Ezra Pound, T. S. Eliot, D. H.

Lawrence, E. M. Forster, H. G. Wells, Harley Granville Barker, and George Moore: "A kind of inner belief pervades their writings, that the transcendent is immanent in the earthy, that to go down far enough is to go up." All these writers used literature to spiritualize the mundane, to find what Granville Barker called "the prose for God"[38] or what D. H. Lawrence described as a "religious Agnosticism."[39] Each of them (to quote Joyce) wrote as "a priest of eternal imagination, transmuting the daily bread of experience into the radiant body of everliving life."[40]

Although Joyce abandoned Roman Catholicism (with immense relief) as an adolescent, he retained an essentially catholic mentality. "Your mind is supersaturated with the religion in which you say you disbelieve," Cranly tells Stephen Dedalus in *A Portrait of the Artist as a Young Man* (1904–1914). Stephen demands a system of belief with the same internal unity as Catholic theology, not the "sectarianism" and "turbulent schisms" of Protestantism: "What kind of liberation would that be to forsake an absurdity which is logical and coherent and to embrace one which is illogical and incoherent?"[41] Joyce rejected Theosophy as a substitute faith, although he was attracted to the idea that all religions are rooted in one primeval parent cult. He seized instead on the sixteenth-century heresy of Giordano Bruno, which he summed up as "a kind of dualism—every power in nature must evolve an opposite in order to realise itself and opposition brings reunion."[42]

The reunion of opposites was an obsession with Joyce. "Do I contradict myself? Very well then, I contradict myself," says Buck Mulligan, quoting Walt Whitman.[43] (The model for Mulligan was the Dublin writer Oliver St. John Gogarty, who scrambled nature worship and supernatural religion in a lusty dialectic: "One becomes many, God becomes man, Being becomes appearance, the Root puts into Leaf . . . the Soul makes the Body.")[44] *Ulysses* (1914–1921) connects all things in an impossibly abstruse but perfectly harmonious matrix. From Homer, Joyce adapted an "all-embracing" story and the most "complete man" in literature. Odysseus becomes a Jew who has been baptized as a Catholic and as a Protestant but who obviously has no religion other than an intuition that all humanity is united by some sort of spiritual bond. The novel works through several consonant sets of symbols simultaneously—colors and hours and organs of the body—"from eighteen different points of view and in as many styles." Male and female, classicism and modernity, the heroic and the comic, dream and reality, mythology and realism all coexist in a seamless fusion. For Joyce, they fitted together as closely as Catholic theology: "Each adventure (that is, every hour, every organ, every art being interconnected and interrelated in the structural scheme of the whole) should not only condition but even create its own technique. Each adventure is so to say one person although it is composed of persons—as Aquinas relates of the angelic hosts."[45]

The meeting of Bloom and Stephen Dedalus may well be Joyce's resolution of the antithesis set up in *Culture and Anarchy*—the union of Jew and Greek, of Hebraism and Hellenism, of moral strictness and aesthetic passion. Or it may be that the synthesis is trinitarian: some critics see Simon Dedalus, Stephen, and Bloom as Father, Son, and Holy Ghost, not necessarily in that order.[46] In any case, when Stephen and Bloom come together, in the penultimate episode, the novel vaults into the celestial realm of scientific precision. Then, finally, heaven touches the earth, as all the strands of the story are funneled into Molly Bloom, Joyce's profane nature goddess.

The artist of *A Portrait* is himself a sort of secular god. He creates a unified cosmos on paper, charging literature with an aura of religion. When Stephen is struck by poetic inspiration, Joyce illuminates the event with a blaze of imagery taken from the Immaculate Conception. In this vision, the earth itself is transformed into "a swinging smoking swaying censer," nicely fusing the worldly and the sacramental.[47] Joyce's sanctification of the mundane is reflected in his special definition of the term *epiphany*, which he used to describe "a sudden spiritual manifestation" revealing the aesthetic quality in an everyday incident or object.[48] Other Edwardian writers arrived independently at that approach to literature, among them G. K. Chesterton, who began drifting toward the Catholic church just as Joyce was leaving it. In a 1909 volume aptly titled *Tremendous Trifles*, Chesterton proclaimed that spiritual-aesthetic visions could be found in mail boxes, advertisements, and railway stations.[49]

Epiphanies also illuminate the work of Virginia Woolf, restoring unity to a universe bereft of God. As a young girl (the exact date is unclear, but it would appear to be around 1890) she was precipitated into a spiritual crisis by two shattering revelations. The first came while she was tussling on the front lawn with her brother Thoby: she abruptly asked herself what right she had to hurt people and, unable to find an answer, immediately lost the will to defend herself. The second shock was her discovery of death when she overheard that a recent visitor to the Stephen household had committed suicide. All children must at some point face the disturbing questions of morality and mortality, and in most Victorian homes religion provided reassuring answers. But the daughter of Leslie Stephen, the agnostic philosopher, did not have that solace. She had to suffer through a period of depression and paralysis until, at last, she stumbled across a metaphysic in the family garden.

> I was looking at the flower bed by the front door; "That is the whole", I said. I was looking at a plant with a spread of leaves; and it seemed suddenly plain that the flower itself was a part of the earth; that a ring enclosed what was the flower; and that was the real flower; part earth; part flower. It was a thought I put away as being likely to be very useful to me later.

That vision revealed to her the sense of universal order that, for the Victorians, had been provided by religion. This was a wonderfully comforting discovery, one that lifted her clear out of her spiritual depression. It provided the faith that sustained her as a writer, a secular faith in the connectedness of all things. She wrote novels to make the connections plain, to place each part in the context of the whole. Toward the end of her life, she recalled that her epiphany in the garden had taught her that the "shock" of losing faith is never

> simply a blow from an enemy hidden behind the cotton wool of daily life; it is or will become a revelation of some order; it is a token of some real thing behind appearances; and I make it real by putting it into words. It is only by putting it into words that I make it whole; . . . it gives me . . . great delight to put the severed parts together. Perhaps this is the strongest pleasure known to me. It is the rapture I get when in writing I seem to be discovering what belongs to what; making a scene come right; making a character come together. From this I reach what I might call a philosophy; at any rate it is a constant idea of mine; that behind the cotton wool is hidden a pattern; that we—I mean all human beings—are connected with this; that the whole world is a work of art; that we are parts of the work of art. *Hamlet* or a Beethoven quartet is the truth about this vast mass that we call the world. But there is no Shakespeare, there is no Beethoven; certainly and emphatically there is no God; we are the words; we are the music; we are the thing itself. . . .
> This intuition of mine . . . has certainly given its scale to my life ever since I saw the flower in the bed by the front door. . . . It proves that one's life is not confined to one's body and what one says or does; one is living all the time in relation to certain background . . . conceptions.[50]

Mrs. Woolf summed up her novel *Night and Day* (1919) as an attempt to reconstruct faith, to "piece together in a laborious and elementary fashion fragments of belief, unsoldered and separate, lacking the unity of phrases fashioned by the old believers." She wrote to refute the heresy "that the world is composed entirely of vast blocks of matter, and that we're nothing but patches of light"—the dismal materialism that Rachel Vinrace grapples with in *The Voyage Out* (1915). Virginia Woolf found a secular religion—a reconciliation of "fact" and "vision," as she liked to put it—simply by chronicling everyday life and the epiphanies she found therein: "One thing led to another and by degrees something had formed itself out of nothing, and so one reached at last this calm, this quiet, this certainty, and it was this process that people called living. . . . Things formed themselves into a pattern . . . and in that pattern lay satisfaction and meaning."[51]

The Social Gospel

For clergymen working in the slums of Edwardian England, the decline of religion was a more immediate problem. Richard Mudie-Smith's 1903 survey of London churches confirmed what had been generally recognized for decades: most urban workers had lost the churchgoing habit. Religion was still a potent force in rural Britain, where a laborer could not avoid church without attracting the notice of his neighbors, the village minister, and the local squire. Industrialization, however, had brought millions of country workers into new, raw, anonymous city slums, where they found few churches but plenty of pubs, music halls, secularist agitators, and labor organizations competing for their free Sundays. Many workingmen had come to feel, with justification, that the major religious denominations served the middle classes more than the poor and were preoccupied with rewards in heaven rather than injustice on earth.

Reformers in all classes responded to this crisis by redirecting their religious energies into political activism. They warned that the churches had become too elitist and "otherworldly" and could only win back their proletarian flock by bringing religion to bear on the worldly problem of poverty. The Christian socialist Percy Alden called for the "application of Christianity to the social conditions of our common life," to slum housing and public health and industrial organization, for politics, "rightly understood, is only applied religion. . . . I see no need for the perpetual warfare between those who advocate care for the body and those who think only of the soul," Alden added; "men and women are flesh and blood, and not disembodied spirits; we have no right to talk as though they could be separated off into departments." Like other forms of Edwardian secular religion, the social gospel erased the boundary between the sacred and the mundane. "Business must be spiritualised, the State Christianised, and religion humanised," was Alden's way of saying it.[52] In a 1906 editorial "The Church and the World," the *Hibbert Journal* found no "*ethical* difference sufficiently marked to justify the opposition of the two. . . . There is no single place of origin for the things of the spirit; no exclusive home for what is best in life; no privileged foundation of goodness and truth; no eminence where the virtues sit apart, like the gods on Olympus."[53] The *Hibbert Journal* therefore published a wide range of social reformers (Edward Carpenter, J. A. Hobson, C. R. Ashbee, W. R. Lethaby, and Helen Bosanquet) on the relevance of religion to questions of socialism, the labor movement, and women's suffrage. The ideal, as one contributor to Mudie-Smith's survey stated, was simply "to make life and religion one."[54]

Much of the Edwardian social gospel was rooted in the Idealist philosophy of T. H. Green, which was itself an attempt to salvage religion through synthetic thinking. Green, who taught philosophy at Balliol from 1870 to 1882, reconnected theology with social justice through a straightforward Hegelian dialectic. He rejected laissez-faire economics: the very existence of society, he reasoned, is a tacit admission that man is a social animal and that the state can and should promote the common good. Green used a similar logic to attack the empiricism that had dominated British philosophy for the past two hundred years. Following Kant, he argued that the presence of ideas in the mind implies some innate "unifying principle which . . . unites them in relation to each other." Green objected to the unconnectedness of unregulated capitalism and empirical philosophy: the first reduced individuals to free competitive units without social ties, the second reduced the mind to a recording device that collected perceptions without fitting them together. Thought and society, Green concluded, must logically have a uniting focus. That focus he identified as God, or at any rate something very like God—a "spiritual principle," a "self-distinguishing consciousness," an "eternal intelligence."[55]

This philosophy made God the practical equivalent of man's social and intellectual achievements. He was therefore a finite and evolving God, continually enhanced by human progress, a God incarnated in history and immanent in all things. By founding his God on logic and stripping Him of all supernatural attributes, Green rendered Him immune to biblical criticism and entirely compatible with Darwinian evolution. Green further argued that since God is manifest in human political institutions, one can serve Him by working to improve society. And since every individual is a part and a product of the society in which he lives, social work can also be a means of serving oneself, of achieving true "self-realization." Thus, at a stroke, Green reversed all the centrifugal tendencies of Victorian thought. He merged opposing beliefs in a Neo-Hegelian Ideal, and he demonstrated that the apparent conflicts between science and religion, the secular and the spiritual, and society and the individual were really "false antitheses."

British empiricism was, for a generation, routed by Green and his students. From 1895 to 1914 Idealists dominated the philosophy faculties of every English and Scottish university except Cambridge, and even there J. M. E. McTaggart and James Ward maintained a strong Idealist presence. Several academic Idealists, including Bernard Bosanquet, J. H. Muirhead, Edward Caird, and William Wallace, extracted a substitute for theology from Green's philosophy: they founded the London Ethical Society, which maintained that the morality of religion was "in no way dependent upon belief in a system of supernatural rewards and punishments." Green always denied that he was trying to set up a surrogate religion,[56] but he did tell Henry Sidgwick "that religious men, who have broken with dogmatic Xtianity *as dogmatic*, should come to some mutual understanding, so as to have a chance of reorganizing worship & religious beneficence when the present fabrics break up, as (tho' I am not impatient for it) I suppose they soon must."[57] It is fair to say that Green and his followers were working to restore the metaphysical unity once provided by religion. The Idealists, to quote James Ward, viewed all history as an ongoing "creative synthesis" that would lead to "the final goal of evolution . . . the eventual consummation of a perfect commonwealth, wherein all cooperate and none conflict, wherein the many have become one, one realm of ends."[58]

In pursuit of that perfect commonwealth, Green laid the philosophical foundations of the New Liberalism—the welfare liberalism of Edwardian Britain. Green introduced the concept of "positive freedom" into the English political vocabulary, thus reconciling individualism and social justice. He argued that the "negative freedom" of laissez faire often had the practical effect of limiting the liberty of the poor, who could not fully exercise their rights as freeborn Englishmen without adequate education, housing, and sewers. A certain amount of social legislation was therefore necessary to permit the free play of individualism. As Green's student Bernard Bosanquet concluded in *The Philosophical Theory of the State* (1895),

> the conceptions of Society and the individual are correlative conceptions through and through; . . . to distinguish the one element from the other as superior from inferior, or as means from end, becomes a contradiction in terms. . . . There are not two opposable sets of contents concerned in the matter at all; but a single web of content which in its totality is society and in its differentiations the individuals. To make the totality the means to the differentiations or *vice versa* is like making a drama the means to the characters, or the characters to the drama.[59]

Green himself did not carry his collectivism very far. He accepted economic inequality, and he only wanted to regulate free enterprise to ensure that every individual had an opportunity to acquire personal wealth. His "social programme" consisted simply of factory legislation, public health and housing regulations, universal primary education, reform of the land laws, and temperance measures—nothing that would have shocked a mainstream Liberal of the 1870s. Nevertheless, Green affirmed that all British subjects were united by a common bond of "citizenship" and therefore entitled to a share of the common wealth. By making a philosophic break with laissez faire, he left an opening to reformers who wanted to transfer wealth from the rich to the poor, including New Liberal theorists like D. G. Ritchie, L. T. Hobhouse, J. A. Hobson, and Graham Wallas. The Liberal government of 1905–1915, which enacted old age pensions (1908), unemployment insurance (1911), and national health insurance (1911), included at least four ministers who had been influenced by Idealist philosophy. Green had tutored H. H. Asquith and had been a friend of James Bryce; Herbert Samuel had published *Liberalism*, an interpretation of Green, in 1895; and R. B. Haldane was a Neo-Hegelian philosopher in his own right.[60]

Green was also the chief inspiration behind the Christian Social Union, founded in 1889 by Henry Scott Holland (one of his pupils), Charles Gore, and J. R. Illingworth. Of fifty-three Anglican bishops appointed between 1889 and 1913, sixteen belonged to the CSU, which in 1895 had 2,600 members.[61] Many of them were High Churchmen or Anglo-Catholics, but there were striking differences between the CSU and the Oxford Movement of the 1840s, differences that reflect Green's influence and the reconciling tendencies of the times. For one, the CSU accepted modern science as compatible with Christianity, borrowing Green's argument that human knowledge and the progress of evolution are manifestations of God's will to perfection. "Truth is One," Charles Gore affirmed. "There can be no conflict between matters of faith and the conclusions of knowledge."[62] Gore, who corresponded with Oliver Lodge on psychical research, conceived of Christianity as a "Liberal Catholicism" that incorporated all the partial truths contained in other religions. Through his theory of "kenosis," which had a far-reaching impact on Anglican theology, Gore reconciled the historical Christ with the holy Christ: he postulated a divine Jesus who had assumed humanity and all its limitations, including fallibility, during his sojourn on earth.[63]

The social gospelers, who agitated in all of the major religious denominations, generally stressed the immanence of God in all creation. They did not necessarily reject the idea of a transcendent deity: J. R. Illingworth drew on Idealist philosophy to argue that God is at once transcendent and immanent. The CSU was immanentist insofar as it aimed to apply Christianity to secular social problems, "to present Christ in practical life as the living Master and King, the enemy of wrong and selfishness, the power of righteousness and love."[64] For Charles Gore, this "social religion" was symbolized in the Eucharist, in which man assimilated God and achieved a "union of the divine and earthly."[65] In that sense, the CSU was catholic: it embraced a range of doctrines and engaged itself in all aspects of secular life.

In 1908 the CSU persuaded the Anglican bishops to endorse a moderate program of social reform, but some religious activists were more radical in their politics. In 1906 the Church Socialist League was organized by left-wing Anglican clerics like F. L. Donaldson (later canon of Westminster) and William Temple. The CSL denounced the moderation of the Parliamentary Labour Party and proposed to give workers control over their own industries through a network of worker-run guilds. The guild socialist movement, which was active between 1904 and 1923, also had a strong High Church or Catholic element, as represented by A. J. Penty, R. H. Tawney, and Maurice Reckitt. Penty invented the guild ideology to return society to the Middle Ages, which he admired because it possessed an intellectual unity based on the teachings of the Catholic church.[66] There were also agnostic guild socialists, like G. D. H. Cole and A. R. Orage, but both of these men manifested some interest in unifying surrogate religions: Cole passed through a brief

Idealist phase as an Oxford undergraduate; Orage was a member of the Theosophical Society and, after 1919, a disciple of the Armenian mystic G. I. Gurdjieff.

In 1888 the architect and designer C. R. Ashbee founded the Guild of Handicraft, a school and workshop in the East End of London dedicated to the revival of traditional artisanship. Ashbee later worked at restoring churches, and he lived in a chapel he had converted into a house in 1905; there was, in fact, a great deal of restored, converted religion in his art and his guild. Ashbee's father, an atheist, had taken his son to attend the services of various religious sects in order to show that a God whom everyone described differently could not possibly exist. But young Ashbee drew precisely the opposite conclusion—that all religions must contain a common element of truth. When he organized his Guild of Handicraft, he experienced a wonderfully eclectic mystical vision, as if the mind, unable to tolerate the vacuum of materialism, was reaching out to all conceivable myths and drawing them into a whole. He imagined a collective Second Coming of Jesus, the Messiah, Mary, the "Great Moor" of Granada, Charlemagne, King Arthur, and Quexacoatil—"All the Christs long expected shall come," he wrote. "All the inconsolidated ideas of the World shall in that hour consolidate," and "the Idea of Unity" would be realized. Ashbee, who had joined the Cambridge branch of the Society for Psychical Research, believed that the arts needed religion as a source of inspiration and symbolism. But it would have to be a truly "catholic" religion, embracing all classes and sects and incorporating the discoveries of modern science and biblical criticism. He founded his guild as a practical exercise in Christian social ethics, "a reaction against the anti-religious, the materialistic view of life held in the Victorian age."[67]

The Fabian Society also preached a quasi-religious gospel of social reform—an Evangelicalism broadened, secularized, and modernized. Most of the founding Fabians were former Anglican Evangelicals, whereas the working-class provincials who poured into the society around 1890 were mainly Nonconformists, often former lay preachers. Fabian proselytizers like Ramsay MacDonald, Robert Blatchford, Bruce Glasier, and Kate Conway used revivalist rhetoric to promote socialism, which they explicitly preached as a new "religion." The society always attracted large numbers of Christian socialist lay people, including Percy Alden, H. B. Holding, and Mary O'Brien, author of the first publication of the Socialist Quaker Society, "The Oneness of Religious and Secular Life" (1898). There were also at least twenty-five reverends on the 1894 Fabian membership list, among them John Trevor and Stewart Headlam. Perhaps the most celebrated Fabian cleric was the Reverend R. J. Campbell of the City Temple, who drew overflow audiences from the financial community with sermons on the social gospel and immanentist theology ("There is nothing that is not God").[68] In 1893 there was even talk of founding a "Fabian church" in Hampstead, dedicated to the quintessentially Fabian ideal of "a level-headed enthusiasm," but it never materialized.[69]

The Fabian Society evolved out of the welter of unconventional religious sects that arose in London after 1870, each of them attempting to fill the gap left by the rejection of traditional Christianity. Sydney Olivier and Sidney and Beatrice Webb came to Fabianism after toying with the Positivist theology of Auguste Comte.[70] William Clarke, Percival Chubb, and Ramsay MacDonald were involved in the Ethical Culture movement; and the large Ethical congregations at South Place and Bayswater were led for a time by another Fabian, Dr. Stanton Coit.[71] The sect from which the Fabian Society sprang directly was the Fellowship of the New Life, organized in 1883 around the mystical philosopher Thomas Davidson. Davidson preached a "pantheistic monism" postulating a single immanent deity uniting the entire material universe; he also proposed to establish monastic communities dedicated to education, moral improvement, and "fellowship." Some future Fabians, particularly William Clarke and Percival Chubb, were attracted to Davidson, at least for the moment. But others—Edward Pease, Hubert Bland, and Frank Podmore—broke away from Davidson's group in 1884 to found the Fabian Society, which took a more practical approach to social reform. The Fellowship of the New Life continued until 1896; its members (many of whom were also Fabians) included Havelock Ellis, Henry Salt, and Ramsay MacDonald.[72]

The son of Anglican minister, Sydney Olivier worked for Stewart Headlam's *Christian Socialist* magazine and then gravitated to the Fabian Society. As he explained in 1884, he was looking for a broader religion than his father's dogmatic theology.

> It is not enough for me that men can find perfect satisfaction for their nature in one line and religion, say Christianity, the Salvation Army, Socialism, Art. What I want to know is what is the common element in all these? Hence I am full of desire to investigate all forms of religion and thought and feeling.[73]

Eventually Olivier worked out a unifying religion of social responsibility that promised "Providence for *my* spirit, with the corresponding condition of service, and doing of God's will on my part."[74] Bernard Shaw, in 1896, proclaimed an equally catholic gospel: "I am a resolute Protestant; I believe in the Holy Catholic Church; in the Holy Trinity of Father, Son (or Mother, Daughter) and Spirit; in the Communion of Saints, the Life to Come, the Immaculate Conception, and the everyday reality of Godhead and the Kingdom of Heaven."[75] All these paradoxes reflect Shaw's spiritualization of the mundane: everyone is the Son (or Daughter) of God, all conceptions are immaculate, and the Communion of Saints, apparently, is the Fabian Society, working toward the Kingdom of Heaven through incremental reform. By demanding (as many Christian socialists did) that the churches open their doors to all regardless of creed and allow complete intellectual freedom, Shaw reconciled the protest of Protestantism with the catholicity of Catholicism. In *Man and Superman* (1901–1903), Don Juan predicts that

> every idea for which Man will die will be a Catholic idea. When the Spaniard learns at last that he is no better than the Saracen, and his prophet no better than Mahomet, he will arise, more Catholic than ever, and die on a barricade across the filthy slum he starves in, for universal liberty and equality. . . . Later on, Liberty will not be Catholic enough: men will die for human perfection, to which they will sacrifice all their liberty gladly.[76]

That catholicity is powerfully proclaimed in *John Bull's Other Island* (1904), where Father Keegan describes his trinitarian vision: "In my dreams it is a country where the State is the Church and the Church the people: three in one and one in three. . . . It is a temple in which the priest is the worshipper and the worshipper the worshipped: three in one and one in three. It is a godhead in which all life is human and all humanity divine: three in one and one in three."[77]

Beatrice Webb was gripped by passionate religious feelings all her life, and her loss of faith, at about the age of sixteen, left a gnawing emptiness. Determined to "find a firm belief of my own," she investigated the Bible, Plato, Diderot, Voltaire, Goethe, Balzac, Matthew Arnold, Catholicism, Positivism, spiritualism, and a variety of unconventional cults, none of which proved satisfactory. In 1883 she at last found some comfort in the sociology of Herbert Spencer, a family friend who became her guide and tutor. Scientific social work provided an outlet for the altruistic impulses of religion, so she plunged into the study of slum conditions. She later described her conversion as "the flight of emotion away from the service of God to the service of man,"[78] but she would have been more accurate if she had written that "the service of man is the service of God" (to quote the *Hibbert Journal*),[79] for later in life she gradually picked up all the accoutrements of religion. She found solace in prayer, often attended services at St. Paul's, vigorously supported state-funded religious education, and fasted to attain mystical communion with the universal ether.[80]

Sociology likewise served Charles Booth as a form of what he called "diffused religion."[81] Darwinism destroyed Booth's faith in God early in life, and he consequently rejected the Victorian assumption that poverty was an act of divine will. Booth concluded that social science could discover ways to eliminate poverty, but he did not believe that science alone would actually motivate people to reform society. That would require some sort of religious impulse, a system of belief that would combine scientific sociology with spiritual fervor. No conventional theology, including the Unitarian faith in which he had been raised, effected that fusion, so Booth turned for a time to the "scientific" religion of Comtean Positivism.[82] "The old forms of religion, divorced by their dogmatic teaching from modern thought and science, are powerless. To whatever extent they have hold of the moral truths which we need to act up to, they are still powerless to use them, for no man listens to what they say," he wrote in 1870. "Thus we need a philosophy which can embrace all things human and divine, so far as knowledge goes or can go," and at the same time provide for "the direction of the moral half of human nature in some organised or, at least, intelligible way."[83] Booth declared himself a follower of Comte in 1883,[84] but he eventually settled on a even broader theology: "Everything is religious that is not irreligious."[85]

Booth brought that unifying turn of mind to late Victorian sociology, which, like late Victorian religion, was having difficulty reconciling conflicting intellectual claims. Nineteenth-century social investigators generally recognized that a true sociology would have to offer general theories of society and scientific prescriptions for social reform, all derived from a hard statistical base, but by the 1880s it was evident that these objectives were simply not coming together. The Statistical Society of London had been collecting masses of data since 1834 without discovering any clear solutions to poverty and other social ills. Impatient reformers could publish sensational impressionistic reports on slum

life, like *The Bitter Cry of Outcast London* (1883), but they could not agree
on policies for attacking poverty, nor could they produce anything like a
scientific sociology. Booth's response to this impasse was his *Life and
Labour of the People in London* (published 1889–1903), a comprehensive
survey of the whole metropolis as a complete social organism. It combined studies of home life and of the workplace, statistics and personal observation, each cross-verifying the other. As an attempt at a
grand sociological synthesis, *Life and Labour* was less than successful:
Booth had difficulty drawing conclusions from his sixteen volumes of
data. Nevertheless, the work served as a model for numerous parliamentary blue books published between 1900 and 1914, as well as for the
Edwardian sociology of A. L. Bowley, Seebohm Rowntree, and Sidney
and Beatrice Webb.[86] As Booth explained to the future Mrs. Webb in
1886, his sociology was based on a habit of "relative" thinking so deeply
ingrained in his mind that he could not use single facts or methods in
isolation.

> It is this relative character or *proportion* of facts to each other, to us, to others,
> to society at large and to possible remedies that must be introduced if they
> are to be of any value at all in social diagnosis.
>
> Both single facts and strings of statistics *may* be true, and clearly demon-
> strably true, and yet entirely misleading in the way they are used. . . .
>
> As to the deductive and inductive methods, I seem to need both eternally
> and never could separate them in my mind nor decide which moved first. No
> induction is possible (I should say) without preceding deduction, nor any
> deduction without preceding induction. If induction does not promptly lead
> to deduction it is barren, and if deduction be not very humble and modest
> leaning on induction past and demanding increasingly inductive proof for
> every step it makes forward, it will assuredly go wrong.[87]

Seven volumes of *Life and Labour* surveyed religious activity in London
between 1897 and 1902. Booth reported that many observers who
worked with slum dwellers perceived among them a "latent," secular
religion.

> According to many, including not a few of the clergy themselves, every-
> thing that is beneficial may be brought under the aegis of religion. "Only
> that which is harmful is irreligious," says one, while some go so far as to
> "recognise no distinction between the sacred and the secular," in which case
> all moral life could be accepted as religious, and of moral conscientious life
> in London there is much.

Booth conceded that this might be too broad a definition of religion, but he insisted that religious belief could often manifest itself simply as "an impulse and a persistent attitude, an intimate possession of the soul, perhaps not understood even by the individual, and very difficult of interpretation by others. . . . In this sense men are often more religious than is known."[88]

Perhaps, but this was mostly speculation. Booth may have been projecting his own secularized religion on the working people he was studying. It is certainly true that conventional religion was losing its hold on urban workers; so, for that matter, was the militant atheism of Charles Bradlaugh, who had a large proletarian following between 1870 and 1890.[89] But does it follow that Edwardian workers had arrived at a midpoint between the two, or were they (as most contemporary observers believed) simply indifferent to religion? When C. F. G. Masterman took up settlement work in the slums of Camberwell in 1898, he expected "that the widespread break-up of faith and the influence of destructive criticism would have created a large class of persons unable conscientiously to attach themselves to church or chapel, but eager for ethical progress and the assertion of the supremacy of the things of the spirit. But," he concluded in 1903, "all experience has failed to discover any number of such individuals. . . . The man who will abstain from church-going, and informs you with complacency that his religion is that of the Sermon on the Mount, is usually distinguished by little but an amiable unwillingness to do conscious injury to those who have not injured him, and by a determination at least not to love himself less than his neighbour." Masterman concluded that British workers followed either an orthodox religion or (more likely) none at all, and that liberal or "undenominational" churches (as Booth conceded) utterly failed to interest them.[90]

It is difficult to say how many Edwardian working people embraced any form of secular religion. It was a subtle and often private theology, and its popularity among great masses of people is not easily measured. Spiritualism, however, does seem to have attracted a considerable proletarian following in the industrial cities of the North and in London slums like West Ham and Camberwell, where Mudie-Smith's survey found six Spiritualist churches.[91] The social gospel also clearly commanded broad respect among the working classes. Charles Booth noted "The success at the polls, whether for Boards of Guardians, Borough Councils, or the School Board, of men and women who in the name of religion are giving their lives to the service of the people"—one of whom was C. F. G. Masterman, elected member of Parliament for West Ham North in 1906. A layman familiar with the slums told Booth that "among working men a kind of sublimated trades' unionism is the most prevalent gospel: a vague bias towards that which is believed to be good for one's fellow man."[92] Many organizers of the Independent Labour Party, especially in the north of England, were former Methodist lay preachers; they worked Christian imagery and metaphors into their socialist oratory and built the ILP along Methodist lines of organization.[93] Beginning in 1910, Labour MPs held annual religious lectures at the Robert Browning Settlement House in Walworth, and they often defined socialism simply as "applied Christianity."[94] Philip Snowden was an organizer of the Free Church Socialist League, and in his 1905 ILP pamphlet *The Christ That Is to Be* he preached a new "political religion" that would synthesize "all the great ethical religions of the world."[95]

Socialism became a religion unto itself in the Labour church movement, founded by the Fabian socialist John Trevor. Raised by Calvinist grandparents, who terrified him with the prospect of eternal damnation, Trevor abandoned religion entirely in 1877, but he needed some sort of faith and eventually became a Unitarian minister. In 1891, inspired by Ben Tillett, he organized the first Labour church; there were fifty-four of them in Great Britain by 1895, when the movement reached its peak. It was a liberal, undoctrinal religion with no distinctive creed beyond the statement "that the Labour Movement is a Religious Movement." Few of the Labour churches survived the First World War,[96] but they and the various other forms of Edwardian labor gospel represented the beginnings of what Richard Hoggart calls the "primary religion" of the British working class in the twentieth century, a "practical Christianity" that emphasizes charity and brotherhood rather than doctrine or churchgoing.[97]

Only Connect

One result of the Edwardian effort to connect the sacred and the secular was a tendency to connect everything else, as if by reflex. The paradoxes of Bernard Shaw, the mystical poetry of W. B. Yeats, the densely interwoven fiction of James Joyce, and the harmonizing philosophy of the Neo-Hegelians all manifest a remarkable talent for lateral thinking—an ability to veer off at right angles to conventional trains of thought, cross the boundaries of discipline and genre, and link ideas that seem to have nothing in common.

With Alfred North Whitehead, this connecting impulse grew out of religious conflicts and found an outlet in mathematics. The son of an Evangelical Anglican clergyman, Whitehead frequently discussed religion and missionary work as a Cambridge undergraduate. He wanted to find "unity in the universe," Bertrand Russell recalled, and "as a young man, he was all but converted to Roman Catholicism by the influence of Cardinal Newman." In the 1890s Whitehead read dozens of theological volumes—and then sold them all to a Cambridge bookstore. Russell describes the Whitehead he knew between 1898 and 1912 as "very definitely and emphatically agnostic," and Whitehead in fact wrote no major work on religion until 1925.[98]

Whitehead's first book was an attempt to restore faith, not in Christ, but in Euclid, who in the nineteenth century had been challenged by the non-Euclidean geometries of Lobachevsky, Bolyai, Gauss, and Riemann. In *A Treatise on Universal Algebra* (1898), Whitehead delineated a new algebra that could serve as the basis of all forms of geometry. "Unity of idea" was the declared aim of that book.

> The ideal of mathematics should be to erect a calculus to facilitate reasoning in connection with every province of thought, or of external experience, in which the succession of thoughts, or of events can be definitely ascertained and precisely stated. So that all serious thought which is not philosophy, or inductive reasoning, or imaginative literature, shall be mathematics developed by means of a calculus.[99]

"In pursuit of that," as Victor Lowe notes, Whitehead "breaks out of boundaries and surprises the professions, not entirely to their pleasure."[100] In 1905 Whitehead attempted a daring leap to physics, suggesting that geometry might provide a unified field theory applicable to all the sciences. Space, time, and matter, which classical science had presumed to be the three irreducible elements of physics, were now further reduced by Whitehead to a single factor: geometric lines of force. "From such a hypothesis the whole electromagnetic and gravitational laws might follow with the utmost simplicity," he assured the Royal Society.[101] Then in 1910, with Bertrand Russell, Whitehead published the first volume of *Principia Mathematica*, which attempted to prove that all pure mathematics could be deduced from logic. Whitehead and Russell described the book as an exhaustive cross-disciplinary effort to enlarge "the scope of mathematics . . . by a backward extension into provinces hitherto abandoned to philosophy."[102]

In all his work Whitehead was obsessed with connections—this may explain why he was attracted to the study of geometry, which he defined as "the investigation of the morphology of nexūs."[103] His was a geometer's universe, in which all things were linked and no thing could enjoy a perfectly independent existence. In 1919 he defined philosophy as the search for "some unifying concept which will set in assigned relationships within itself all that there is for knowledge, for feeling, and for emotion."[104] The unifying vision of Idealism may have influenced Whitehead: he found Hegel unreadable, but he absorbed some Hegelianism from secondary works and from discussions with J. M. E. McTaggart and R. B. Haldane.[105]

Idealism also had an impact on Bernard Shaw via his friend Ernest Belfort Bax. A Marxist and a Hegelian lay philosopher, Bax preached socialism as a new "religion" that would supersede Christianity and effect a "synthesis of human solidarity and human freedom."[106] Shaw credited Bax with being a source of inspiration for *Major Barbara* (1905), which unites the Salvation Army and the munitions industry in a common mission to carry out the will of God. Gilbert Murray told Oliver Lodge that an early version of the play concluded with Barbara bereft of faith, but this ending left Shaw and Murray "dreadfully disappointed. . . . It was necessary, after the failure of the Salvation Army, to invent a new religion for Barbara and Cuzens [*sic*] which would really stand."[107] In the revised final act, they discover a new faith in the paradoxical marriage of religion and the arms industry: "The way of life lies through the factory of death." By uniting the sacred and the profane— "through the raising of hell to heaven and of man to God, through the unveiling of an eternal light in the Valley of The Shadow"—Barbara reconciles guns and gospel. Both are weapons to be grasped and used by the righteous, transcending any crude antithesis of good and evil. "There is no wicked side" of life, Barbara proclaims; "life is all one."[108]

Gilbert Murray, a former Catholic and a future president of the Society for Psychical Research, was written into *Major Barbara* as Adolphus Cusins, a "collector of religions" who is capable of believing in every one of them. Murray found his own version of oneness in a form of pantheism, "a Glory, a thing like Heaven or God, of which one can get glimpses in many different ways—music, poetry, mathematics, heroic conduct &c."[109] There was a great deal of pantheistic nature-worship in

Edwardian literature—in the poetry of John Masefield, in the writings of Edward Thomas, in George Moore's 1905 novel *The Lake*. As a pagan deity immanent in all life, Pan attracted a worshipful Edwardian following. Saki called him "the Father of all the Gods": "Other newer Gods have drawn aside his votaries from time to time, but he is the Nature God to whom all must come back at last."[110] The popular novelist Maurice Hewlett wrote *Pan and the Young Shepherd*, an ersatz Elizabethan verse drama of 1898. Hewlett's father had revolted against his evangelical upbringing and imposed no faith on his children. Most of them turned back to orthodox religion, but Maurice took up pantheism: "The root idea, I suppose, is the oneness of creation—man as a natural force, differing in no essential way from plants and animals. Then God is reduced to the same expression, and He and Man, and the Wind and Weather, Trees, Sheep, Love, Life, Death, Fear, all play their parts out and meet and merge, and mate and mingle."[111]

This quest for unity could ultimately manifest itself in what L. P. Jacks called "undenominational religion." In the face of declining church attendance, religious reformers like Percy Alden and Canon Samuel A. Barnett of Toynbee Hall were urging the various sects to put aside their internecine conflicts. "The hope of religion is not in the dominance of any one denomination, but in a unity to which each is necessary," Barnett declared in the *Hibbert Journal* in 1907.[112] In fact, as Helen Meller has noted, the sectarian infighting of the nineteenth century was muted in the Edwardian period, as denominations drew together in a common effort to win back their working-class following.[113] The God of the future, H. G. Wells predicted in 1905, "will be a synthesis," a being "of an endless variety of aspects, to be expressed by no universal formula nor approved in any uniform manner," but worshiped variously according to "every man's individuality."[114]

Things Fall Apart

Secular religion was a broad, pervasive, and vigorous trend in Edwardian culture, but it would be reckless to conclude that it had become the British national faith. Orthodox forms of Christianity, which sharply distinguished between the sacred and the not sacred, were still being preached by thousands of clergymen and practiced by millions of their parishioners. The Catholic church in particular resisted the tendency to secularize religion. The Jesuit father George Tyrrell tried to work out a Catholic modernism that would accept biblical criticism and balance "authority & liberty, or Catholicism & Protestantism," but he was excommunicated in 1907.[115] As lower-case catholics outside the church, Bishop Gore and G. K. Chesterton were only prepared to carry the quest for oneness so far: both of them denounced the Edwardian slide toward pantheism and pure immanentism.[116]

Even among "advanced" intellectuals, there were some who resisted alluring visions of cosmic harmony. Bertrand Russell could only shake his head at the beautiful metaphysical systems constructed by his friends Alfred North Whitehead and Goldsworthy Lowes Dickinson. He often wounded the latter "by my somewhat brutal statement of unpleasant truths": "To Hell with unity, and artistic serenity, and the insight that perceives the good in other people's Pain—it sickens me." Russell wanted "to treat the religious instinct with profound respect," but he felt compelled "to insist that there is no shred or particle of truth in any of the metaphysics it has suggested."[117] He repudiated the fashionable Idealist philosophy of his day: "The apparent oneness of the world is merely the oneness of what is seen by a single spectator or apprehended by a single soul." Russell devised a philosophy of his own

> called logical atomism or absolute pluralism, because while maintaining that there are many things, it denies that there is a whole composed of those things. . . .
>
> The essence of philosophy as thus conceived is analysis, not synthesis. To build up systems of the world, like Heine's German professor who knit together fragments of life and made an intelligible system out of them, is not, I believe, any more feasible than the discovery of the philosopher's stone.[118]

It was partly to escape the chaos of the material universe that Russell turned his attention to mathematics, the only area of study where he could find absolute harmony, "an ideal world where everything is perfect and yet true."[119]

Both Russell and his colleague G. E. Moore had passed through an Idealist phase in their youth, but by 1903 they had become ruthless skeptics, disdaining overarching syntheses in favor of rigorous scientific analysis of philosophical language and principles. The quotation from Bishop Butler that opens Moore's *Principia Ethica* (1903)—"Everything is what it is, and not another thing"—is a direct repudiation of Edwardian synthetic philosophy, which tried to make everything a part of everything else. Moore criticized the Idealist vision of absolute oneness as the product of muddled thinking and a sloppy vocabulary: "To search for 'unity' and 'system,' at the expense of truth, is not, I take it, the proper business of philosophy, however universally it may have been the practice of philosophers."[120]

By 1914 T. E. Hulme had developed a hard analytical philosophy based on the work of Moore and Russell, but going further than either of them.

> The absolute is invented to reconcile conflicting purposes. But these purposes are necessarily conflicting, even in the nature of Truth itself. It is so absurd to construct an absolute which shall at each moment just manage by artificial gymnastics to reconcile these purposes.
>
> Philosophical syntheses and ethical systems are only possible in arm-chair moments. They are seen to be meaningless as soon as we get into a bus with a dirty baby and a crowd.[121]

The universe, as Hulme perceived it, was an "ash-pit of cinders" without connection or order. Unity could only be attained by imposing artificial rules and coordinates on the chaos, like "a kind of manufactured chess-board laid on a cinder-heap."[122] Hulme therefore demanded the creation of absolute ethical values. He admired Moore and Russell for attempting to build a moral system on the objective ground of logical analysis, but he believed that a more solid basis for ethics could be provided by religion—not the New Theology, which erased the division between the secular and the divine, but a rigidly orthodox and transcendent religion that maintained "an *absolute* division" between the two. Hulme deplored the contemporary trend toward "the elaboration and universal application of the principle of *continuity*," and he urged "the re-establishment of the temper or disposition of mind which can look at a *gap* or chasm without shuddering."[123]

After the First World War, Idealism would be swept aside by the analytical philosophies of Logical Atomism and Logical Positivism, and orthodox Christianity would stage something of a comeback, championed by T. S. Eliot, Ronald Knox, and C. S. Lewis. In such a light, it is tempting to see Moore, Russell, and Hulme as the cutting edge of a wedge that would inexorably split apart the Edwardian synthesis of reason and religion. Historians are now in the habit of saying, with George Dangerfield, that the postwar era began as early as 1910, that "the war hastened everything . . . but it started nothing."[124] This, however, may be reading history backward. If one searches hard enough, it is always possible to find traces of one period in a preceding period, but it does not follow that postwar Britain would have materialized without the war or that Edwardian secular religion was disintegrating before August 1914. T. E. Hulme's only book, *Speculations*, was written before the war but not published until 1924, when T. S. Eliot accurately described it as the product of "the antipodes of the eclectic, tolerant, and democratic mind of the end of the last century."[125] Moore and Russell certainly presented a formidable challenge to the Idealist school, but Neo-Hegelians continued to dominate British academic philosophy right up to the war. In 1914 Russell was still complaining that "the oneness of the world is an almost undiscussed postulate of most metaphysics. 'Reality is not merely one and self-consistent, but is a system of reciprocally determinate parts'—such a statement would pass almost unnoticed as a mere truism."[126]

It should be noted, moreover, that in spite of their hostility to synthetic philosophy, Russell, Moore, and Hulme were all susceptible to other unifying secular faiths. Russell and Moore both embraced a gospel of human relations (discussed in chapter 2), and Hulme briefly found a replacement for religion in the vitalism of Henri Bergson (discussed in chapter 3). The fact that secularized spirituality could infect even its critics goes to show how compelling a movement it was in Edwardian Britain.

Ultimately, the reconciling trends in Edwardian intellectual life were reversed only by the world war and the epidemic of civil strife that followed it. Protracted warfare, as Paul Fussell has noted, tended to fix the minds of combatants and civilians in "binary deadlock": they came to see "simple antithesis everywhere," convinced that the opposing trenches were, as one soldier put it, "peopled by men whose way of thinking was totally and absolutely distinct from our own." Fussell points out that

> the mode of gross dichotomy came to dominate perception and expression elsewhere, encouraging finally what we can call the modern *versus* habit: one thing opposed to another, not with some Hegelian hope of synthesis involving a dissolution of both extremes (that would suggest "a negotiated peace," which is anathema), but with a sense that one of the poles embodies so wicked a deficiency or flaw or perversion that its total submission is called for.[127]

In that atmosphere of extreme polarization, the harmonizing philos-

ophy of the Idealists rapidly lost favor in British universities. It did not
help matters that Idealism had a German pedigree, for the war produced
a hysterical reaction against all aspects of Teutonic culture. From every
side, observed Bernard Shaw, came "frantic denunciations of German
chemistry, German biology, German poetry, German music, German
literature, German philosophy, and even German engineering, as ma-
lignant abominations standing towards British and French chemistry
and so forth in the relation of heaven to hell."[128] R. B. Haldane, whose
army reforms probably saved the Allies from defeat in the opening
weeks of the war, was hounded out of office in 1915 partly because he
had long professed a fondness for Neo-Hegelian philosophy.[129]

As late as the summer of 1915, a young friend of the Haldane family
named Aldous Huxley held to a faith in metaphysical unity that sounds
very much like Idealism.

> One does feel tremendously . . . that one is part of a larger soul, which
> embraces everything. . . . I think the good will probably win in the end—
> though not necessarily, unless the most persistent and tremendous efforts are
> made. . . . I'm not a pessimist, and I think it will be all right. I think we
> shall ultimately work all the disorder into a single principle, which will be
> an Absolute.[130]

After the war, however, Huxley dismissed all of this as a quaint exploded myth cherished only by members of the older generation, like
Rosie Shearwater's father in *Antic Hay* (1923), who used to read the
Hibbert Journal aloud to his family.[131] Now there was no hope of reconciling religion and reason: there was "God as a sense of warmth about the
heart," and then there was "God as 2+2=4," but there were no "bridges
to join the two worlds."[132] Universal discordance is suggested in the
very title of *Point Counter Point* (1927–1928), particularly in the concert
at Lord Tantamount's, playing Bach's Suite in E Minor.

> The parts live their separate lives; they touch, their paths cross, they com-
> bine for a moment to create a seemingly final and perfected harmony, only
> to break apart again. Each is always alone and separate and individual. "I am
> I," asserts the violin; "the world revolves around me." "Round me," calls
> the cello. "Round me," the flute insists. And all are equally right and equally
> wrong; and none of them will listen to the others.[133]

Dissonance is embodied in the structure of the novel, with its several
characters and stories and themes crossing paths randomly and point-

lessly, and never tied together. In contrast, Richard Ellmann has noted the Edwardian fashion of winding novels tightly around a unifying theme or title—*A Room with a View, The Man of Property, The Golden Bowl, The Rainbow, A Portrait of the Artist as a Young Man.*[134] There is nothing in prewar literature that has the fragmentary structure of *The Waste Land* (1922), where T. S. Eliot found that "I can connect/Nothing with nothing."[135] W. B. Yeats, who had searched all his adult life for unity, was overwhelmed by the tidal wave of violence that swept over Europe and Ireland, and in "The Second Coming" he saw that unity spinning apart.

> Turning and turning in the widening gyre
> The falcon cannot hear the falconer;
> Things fall apart; the centre cannot hold;
> Mere anarchy is loosed upon the world,
> The blood-dimmed tide is loosed. . . .[136]

In reaction to that postwar disorder, some writers of the older generation produced secular versions of the Bible: a last great effort at a comprehensive synthesis of the universe. Yeats summed up his occult metaphysics in *A Vision*, written and rewritten continually from 1917 to 1937. In August 1918 H. G. Wells conceived the idea of writing a modern "Bible of Civilization," and by the end of 1919 he had completed *The Outline of History*, a universal record of mankind that became one of his most popular works. Bernard Shaw wrote his "Metabiological Pentateuch," *Back to Methuselah*, between 1918 and 1920, and in 1922 James Joyce began "a history of the world" that would eventually become *Finnegans Wake*. At least some of these secular scriptures, however, were cries in the dark, wishful attempts to find harmony where there was no harmony. Yeats admitted that *A Vision* was "a last act of defence against the chaos of the world," and Shaw acknowledged that he had written *Back to Methuselah* to avoid sinking into "the bottomless pit of an utterly discouraging pessimism."[137]

Alfred North Whitehead, whose son Eric had died in the war, found some solace in an all-embracing "philosophy of organism." He depicted the entire cosmos as a fusion of paired opposites: God became an immanent spiritual ideal interacting with the material universe in an endless creative dialectic.[138] But in *Process and Reality* (1929), Whitehead revealed that he had constructed this system because he could no longer live without some kind of faith.

Religion is an ultimate craving to infuse into the insistent particularity of emotion that non-temporal generality which primarily belongs to conceptual thought alone. In the higher organisms the differences of tempo between the mere emotions and the conceptual experiences produce a life-tedium, unless this supreme fusion has been effected. The two sides of the organism require a reconciliation in which the emotional experiences illustrate a conceptual justification, and conceptual experiences find an emotional illustration.[139]

The war put a terrific strain on the Edwardian synthesis of secular theology. On the one hand, the holocaust completely destroyed the faith of many and accelerated the decline of churchgoing and organized religion. Others, particularly among the bereaved, retreated to a self-deluding belief in life after death, as reflected in the postwar proliferation of phony mediums, in sentimental plays like J. M. Barrie's *Mary Rose* (1920), and in the growth of the spiritualist movement, which enjoyed its greatest popularity in the interwar years.[140] Anxious to comfort grieving families and often themselves, many psychical researchers relaxed their investigative standards: their quest for a scientific religion lapsed into credulous table rapping. When his son Raymond was killed in France, Sir Oliver Lodge abandoned his serious work in physics and devoted the rest of this life to exploring communication with the dead. He claimed to have contacted his son in *Raymond* (1916), a pitiable book by any scientific standard, but one that enjoyed a huge readership.[141] Also in 1916 Arthur Conan Doyle frankly renounced rational religion for faith pure and simple.

In the presence of an agonized world, hearing every day of the deaths of the flower of our race in the first promise of the unfulfilled youth, seeing around one the wives and mothers who had no clear conception whither their loved ones had gone to, I seemed suddenly to see that this subject with which I had so long dallied was not merely a study of a force outside the rules of science, but that it was really something tremendous, a breaking down of the walls between two worlds, a direct undeniable message from beyond, a call of hope and of guidance to the human race at the time of its deepest affliction. The objective side of it ceased to interest, for having made up one's mind that it was true there was an end of the matter. The religious side of it was clearly of infinitely greater importance.[142]

After the war, having abandoned its earlier rigor, the Society for Psychical Research ceased to attract the distinguished intellectuals—the bishops, psychologists, and fellows of the Royal Society—who had flocked to it before 1914.

This postwar reversion to blind faith reveals the weak link in Edwardian secular religion—an unwillingness to let go of old beliefs, a wishful insistence that those beliefs were consonant with new realities. To say that all things are one and that all points of view are compatible is, after all, a neat way of avoiding difficult choices. John Galsworthy could rationalize it all with Panglossian ease—and a touch of self-satire. Every smudge of ugliness, he assured his readers, is "in harmony with Design—a tiny thread on the miraculous quilt." Every injustice "is a little bit of continuity, as perfectly logical an expression of a necessary phase or mood of existence as I myself am." All things good and evil are "fit expressions of the separate moods of a great underlying Mood or Principle, which must be perfectly adjusted, volving and revolving on itself. For if It did not volve and revolve on Itself, It would peter out at one end or the other, and the image of this petering out no man with his mental apparatus can conceive."[143]

Lord Quinton notes that Edwardian Idealism could degenerate into "a kind of edifying eclecticism which argued on idealist principles, not to establish hard and painful truths, but rather to express common beliefs about men and the world in a cheerful, boneless idiom in which all conflicts were ultimately resolved, all apparent set-backs and disasters seen as merely circuitous paths to final perfection." (Quinton specifically blames Edward Caird and his followers, such as J. S. Mackenzie and Sir Henry Jones, for promoting this soft version of Idealism.)[144] Psychical research could provide the same cozy ecumenicism to intelligent, educated men and women who would not deny the facts of science and yet could not face the fact of death and the prospect of a godless universe. Spiritualism pointed toward a new religion far more easygoing than the old Christianity—a Christianity stripped of all its unpleasantness, moral strictures, and demands of faith. There was no clear idea of hell in Oliver Lodge's cosmology, but there was a very English heaven, like a celestial West End club, where the spirits of the dead could order themselves ectoplasmic cigars and whiskey sodas.[145] In psychical research Conan Doyle found an "extraordinarily comforting" religion and a hereafter that kept out bores.

> When once you are convinced of its truth this world holds no terrors for you, and you look into the future unafraid, with no fear of death. It tells of a

really merciful God, whose rewards are immense, and whose judgments are mild; of a new world which contains that work and those pleasures which are most congenial to us, of a gradual evolution from a lowly paradise to the higher ones, and the development of our own natural faculties, of homes and family circles and the reunion of all who love, even of the lowly animal world, with the exclusion of all who jar.[146]

One thing should be said in defense of this Edwardian latitudinarianism: it represented an understandable reaction against the suffocating dogmatism of the nineteenth century. Raymond Williams, John Lester, and Frank Miller Turner have all pointed out the "mechanical" bent of Victorian thought, the habit of fixating on a single idea or ideology. Walter Houghton concluded that,

> by and large, the Victorian mind was rigid. It tended to follow one line of thought, to look at objects from a single point of view, to shut out wide interests. It was marked, in Matthew Arnold's analysis, by a "want of flexibility," an "inaptitude for seeing more than one side of a thing," an "intense energetic absorption in the particular pursuit" it was engaged in.[147]

This was the sort of one-track thinking that Arnold attacked in *Culture and Anarchy*, that John Stuart Mill criticized in his essays on Bentham and Coleridge. The Edwardians may have mixed their science and religion too easily, but in 1852 the Unitarian philosopher James Martineau (who later became the oldest member of A. J. Balfour's Synthetic Society) noted that Victorian theologians and scientists had both trapped themselves in linear chains of logic.

> There is . . . a certain secret affinity of feeling between a Religion which exaggerates the functions and overstrains the validity of an external authority, and a Science which deals only with objective facts, perceived or imagined. . . . Both rest upon *hypotheses*, which it is beyond their province to look into, but after the assumption of which, all room for opinion is shut out by a rigid necessity. *Once get* your infallible book, and (supposing the meaning unambiguous) it settles every matter on which it pronounces; and once allow the first principles and definitions in geometry to express truths and realities, and you can deny nothing afterwards.[148]

Of course, Martineau was exaggerating: as Walter Houghton acknowledged, there were some open-minded Victorians.[149] But there was also an oppressive sectarianism in Victorian politics, religion, and irreligion, and that was what the Edwardian generation revolted against. Virginia Woolf satirized Victorian one-dimensional thinking in *To the Lighthouse* (1927–1928), where Mr. Ramsay treats philosophy like the alphabet, plodding through it letter by letter and always getting stuck at Q. The essential thing, wrote Mrs. Woolf, was to grasp the universe as a whole, to "lump all the letters together in one flash—the way of genius."[150]

2. Personal Relations

The Edwardian urge to reconcile things applied not only to ideas: it extended to people as well. It often took the form of a cult of human relations, which, like so many other movements in Edwardian culture, served as a substitute for a lost religion. Where some post-Victorians searched for new connections between faith and reason, others found the same reassuring sense of connectedness in idealized personal relationships. Like Virginia Woolf, they perceived individuals "to be more than individuals; to be made of many different things in cohesion," and thus they arrived at "a vision of an orderly world."[1] Even those Edwardians who did not see the world as an orderly place could find a refuge from metaphysical chaos in the communion of kindred souls. Religion might be a lie, the existing social order might be corrupt and cruel, but within a circle of close friends all things could be true, just, and beautiful. There were also many social reformers who saw personal relations as a means of overcoming class barriers. They tried to create bonds of friendship between rich and poor—like the Cambridge undergraduate in E. M. Forster's *Howards End* (1910), who meets the clerk Leonard Bast on a train and invites him up to his rooms for coffee. Among the Edwardians, Forster recalled in 1939, personal relations were frequently

> exalted into something political, and it was felt that if they were solved the problems of civilization would be solved too. . . . I remember so well my first visit to India in 1912, when I thought that if the English would only behave more politely to the Indians, the difficulties between the races would be solved. Good manners were to do the trick. I see now how superficial my conclusion was: I was completely ignoring the economic factor for instance. But my mistake is typical of the period. We deified personal relationships and expected them to function outside their appropriate sphere.[2]

Moore and His Apostles

Much of the credit and blame for this Edwardian sanctification of personal relations is commonly assigned to G. E. Moore and his treatise

Principia Ethica. Although Moore criticized Idealist philosophers for seeing oneness everywhere, he shared that unifying predisposition, particularly as it applied to human intimacy. In *Principia Ethica* he proposed a theory of "organic unities," which postulated that the value of a whole can be enhanced by the interconnectedness of its parts. According to this principle, an aesthete and a Grecian urn, each in isolation, are nothing more than an aesthete and a Grecian urn, a simple sum of parts. But an aesthete appreciating a Grecian urn is something far more valuable, and two aesthetes appreciating each other are more valuable still, by virtue of the intimate reciprocal connection between the two. Thus, Moore concludes, "By far the most valuable things, which we know or can imagine, are certain states of consciousness, which may be roughly described as the pleasures of human intercourse and the enjoyment of beautiful objects."[3]

Among his friends in the Bloomsbury Group, Moore was a revered and charismatic figure. Indeed, Quentin Bell has it that of the entire Bloomsbury Group, only Vanessa Bell, Roger Fry, Duncan Grant, and Adrian Stephen were *not* disciples of Moore.[4] But Bloomsbury's fascination with personal relations did not begin with Moore. Well before the publication of *Principia Ethica*, it was a favorite topic of conversation among the Cambridge Apostles, the select philosophical society that included Moore and the men who later became the nucleus of the Bloomsbury Group. Platonic love was the highest ideal of Lowes Dickinson and J. M. E. McTaggart, the two Cambridge dons who were the most influential teachers of Moore and the Bloomsbury Apostles. Far from being inspired by *Principia Ethica*, many of the Apostles (like John Maynard Keynes and Lytton Strachey) only skimmed Moore's hard philosophy and seized upon the twenty-odd pages in the final chapter where Moore discussed—almost as an incidental, illustrative point—the value of human relationships.[5] E. M. Forster always insisted that he had never read *Principia Ethica*, but he was a member of the Apostles and participated enthusiastically in their talks on personal relations, so it is not surprising that he seems to echo Moore on this subject.[6]

Bloomsbury was drawn to the gospel of human relations not so much by G. E. Moore as by the vacuum of post-Victorian skepticism. In a paper read to the Apostles in December 1900, three years before the publication of *Principia Ethica*, Desmond MacCarthy noted a critical change in attitude among educated people and the Apostles in particular over the preceding thirty years. "It seems that we take everything much more *personally* than our predecessors," MacCarthy observed. "It is much more difficult for *us* to feel things in various capacities, from citizenship or membership of the University to membership of the [Apostles]." This, he argued, was a result of living in "a self-conscious analytical age. Intellectual speculation is commoner . . . between friends than it was." Because the Victorian Apostles enjoyed a greater sense of philosophic certainty, they concentrated their energies on practical and worldly affairs. "In proportion to their other aims in life, the state of personal relations *at any particular time* was not so important to them as it it to us. . . . They had their keen interests and therefore their attention was fixed on other things." The nineteenth century had clear standards for judging persons and ideas, but since then "all institutions, the family, state, laws of honour, etc., which have a claim on the individual [have] been asked to produce their warrants, and [have] failed to produce convincing proofs of their authority." Since no other criteria could be trusted any longer, MacCarthy concluded, the Apostles had decided that the only way to measure the worth of a human being was to "trust your personal feelings towards him."[7]

To this extent, Moore's philosophy served as a substitute for religion. The Bloomsbury Group was in revolt against the various faiths of its ancestors, whether they were Quakers (Moore and Fry), Unitarians (the Stracheys and the Trevelyans), Anglican Evangelicals of the Clapham Sect (Forster and the Stephens), or Jews (Leonard Woolf). According to Maynard Keynes, the Edwardian Apostles were generally agnostics, and they hailed the doctrines of *Principia Ethica* "as entirely rational and scientific in character." Leonard Woolf, for example, congratulated Moore for sweeping away the "cobwebs" of theology. The Apostles, wrote Keynes, would have been indignant if anyone had called this philosophy of personal relations a "faith" or a "religion"—and yet, these are precisely the words that Keynes used to describe it. He specifically compared it to English Puritanism, "being chiefly concerned with the salvation of our own souls."[8]

There is consequently a thick haze of religiosity surrounding Bloomsbury writing on personal relationships, as in E. M. Forster's novel *A Room with a View* (1908). It begins, as do all his novels, with two sets of characters in separate social compartments, in this case two tourist parties staying at the same Italian *pensione*. Lucy Honeychurch and her chaperone, Charlotte Bartlett, are far too proper to respond to the overtures of George Emerson and his socialistic, embarrassingly affable father. Emerson Senior is a happy materialist, not in the least bothered by the notion "that all life is perhaps a knot, a tangle, a blemish in the eternal smoothness," that he himself may be nothing more than a chance collection of atoms.

> From far, from eve and morning,
> And yon twelve-winded sky,
> The stuff of life to knit me
> Blew hither: here am I.

But it does bother his son. His secularist upbringing has left him with "an enormous note of interrogation," a painful sense that "things won't fit." Later, a street brawl, in which an Italian is killed, literally drives Lucy into George's arms, and they experience an epiphany, an uncanny sense that they have "crossed some spiritual boundary."[9] In fact, Italy does shake some of the English reserve out of Lucy. She learns to approach strangers openly and to leap over class boundaries "just as you jump into a peasant's olive-yard in the Apennines, and he is glad to see you" (*Room* 171–72).

A religious conflict, however, obstructs a final reconciliation between Lucy and George. The Reverend Cuthbert Eager, a narrow-minded clergyman, delivers a stunning accusation: Mr. Emerson "has practically murdered his wife in the sight of God." The facts of the matter are that George, as a boy, contracted typhoid, and Rev. Eager took advantage of this opening to pry Mrs. Emerson away from atheism. He persuaded her to baptize her son, but Mr. Emerson forbade it, and although George recovered, his mother died, borne down by the consciousness of sin. Bigoted religion and bigoted irreligion, then, are equally implicated in her death. Eager is a blinkered sectarian, but so is Emerson, who can think only of the exploitation of medieval workmen when he views a Florentine church. Giotto's fresco "The Ascension of St. John" is, for Emerson, only a fantastic cartoon of a "fat man in blue . . . shooting into the sky like an air-balloon," but his son can see the element of truth in it—not literal truth, perhaps, but a true expression of religious emotion (*Room* 43–44, 89–90).

As Forster later affirmed in *Howards End*, it is "personal intercourse, and that alone, that ever hints at a personality beyond our daily vision"—and perhaps "will win us immortality."[10] When Emerson finally admits the claims of the spirit and persuades Lucy to marry his son, she experiences a revelation in which all things are spiritualized and harmonized through human love. Suddenly she has "a sense of deities reconciled, a feeling that in gaining the man she loved, she would gain something for the whole world. . . . [Emerson] had robbed the body of its taint . . . ; he had shown her the holiness of direct desire. . . . It was as if he had made her see the whole of everything at once."

In marriage, Lucy and George find connubial "passion requited, love attained. But they were conscious of a love more mysterious than this"—the spiritual love preached by G. E. Moore (*Room* 303–11, 318). In 1911 Forster described himself as an agnostic, but, he added, "I should say that I have more sense of religion now than in the days of my orthodox Xtianity."[11]

Forster's religion of personal relations was a means of synthesizing many partial truths into the Whole Truth. That, in a sentence, is the backbone of each of his prewar novels. A confrontation is set up between antithetical characters, each of them limited and one sided, prevented from coming together by class, nationality, belief, habit, convention, or circumstance. Ultimately a sudden death—a reminder of mortality—breaks down these barriers, and there is a spiritual union of minds as well as of persons. "Only connect" people, and we also connect ideas to form a balanced system of belief.

Virginia Woolf, who did not care either for conventional theology or for her father's chilly unspirituality, found an alternative to both in a Moorean sanctification of human relations. She regarded the Cambridge Apostle as "probably the highest type in the world, and it solves all my religious feelings." Although she was never actually a part of it, she always "felt a kind of reverence for . . . old Cambridge, as we knew it, in the days of 'personal emotions.' "[12] She worshipped G. E. Moore as much as anyone in Bloomsbury did: *Principia Ethica* is directly quoted in *The Voyage Out*,[13] which deals with the same problem of human connections. "Here I sit; there you sit; both, I doubt not, chock-full of the most interesting experiences, ideas, emotions; yet how communicate?" as Richard Dalloway puts the question to Rachel Vinrace (*Voyage* 68).

In church Rachel senses that the answer may lie in a spiritual vision transcending Christianity and every other organized religion: "All round her were people pretending to feel what they did not feel, while somewhere above her floated the idea which they could none of them grasp, which they pretended to grasp, always escaping out of reach, a beautiful idea, an idea like a butterfly." Even the dull clergyman in the pulpit makes a clumsy attempt to define this vision, which is essentially the vision that Virginia Stephen once found in her garden: that our surroundings are a part of us, that everything we do affects everything else in the universe (*Voyage* 228–32). Groping toward the same idea, Terence Hewet mumbles

> "something about bubbles—auras—what d'you call 'em? You can't see my bubble; I can't see yours; all we see of each other is a speck, like the wick in the middle of that flame. The flame goes about with us everywhere; it's not ourselves exactly, but what we feel; the world is . . . people mainly; all kinds of people. . . . And supposing my bubble could run into some one else's bubble—"
>
> "And they both burst?" . . .
>
> "Then—then—then— " pondered Hewet, as if to himself, "it would be an e—nor—mous world." (*Voyage* 109)

Once Rachel grasps this truth, she plunges into that favorite Bloomsbury pastime, a frank discussion "about the relations between the sexes" (*Voyage* 162–63). She hates all "divisions" and "curtains," but when she becomes engaged to Hewet "the divisions disappeared, and it seemed as if the world were once more solid and entire" (*Voyage* 302–3). Even the coldly analytical St. John Hirst comes to realize that "the whole meaning of life" is "love. . . . It seems to me to explain everything." But the love of Rachel and Hewet is "not the love of man for woman"; it is the platonic love of G. E. Moore, "where people knew each other intimately and thus judged each other by what was good, and never quarrelled" (*Voyage* 290, 312–15).

Human relations were essential to Virginia Woolf's sanity, for one symptom of the psychosis that plagued her at intervals all her life was complete dissociation from external reality and other people. In order to maintain these contacts, she wrote volumes of correspondence— "Life would split asunder without letters," she declared in *Jacob's Room* (1922). Bank holidays were an ordeal for her because there were no mail deliveries, and the very fabric of human relations appeared to dissolve. "There should be threads floating in the air, which would merely have to be taken hold of, in order to talk. You would walk about the world like a spider in the middle of a web. In 100 years time, I daresay these psychical people will have made all this apparent—now seen only by the eye of genius."[14]

Edwardian authors and psychical researchers were both searching for some spiritual connection between human beings. Oliver Lodge resorted to telepathic experiments to find a "community of life or family relationship running through all living beings"[15]; Virginia Woolf used the novel and G. E. Moore for the same purpose. A devout Christian is constantly reminded that he is never alone, that God is always with him, that he is a member of a like-minded congregation, that even after death he may be reunited with his loved ones. Victorian and Edwardian unbelievers, however, had to endure the awful metaphysical loneliness of living in a godless universe, as well as the social isolation of living in a country where agnosticism was not yet respectable. An extreme skeptic might begin to doubt the very existence of other people and slip into total solipsism. The late Victorian poet F. W. H. Myers was terrified of death because it meant not only personal annihilation but also eternal separation from those he loved. "Love and religion are thus *continuous*," Myers affirmed, and in the SPR he investigated telepathy "as the scientific or objective expression of what was emotionally and subjectively felt as love."[16] For Myers, love was the source of all unity and order in the universe, "the energy of integration which makes a Cosmos of the Sum of Things."[17] Virginia Woolf embraced a similar metaphysic and even suggested that human intimacy could transcend the grave. Like Mrs. Flushing in *The Voyage Out*, "She refused to relinquish her friends to death." If we are a part of our surroundings, then a part of us lives on in everything and everyone we have touched. Rachel Vinrace dies, but a casual glance at a photograph she once handled recalls her presence vividly, and the very act of dying binds her forever to Terence Hewet.

> They seemed to be thinking together; he seemed to be Rachel as well as himself; and then he listened again; no, she had ceased to breathe. So much the better—this was death. It was nothing; it was to cease to breathe. It was happiness, it was perfect happiness. They now had what they had always wanted to have, the union which had been impossible while they lived. (*Voyage* 353–54, 359, 364)

Among Victorian skeptics, this transference of religious emotion to human relations was anticipated by none other than Leslie Stephen, an early member of the Society for Psychical Research. Julia Duckworth, his second wife and Virginia's mother, served him as "a living image before whom he could pour out the flood of devotion that could find no outlet in religion," to quote Lord Annan. "You must let me tell you that I do and always shall feel for you something which I can only call reverence as well as love," Stephen wrote in one of his courting letters, adding, rather poignantly, "You see, I have not got any saints and you must not be angry if I put you in the place where my saints ought to be."[18] "Though [Leslie Stephen] was an agnostic," Virginia Woolf later recalled, "nobody believed more profoundly in the worth of human relationships."[19] Like Desmond MacCarthy, she understood that loss of belief turns people toward one another: human beings "live in a state of perpetual uncertainty, knowing nothing, leaping from moment to moment as from world to world," and they cluster together for security like cows in a pasture or ships at sea (*Voyage* 127). As Matthew Arnold had lamented back in 1851, the ebbing of "The Sea of Faith" left only one rock to cling to: "Ah, love, let us be true/To one another!"[20]

It was the loneliness of irreligion that led Bertrand Russell to a spiritualized view of human relations. Russell grew up in an atmosphere of dissolving religious belief: his father was an atheist, his elder brother Frank joined the SPR and became a Buddhist, and Bertrand was raised chiefly by a Presbyterian grandmother who became a Unitarian and an uncle who wrote scientific psalms to the universal ether.[21] At age eighteen, after reading Mill's *Autobiography*, Russell became an atheist, and for eleven years he lived comfortably without religion. Then, in 1901, the wife of his friend Alfred North Whitehead was struck down by a prolonged and excruciating heart seizure, and Russell was precipitated into a spiritual crisis by the problem of pain and human isolation.

> She seemed cut off from everyone and everything by walls of agony, and the sense of the solitude of each human soul suddenly overwhelmed me. . . . The ground seemed to give way beneath me. . . . Within five minutes I went through some such reflections as the following: the loneliness of the human soul is unendurable; nothing can penetrate it except the highest intensity of the sort of love that religious teachers have preached; whatever does not spring from this motive is harmful, or at best useless; it follows that war is wrong, that a public school education is abominable, that the use of force is to be deprecated, and that in human relations one should penetrate to the core of that loneliness in each person and speak to that.

After that experience, Russell for a time believed that he had actually established a "sort of mystic" connection with other minds.

> I felt I knew the innermost thoughts of everybody that I met in the street, and though this was, no doubt, a delusion, I did in actual fact find myself in far closer touch than previously with all my friends, and many of my ac-

quaintances. . . . The mystic insight which I then imagined myself to possess has largely faded, and the habit of analysis has reasserted itself. But something of what I thought I saw in that moment has remained always with me.[22]

What remained was a painful consciousness of "the loneliness which I had perceived . . . to be the essential lot of man" (*Autobio.* 152) and a determination to assuage that loneliness through a quasi-religious form of love. That, Russell declared in his autobiography, was one of the great passions of his life.

I have sought love, first, because it brings ecstasy—ecstasy so great that I would often have sacrificed all the rest of my life for a few hours of this joy. I have sought it, next, because it relieves loneliness—that terrible loneliness in which one shivering consciousness looks over the rim of the world into the cold unfathomable lifeless abyss. I have sought it, finally, because in the union of love I have seen, in a mystic miniature, the prefiguring vision of the heaven that saints and poets have imagined. (*Autobio.* 9)

Russell was closely involved with the Bloomsbury Group, but he sharply criticized the Bloomsbury conception of personal relations as precious and cliquish (*Autobio.* 67–68). In fact, Bloomsbury was divided between at least two approaches to friendship—one was philanthropic and all-embracing, a desire to love and be loved by everybody, whereas the other was highly exclusive, limited strictly to a close circle of like-minded souls. In a paper read to the Apostles in 1903, John Sheppard argued that these rival mentalities were inculcated by the two Cambridge colleges from which most of the Apostles were drawn—King's stressed the fellowship of man, but Trinity was far more selective. In most cases the rule applies: Lowes Dickinson, Roger Fry, E. M. Forster, and Sheppard were all King's men, whereas Lytton Strachey, Moore, and Keynes attended Trinity (so had Russell, but his spiritual crisis apparently cured him of his Trinitarian snobbery). Sheppard closed his paper with a few lines from Shelley's *Epipsychidion*—the same lines that Forster would use to open *The Longest Journey* (1907), which contrasts the attitudes of King's and Trinity and comes down firmly on the side of Forster's old school.

I never was attached to that great sect
Whose doctrine is, that each one should elect
Out of the world a mistress or a friend,
And all the rest, though fair or wise, commend

To cold oblivion, though it is in the code
Of modern morals, and the beaten road
Which those poor slaves with weary footsteps tread,
Who travel to their homes among the dead
By the broad highway of the world, and so
With one chained friend, perhaps a jealous foe,
The dreariest and the longest journey go.[23]

Hanging Together

At a time of religious uncertainty, the craft of the novel could itself be a means of creating truth, oneness, and comradeship. "Art is the one form of human energy in the whole world, which really works for union, and destroys the barriers between man and man," wrote John Galsworthy. "It is the continual, unconscious replacement, however fleeting, of oneself by another; the real cement of human life."[24] Joseph Conrad, in his preface to *The Nigger of the "Narcissus"* (1897), defined the novel as "a single-minded attempt to render the highest kind of justice to the visible universe, by bringing to light the truth, manifold and one, underlying its every aspect." This truth is absolutely permanent, proof against "the changing wisdom of successive generations [that] discards ideas, questions facts, demolishes theories," for the novelist appeals to man's timeless need for community.

> He speaks . . . to the latent feeling of fellowship with all creation—and to the subtle but invincible conviction of solidarity that knits together the loneliness of innumerable hearts, to the solidarity in dreams, in joy, in sorrow, in aspirations, in illusions, in hope, in fear, which binds men to each other, which binds together all humanity—the dead to the living and the living to the unborn.[25]

More than any native-born English author, Conrad was oppressed by the intellectual disintegration of the late nineteenth century—by Darwinism, by the threat of anarchism (reflected in *The Secret Agent*, 1907), and by the Decadent movement in literature. He descended for a time into the sort of nihilism that torments and immobilizes Axel Heyst in *Victory* (1914). Conrad's ideological parentage is personified in Heyst's father, who stands for all the dissolving ideas of the late Victorian period—the gospel of "universal nothingness," the "contemptuous, inflexible negation of all effort."[26]

That spiritual rootlessness was aggravated by physical loneliness.

Conrad was a Polish expatriate and a former merchant seaman pursuing the most solitary of professions, that of an author writing in a foreign language. His letters reveal the isolation and uncertainty he suffered as he struggled with the manuscript of *Lord Jim* (1900). "It seems to me I am looking at the rush and recoil of the waves at the foot of a cliff," he wrote, recalling an image out of "Dover Beach": "I am like a man who has lost his gods." He felt dissociated from reality and other people, a "desolate Shade" wandering in a fictional world "peopled by shadows." In his new novel, he protested, "every image floats vaguely in a sea of doubt . . . unrelated to anything in heaven and everything under heaven is impalpable to the touch like shapes of mist." He labored on, "solitary as a mole . . . without ever arriving at seeing anything clearly."[27]

What Conrad ultimately arrived at was a novel in which no individual has an identity except in relation to other individuals. When Jim commits "a breach of faith with the community of mankind" by abandoning the *Patna*, he loses all sense of self. For a time he is forced to endure the loneliness that Conrad describes as "a hard and absolute condition of existence; the envelope of flesh and blood on which our eyes are fixed melts before the outstretched hand, and there remains only the capricious, unconsolable, and elusive spirit that no eye can follow, no hand can grasp."[28] Jim recovers his identity by committing himself to the natives of Patusan, but as their ruler he becomes increasingly aloof and exalted. He may "love the land and the people," but only "with a contemptuous tenderness" (*Jim* 248). He still thinks of himself as European and superior, and Gentleman Brown uses that opening to seduce Jim away from his flock: "You have been white once, for all your tall talk of this being your own people and you being one with them. Are you?" (*Jim* 381). Jim pressures the natives into releasing Brown, who reciprocates by murdering the son of the local chieftain. Once again Jim has betrayed his community, once again he finds "Loneliness . . . closing in on him," but this time he refuses to abandon his post. Rather than endure another term of exile, he gives himself up to his people to be killed. This is not an act of self-obliteration but an assertion of Jim's "exalted egoism": he affirms his identity by binding and sacrificing himself to others (*Jim* chap. 45).

By giving up her life for Axel Heyst, Lena will find her own sense of self in Conrad's *Victory*. Heyst is "a man of universal scorn and unbelief," and he is consequently "the most detached of creatures in this earthly captivity," living virtually alone on a desolate island. Once, purely as a whim, he saved a man's life and was disconcerted to find that he had "created for myself a tie. . . . One gets attached in a way to people one has done something for." He creates a much deeper tie when he takes Lena under his protection, and in doing so he confirms his own identity: "That human being so near and still so strange, gave him a greater sense of his own reality than he had ever known in all his life."[29] Conrad here asserts what the Idealist philosophers Edward Caird and James Ward called the "social character of self-consciousness."

> It may be truly said that we find ourselves in others before we find ourselves in ourselves, and that the full consciousness of self comes only through the consciousness of beings without us who are also selves. Self-consciousness in one is kindled by self-consciousness in another, and a social community of life is presupposed in our first consciousness of ourselves as individual persons. It is true, indeed, that in his first return upon self, the individual is conscious rather of opposition to, than of community with, the other selves to whom he finds himself in relation. . . . But we should not be misled by self-seeking and self-will, which are the first manifestations of selfhood, so as to forget that the individual's consciousness of himself as an independent self *is* essentially a return upon self from the consciousness of others which it implies.[30]

"We exist only in so far as we hang together"—the very structure of *Lord Jim* embodies that message. We know nothing about Jim except what other characters tell us: "After all," Marlow reminds us, "it is only through me that he exists for you." In Conrad's tropical backwaters, secondhand news could be the only connection between friends, and it is out of such testimony that *Lord Jim* is constructed. Without human contacts, Conrad's characters inexorably slip into a ghostly solipsism. In Patusan, "thinking . . . of the living who [are] buried in remote places out of the knowledge of mankind," Marlow allows "the sense of utter solitude to get hold of me so completely that all I had lately seen, and all I had heard, and the very human speech itself, seemed to have passed away out of existence, living only for a while longer in my memory, as though I had been the last of mankind" (*Jim* 223–24, 323). Jim realizes that the only antidote to this radical nihilism is connection with others, and that is why he stays with the people of Patusan: "I must go on, go on for ever holding up my end, to feel sure that nothing can touch me. I must stick to their belief in me to feel safe and to . . . keep in touch with . . . those whom, perhaps, I shall never see any more" (*Jim* 334).

In a similar way, Henry James would use the novel to restore human relations and provide a replacement for religion. James's father had passed through a crisis of faith and found comfort in Swedenborgianism, but he imposed no theological dogma on his children. They were vaguely told to partake of all faiths, so young Henry found an object of worship in European civilization. Religion as such interested him mainly as a social force, a source of order, continuity, and standards. He was uncomfortable in American society because he felt it lacked those standards, but Europe had its art, its culture, its traditions, its antiquity, and for James these were absolutes as certain as any religion. In the 1880s, he was somewhat disturbed to find this civilization assaulted by socialists, Irish nationalists, and French "decadents," but he was confident that it would be proof against all of them.[31] That optimism is proclaimed in *The Princess Casamassima* (1886), in which an anarchist workingman, sent to assassinate an aristocrat, is overcome by the splendor of Paris and Venice—"the monuments and treasures of art, the great palaces and properties, the conquests of learning and taste, the general fabric of civilization as we know it, based if you will upon all the despotisms, the cruelties, the exclusions, the monopolies and the rapacities of the past." He ultimately renounces his mission to bring down society, filled with "the sense of the wonderful, precious things it had produced, of the fabric of beauty and power it had raised."[32]

On the evening of 5 January 1895, James saw that fabric ripped apart. This was the opening night of his play *Guy Domville*, an ill-conceived bid for popular success, peopled with impossibly poised characters speaking overpolished dialogue. The performance was politely applauded by the literati in the stalls; but when James appeared to take his bows, the gallery let loose with an explosion of abuse and jeered him off the stage. The sensitive author was shattered by the experience, and he endured a period of deep depression. His father and his brother William had both suffered debilitating spiritual crises before him, and now, James realized, he was experiencing a horrifying loss of faith in his religion of culture.

Around 1895 many European intellectuals perceived the growth of a new type of rabble, irrational and destructive, mobilized by the yellow press, eager to trample on civilization. Like Gustave Le Bon in France and Graham Wallas in England, James had come face to face with "The Crowd," and now he saw it everywhere, invading the walled garden of European culture. American tourists on packaged tours were overrunning the continent, hooligans were persecuting Oscar Wilde and Captain Dreyfus, and mob jingoism flared up during the Venezuela crisis (1895–1896), the Spanish-American War (1898), and the Boer War (1899). The popular press, the decadence of fin-de-siècle Paris, the garishness of Victoria's Diamond Jubilee, the vulgarity of Edward VII—all of them were reviled by James as products of a mass-market culture: "The machinery of insistence and reverberation—the newspaper deluge and uproar—deflowers and destroys and maddens."[33]

Living in such a world, James felt unbearably isolated. As an expatriate novelist, he had chosen to lead a solitary and rootless life, carefully avoiding most intimate relationships. He had no one to fall back on after the fiasco of *Guy Domville*, which, he wrote, left him utterly "homeless." Against "*the essential loneliness of my life*," James now sent "the deep counterminings of art" to rebuild a network of social and cultural connections. He broke out of his isolation by constructing novels out of a framework of human relations, in particular the "great relation" of man and woman which, in a decaying culture, he looked to as a source of "constant world renewal." He now based his novels on scenarios in which he plotted out the web of relationships uniting the cast of characters. James finally arrived at the "organic" novel, in which everything is "a sort of indistinguishable part of everything else." The human relations within the tale are the warp and woof of that fabric, crossing and weaving to reveal the story and the interactions among the characters.[34] Only by conveying the story to the reader "in as many ways and on as many sides" as possible, wrote James, can "we enable him to pick and choose and compare and know, enable him to arrive at any sort of synthesis that isn't, through all its superficialities and vacancies, a base and illusive humbug."[35]

The Ambassadors (1903) is a story that Lambert Strether pieces together from several fragmentary versions offered by other characters. He comes to Europe "to find out *all*"; he finds "too many connexions missing"; so he collects and arranges different points of view until "it hung beautifully together."[36] The novel begins on a note of human isolation—Strether's wife and child are dead, Waymarsh is separated from his wife, Chad and his mother are an ocean apart in terms of geography and mentality. But immediately after his arrival in Europe,

Strether begins making connections, first of all with his escort, Maria Gostrey. He breaks out of his long dependence on Mrs. Newsome and builds a circle of human contacts, rejuvenated by "the lives, the conditions, the feelings of other persons" (*Ambass.* 22:51). James worshipped personal relations much as G. E. Moore did—as an ultimate but indefinable Good that could only be understood intuitively. "A personal relation," wrote James, "was a relation only so long as people either perfectly understood or, better still, did n't care if they did n't" (*Ambass.* 21:141). When Strether meets Madame de Vionnet at the Notre Dame, he realizes that their friendship affords her some of the consolations of religion.

> Help, strength, peace, a sublime support—she had n't found so much of these things as that the amount would n't be sensibly greater for any scrap his appearance of faith in her might enable her to feel in her hand. Every little, in a long strain, helped, and if he happened to affect her as a firm object she could hold on by, he would n't jerk himself out of her reach. People in difficulties held on by what was nearest, and he was perhaps after all not further off than sources of comfort more abstract. (*Ambass.* 22:11)

Afterwards they retire to a cafe, which performs much the same function as the cathedral: it is "a place of pilgrimage for the knowing," where people can commune together. James's treatment of human intimacy was, in fact, almost too spiritual for this world. A relation "can't be vulgar or coarse," Strether nervously insists. It has to be a "virtuous attachment," "unassailably innocent," completely "disinterested." There must be "nothing in it for himself," no carnal or mercenary motives. For Strether, that eliminates Madame de Vionnet, Mrs. Newsome, and Miss Gostrey. His conscience finally compels him to renounce all the connections he has made, and he ends the novel impeccably "right," but alone (*Ambass.* ibid.; 21:180–82, 280; 22:10, 60, 326).

The Organic Society

While some Edwardians were preaching intimacy between individuals, others were working for a broader version of that ideal. They wanted to make the whole British nation—perhaps even the whole of humanity—an "organic" community. It is said that Virginia Woolf cared nothing for politics, but this was one political ideology with which she could sympathize. Richard Dalloway sums up that philosophy "in one word—Unity"—and he practices it by attending both Oxford and Cambridge. "A human being," he argues,

> is not a set of compartments, but an organism. . . . Conceive the world as a whole . . . ; conceive the state as a complicated machine; we citizens are parts of that machine; some fulfil more important duties; others (perhaps I am one of them) serve only to connect some obscure parts of the mechanism, concealed from the public eye. Yet if the meanest screw fails in its task, the proper working of the whole is imperilled. (*Voyage* 64–68)

"We are members one of another": Bernard Shaw quoted from the Bible to express that ideal, and William Morris put it in sacramental language: "Fellowship is heaven and lack of fellowship is hell: fellowship is life and lack of fellowship is death: and the deeds that ye do upon the earth, it is for fellowship's sake that ye do them."[37]

The idea of an organic society did not begin with the Edwardians. In *Culture and Society* Raymond Williams traces a long succession of nineteenth-century writers who protested the social atomization, the loosening of traditional loyalties and responsibilities, brought on by laissez-faire industrialism—Robert Southey, Robert Owen, Coleridge, Carlyle, John Stuart Mill, Thomas and Matthew Arnold, Dickens, Disraeli, Charles Kingsley, F. D. Maurice, and A. W. Pugin. Each of these men saw the problem clearly enough, but as Williams notes, none of them had a practical plan for recovering a sense of community. Some suggested that it might be created by an enlightened intellectual elite, by the sort of men that they imagined themselves to be—a "clerisy" (Coleridge), an "organic Literary Class" (Carlyle), a progressive aristocracy (Disraeli and Kingsley), or simply those rare individuals, found in every class, who possessed what Matthew Arnold called "Culture." But what this elite would *do* to create an organic society was never made clear. The clerisy was conceived as a class isolated from the everyday world, a caste of mandarins who, simply by maintaining high cultural standards, would somehow regenerate society without dirtying their hands in the task of social reform.[38]

Toward the end of the century, however, thousands of educated men and women undertook a practical personal commitment to "fellowship." In an effort to bridge class divisions, they went to live and work in the slums of Britain. They too were seeking to replace one of the blessings of religion: to restore the social unity once provided by the national church. As one contributor to Mudie-Smith's religious survey observed, urbanization was a "disintegrating process." Workers had been uprooted from rural England and dumped in the factory districts, where they lost touch with the churches and were segregated from the rest of society. What was needed were "relations between diverse classes . . . brotherhood—an immense trust in the value of human contact, as such. . . . There we find a reverence for man which is the truest living expression of man's reverence for God."[39]

T. H. Green, who had united classes in a common bond of "citizenship," provided a philosophical basis for this ideal, which found expression in the settlement house movement. Green was a close friend of Arnold Toynbee, who inspired the first settlement house, Toynbee Hall, opened in 1885. Mrs. Humphry Ward popularized Green's "secular religion" in her best-selling novel *Robert Elsmere* (1888) and then put it into practice by helping to found the Passmore Edwards Settlement in 1896. By 1913 twenty-seven settlements had been planted in the poor districts of London, including Oxford House (High Church), Bermondsey (Methodist), and the Women's University Settlement in Southwark. Middle-class students took up residence in the settlements for a year or more and provided a range of social services: health care, kindergartens, child-care classes, legal aid, lectures, libraries, concerts, labor exchanges, and recreational and athletic facilities.

Canon Samuel Barnett, the first warden of Toynbee Hall, emphasized that the most important objective of that institution was to promote "friendship" with the poor. "Many have been the schemes of reform I have known," he declared, "but, out of eleven years' experience, I would say that none touches the root of the evil which does not *bring helper and helped into friendly relation.*"[40] The various settlements, wrote Charles Booth in 1902, had "a constant community of aim found in this underlying idea of neighbourliness—the 'making of friendships' which is sometimes spoken of as the fundamental idea of all Settlements alike."[41]

That idea was essentially a transmuted form of religion. Of the 80 settlement workers who took up residence at Toynbee Hall between 1884 and 1894, at least 17 were or became clergymen. In contrast, only 2 of the 129 residents who served between 1895 and 1914 pursued careers in the church, but many among that latter cohort had strong religious motives in taking up settlement work.[42] Charles Booth reported that although the settlements avoided sectarian proselytizing, "most of the residents are religiously-minded men, and if many of them do not attend any place of worship, yet must the self-sacrificing work they do, and the spirit in which it is done, be recognised as a proof of the most real religion and a definite witness to God."[43] C. F. G. Masterman had planned to become an Anglican priest until he matriculated at Cambridge, where his scientific studies clashed with his Evangelical upbringing. He worked briefly with F. W. H. Myers and the Society for Psychical Research, but in social work Masterman found a more satisfying answer to his religious doubts. One of his classmates at Christ's College recalled that, over tea, he talked enthusiastically of organizing "a monastic order . . . for the amelioration of the world." Masterman's work with the Cambridge House settlement in Camberwell did not completely restore his old faith and he never took orders, but for the rest of his life he practiced a High Church social gospel, writing "secular sermons" on the problems of urban poverty.[44] "Religion underlies all," Charles Booth wrote of the settlement movement. "Who can doubt it? But it remains at the bottom. No creed is avowed, no propaganda attempted."[45]

By 1913 universities and religious groups had organized forty-six settlements throughout the United Kingdom, with a total of at least 460 residents (the majority of them women) and 1,744 nonresident workers. In London alone, the settlements were estimated to have reached 100,000 working people.[46] In 1902 Charles Booth reported that Toynbee Hall had exerted a great influence on the training of schoolteachers, reform of local government, poor-law administration, and charity organization. He particularly commended the Women's University Settlement as an unsurpassed training school for social workers and teachers.[47]

Many of the students who passed through the settlements in the 1880s and 1890s had, by the Edwardian period, attained positions of power. From that point of leverage, they were able to redirect public policy and permeate the British ruling class with the gospel of fellowship. Among newspaper editors, J. A. Spender of the *Westminister Gazette* had been a Toynbee resident and E. T. Cook of the *Daily News* served on its governing council. Together with A. G. Gardiner (*Daily News*), H. W. Massingham (*Daily Chronicle* and the *Nation*), and Fabian Ware (*Morning Post*), they staffed their papers with a number of Toynbee alumni. Also associated with the settlement were two innovative administrators at the Board of Trade, Herbert Llewellyn Smith and Ernest Aves, and several important educational reformers: Robert Morant, G. L. Bruce, Cyril Jackson, Bolton King, Arthur Acland, Sir John Gorst, and Michael Sadler. Two Toynbee men, Captain John Sinclair and Vaughan Nash, exercised quiet but commanding influence in the Liberal Party, serving consecutively as private secretaries to Campbell-Bannerman and Asquith. W. H. Beveridge, John Murray MacDonald, R. H. Tawney, J. A. Salter, Clement Attlee, and Gerald Shove of the Bloomsbury Group were among the many notable social reformers who worked at Toynbee Hall. Prominent supporters of the settlement included Lord Milner, Beatrice Webb, Augustine Birrell, Austen Chamberlain, Graham Wallas, Sydney Oliver, Mrs. Charles Darwin, C. S. Loch, J. W. Mackail, Alfred Marshall, Stanton Coit, Roger Fry, St. Loe Strachey, L. T. Hobhouse, Anthony Hope Hawkins, H. W. Nevinson, Arthur Henderson, James Bryce, and (among university dons) J. R. Seeley, Gilbert Murray, A. C. Bradley, Sidney Ball, and R. G. Tatton. Frederick Rogers (the union organizer), J. M. Dent (publisher of Everyman's Library), and Albert Mansbridge (founder of the Workers' Educational Association) also participated in the Toynbee experiment. The settlement made its influence felt by conducting seminars for civil servants and taking Liberal reformers like Lloyd George, John Galsworthy, and C. P. Trevelyan on eye-opening tours of the East End.[48]

This list conveys some idea of the impact of a single settlement on Edwardian opinion. One should also take into account the influence of the polytechnics, founded not only to provide technical instruction but also to bring university-bred instructors into personal contact with working-class students. The polytechnics were launched at about the same time as the settlements, and by 1902 they had a combined enrollment of fifty thousand in London alone.[49] The settlements and polytechnics were all part of what Helen Meller has described as a broad middle-class Edwardian movement to reach out to the poor and provide them with cultural and recreational facilities, a movement based on the principle that all English people shared a common "social citizenship" and were therefore entitled to common social services.[50]

This development reflected a crucial change in attitude toward the poor. Victorian charity was essentially paternalistic, something that the affluent voluntarily bestowed on the "lower orders." The Edwardian middle class treated the poor more as fellows, to be aided not as mendicants but as citizens enjoying a right to a share of the public wealth. Former settlement workers like C. F. G. Masterman and William Beveridge played a central role in drafting the welfare legislation of 1906–1911, which was an unprecedented affirmation of "fellowship" in national social policy. In providing old age pensions, unemployment insurance, and national health insurance, the central government undertook for the first time to make transfer payments to the poor as a right of citizenship, without requiring a means test or making a pauper of the recipient. The Victorians wrote and talked a great deal about the organic society, but the Edwardians did something concrete to bring it closer to reality.

T. H. Green's philosophy of social unity also inspired the Edwardian movement for imperial federation. Green believed that the state was destined not only to assume greater responsibility for its citizens but also to extend citizenship to a broader community. Man's circle of loyalties had continually expanded through history, from family to tribe to city to nation-state, and the trend pointed toward still larger units of government, culminating in "a universal human fellowship."[51] By 1910 a group of young civil administrators who had worked under Lord Milner in South Africa, led by Lionel Curtis and Philip Kerr, had launched the Round Table, a study group that advocated a federal union of the British dominions. Many of the founding members had worked in university settlements—"government by Toynbee" was how they characterized their administrative methods in South Africa—and they were deeply influenced by Green's Idealism. Having merged English and Boer states into the Union of South Africa, they set out to transform the entire British Empire into a "commonwealth of nations." Like Green, the Round Table was careful to avoid the totalitarian tendencies of Hegel: the commonwealth would be a voluntary union of the peoples of the British Empire, in the best traditions of English liberty.[52]

The Christian Social Union also drew on Green's broad conception of citizenship. Although he was an opponent of the Broad Churchmen, Charles Gore proposed to bring "men of all races and classes" into the Anglican church by practicing "toleration in theology, ritual, etc., on all matters which do not touch the actual basis of . . . faith."[53] Many CSU men, like Henry Scott Holland (a founder of Oxford House) and C. F. G. Masterman, were active in the settlement house movement. In 1901 Masterman described the class-segregated London slums as "the ghetto"—he may well have been the first to give the term its twentieth-century meaning—and he warned that "isolated effort after material satisfaction [was] tearing individuals and classes apart, and breaking up the organism into an aggregation of isolated atoms." If only there were "more living intercommunication of class and class," Masterman declared, "the polarisation of society into those who get and those who lack . . . would collapse before the determination that all may be one; the calls of a thousand conflicting sects would merge harmoniously into a universal fellowship 'wide as human life and deep as human need.' "54

Some reformers looked back to the medieval guilds for a model of the organic society. C. R. Ashbee's Guild of Handicraft was closely linked with Toynbee Hall, where Ashbee had once lived as a resident. Like the settlement, the guild was designed to bring educated men into contact with East End workers, in this case through common membership in a cooperative workshop. "Comradeship came with Craftsmanship," as Ashbee recalled in his memoirs. "Unless human intimacies were established all this philanthropizing was but a poking and prying into other people's lives, barren statistics, wasted work."55 "Industrialism is the great solvent that has loosed all existing bonds," he proclaimed in 1908, "and *we need bonds to build up a civilized life once again.*"56 Will Brangwen, in D. H. Lawrence's novel *The Rainbow* (1915), teaches handicraft classes for the same reason: "to be unanimous with the whole of purposive mankind."57

Guild socialism, as formulated by A. J. Penty in 1904, was based on the organic social philosophies of Carlyle, Arnold, Ruskin, Morris, and Edward Carpenter. Penty aimed to promote human fellowship by reducing division of labor, replacing the "cash nexus" with a "personal nexus," and uniting artist, worker, and capitalist in the person of the self-employed craftsman. He proposed that architects be recruited from the ranks of construction workers and trained on the building site, in order to make architecture once again the "great co-operative" enterprise that had built the medieval cathedrals. Penty admired medieval society because it was united by the Church, the guilds, and a common aesthetic vernacular: by laying down strict artistic conventions, the medieval Church made sure that art could be appreciated by all the people, not just an elite of educated aesthetes.58

Another guild socialist, Father J. N. Figgis, drew on the legal history of F. W. Maitland to argue that Western political society had never been a simple field of conflict between individuals and the state, as liberals made it out to be, but rather a "pluralistic" association of groups (families, boroughs, guilds, universities, churches), each with its own special prerogatives and responsibilities. Guild socialism would reunite these groups in an organic corporate state, an idea very attractive to Anglican medievalists. Figgis called for a truly "Catholic Church . . . united by Common Worship, and bound by the one universal tie of love, [in which] there are no barriers of sex or race or age or circumstance." Stewart Headlam emphasized the same principle of religious fellowship when he declared that all participants in Holy Communion were literally "Holy Communists," "pledging to be sharers of their wealth." For Headlam, the word *Mass* implied that all Christians took part in the same essential service, regardless of superficial sectarian differences. The motto of the guild socialists, taken from Ecclesiastes, made no mention of equality (a notable omission for a socialist organization), but it did look forward to an organic society based on a secular religion of craftsmanship: "They shall maintain the fabric of the world, and in the handiwork of their craft is their prayer."[59]

The quest for fellowship carried the sculptor Eric Gill all the way from atheism to Roman Catholicism. In 1899 he began work as an apprentice architect in Westminster, and he shortly became a secularist, a Fabian, and an aesthetic socialist in the mold of Ruskin and Morris, more concerned with comradeship than equality. Gill's employer was the architect to the ecclesiastical commissioners of the Church of England, and his fellow apprentices introduced him to the idea that great art can only arise as a collective expression of a common religion. Later, Gill assimilated the same lesson from William R. Lethaby and Ananda K. Coomaraswami, two leading figures in the Arts and Crafts movement. Coomaraswami pointed to the temples of India and the cathedrals of medieval Europe as the highest examples of collective religious art. "The greatest art is never one man deep, but a thousand men deep," he proclaimed. "It is the creation of a race, unified by a profound impulse." By December 1910 Gill had a vision of a new religion "so splendid and all-embracing that the hierarchy to which it will give birth, uniting within itself the artist and the priest, will supplant and utterly destroy our present commercial age." In April 1911 he tried to bring Augustus John, Jacob Epstein, and Will Rothenstein into an artist's collective, which was supposed to "form the nucleus of a larger and finer cooperation than any that existed, or had existed, since the decline of the Roman Church." By January 1912 Gill was approaching the conclusion that the Roman church itself might serve as a world government. He was attracted to Catholicism not as a theology (he airily dismissed the whole question of miracles as a bore) but as a force for social unity. His conversion in February 1913 was, he said, "a political matter"; he saw the Church as a means of creating what he called "the unanimous society."[60]

Some Edwardians, particularly in the academic world, found that unanimity in a type of ideal intellectual community, like that invented by Henry James in his 1898 story "The Great Good Place." The classicists Goldsworthy Lowes Dickinson, Gilbert Murray, and Graham Wallas all constructed Aristotelian utopias based on a nostalgia for the ancient Greek polis. For Wallas, the son of an Anglican minister, this polity clearly filled a religious vacuum. Wallas read Darwin and lost his faith shortly after entering Oxford in 1877, and for the rest of his life he was, as Harold Laski characterized him, "a bishop *manqué.*" Wallas's religious impulses found an outlet in his work with Toynbee Hall and his vision of an organic society, which would unite science, religion, and fellowship in a common civic creed. He admired the Japanese because he believed they had accomplished this three-way synthesis; later, for the same reason, he became interested in the Zionist movement. He hoped that these national faiths would eventually broaden out into a "world-religion," which would be the spiritual foundation of a world state. He endorsed the trade union movement for promoting comradeship among workers, but he opposed guild socialism, fearing that it would exacerbate conflict between classes and occupational groups. Wallas was a teacher and friend of A. E. Zimmern, whose book *The Greek Commonwealth* (1911) was one source of the British Commonwealth idea developed by the Round Table.[61]

Lowes Dickinson believed that the modern world had produced one community that achieved the perfect fellowship of the polis—Cambridge. He communicated his affection for the university to his students, including the young Apostles and Bloomsbury people who came under his tutelage. One of them, E. M. Forster, extolled Cambridge as the place where all things connect.

> Body and spirit, reason and emotion, work and play, architecture and scenery, laughter and seriousness, life and art—these pairs which are elsewhere contrasted were there fused into one. People and books reinforced one another, intelligence joined hands with affection, speculation became a passion, and discussion was made profound by love. When Goldie speaks of this magic fusion, he illumines more careers than his own. . . . The old dry little upper-class notion of an Alma Mater vanishes, and the University becomes for a moment universal.[62]

Rudyard Kipling found his own version of universality in the Indian Raj. As a Freemason, Kipling took pride in belonging to lodges that had Hindus, Moslems, Jews, and Englishmen as members.[63] In the India of *Kim* (1901), the Grand Trunk Road and the crowded railway trains are social solvents, throwing together people of all castes, colors, classes, and faiths. The heroes of the novel are the Orientalists and ethnologists who move effortlessly across cultural boundaries and perceive the anthropological similarities among various religions. Kipling particularly admired Roman Catholics for their rapport with Eastern faiths. When Kim talks of searching for a river that washes away sin, the Anglican chaplain Bennett hears only "gross blasphemy." But his Catholic colleague is more catholic (he dislikes the parochial qualifier "Roman"), and he sees the affinity with baptism. Kim, on his part, understands that the Virgin Mary is "one with Bibi Miriam" of the Mohammedans, and he receives a Catholic education paid for by a Buddhist lama.[64] The secret to overcoming the thousand social and religious barriers that divide Indians is to be a Briton (or Irishman) born in India—like Kim, like Kipling himself.

Kipling had already taught an analogous lesson in his two *Jungle Books* (1894, 1895), where Mowgli, a boy raised among animals, illustrates the cousinhood of men and beasts. Of course, Kipling was not arguing for equality between humans and lesser breeds, any more than he believed in racial equality, but some Edwardians were prepared to extend the principle of fellowship even unto the animal kingdom. Discussing the "very definite and complete Pantheism" of the ancient Stoics before the South Place Ethical Congregation in 1915, Gilbert Murray, a vegetarian, proclaimed that

> all the world is working together. It is all one living world, with one soul through it. And, as a matter of fact, no single part of it can either rejoice or suffer without the rest being affected. The man who does not see that the good of every living creature is his good, the hurt of every living creature his hurt, is one who willfully makes himself a kind of outlaw or exile: he is blind, or a fool.[65]

Henry Salt, a member of the Fabian Society and the Fellowship of the New Life, organized the Humanitarian League in 1891 to agitate against vivisection, meat eating, and cruelty to animals. From reading Darwin, Salt had concluded that man is an animal like any other, with no special divinely ordained place in the universe. Salt therefore advocated kindness to animals not as an act of charity bestowed on a lower order of beings, as earlier humanitarians had done, but as the right of man's fellow creatures. He attracted the support of Thomas Hardy, Edward Carpenter, John Galsworthy, Keir Hardie, Annie Besant, the nature writer W. H. Hudson, Sydney Olivier, Mahatma Gandhi, and Bernard Shaw. Hardy pitied the fate of dumb (and human) animals in a predatory Darwinian universe—in 1895 he offered the pig-butchering scene in *Jude the Obscure* to an animal rights journal for use in its propaganda[66]—and he immediately grasped Salt's argument.

> Few people seem to perceive that the most far-reaching consequence of the establishment of the common origin of the species is ethical; that it logically involved a readjustment of altruistic morals, by enlarging, as a necessity of rightness, the application of what has been called "the Golden Rule" from the area of mere mankind to that of the whole animal kingdom. While man was deemed to be a creation apart from all other creations, a secondary or tertiary morality was considered good enough to practise toward the "inferior" races.[67]

In pursuit of universal fellowship, Salt took up socialism, the rights of colored peoples, and Esperanto. Edward Carpenter, likewise, supported the rights of women, animals, workers, and homosexuals out of "the intense *consciousness* (not conviction merely) of the oneness of all life." Carpenter identified this consciousness (which he derived from Walt Whitman and the *Bhagavad Gita*) as the fundamental impulse behind all religions, and he spent his life searching for "a great new synthesis," a neo-pagan "world-religion" that would eventually replace Christianity. Ultimately he arrived at what he called "the doctrine of the Universal Self," which held that all individual souls are spiritually connected. This principle, he insisted, could be used to draw science, art, politics, religion, ethics, psychology, and every other field of inquiry into a unified whole. It made Carpenter see unity everywhere, and it led him into nearly every one of the bohemian cults and reform movements that flourished in the Edwardian period.

> The doctrine of the Universal Self is obviously fundamental; and it is clear that once taken hold of and adopted it must inevitably revolutionize all our views of Morality—since current morality is founded on the separation of self from self; and must revolutionize too all our views of Science. Such matters as the Transmutation of Chemical Elements, the variation of biological Species, the unity of Health, the unity of Disease, our views of Political

Economy and Psychology; Production for Use instead of for Profit, Communism, Telepathy; the relation between Psychology and Physiology, and so forth, must take on quite a new complexion when the idea which lies at the root of them is seized. This idea must enable us to understand the continuity of Man with the Protozoa, the relation of the physiological centres, on the one hand to the individual Man and on the other to the Race from which he springs, the meaning of Reincarnation, and the physical conditions of its occurrence. It must have eminently practical applications; as in the bringing of the Races of the world together, the gradual evolution of a Non-governmental form of Society, the Communalization of Land and Capital, the freeing of Woman to equality with Man, the extension of monogamic Marriage into some kind of group-alliance, the restoration and full recognition of the heroic friendships of Greek and primitive times; and again in the sturdy Simplification and debarrassment of daily life by the removal of those things which stand between us and Nature, between ourselves and our fellows—by plain living, friendship with the Animals, open-air habits, fruitarian food, and such degree of Nudity as we can reasonably attain to.[68]

In the case of Carpenter and a number of other Edwardian writers, the sanctification of fellowship was largely an expression of homosexuality. E. M. Forster often sublimated his homoerotic feelings into a yearning for connection, as in the relationship of Rickie and Stephen in *The Longest Journey*. While visiting Edward Carpenter in 1913, Forster experienced a homosexual awakening, and in a few weeks of thrilling activity he dashed off *Maurice*. It was an explicitly homosexual novel, in which a Cambridge graduate takes a workingman as a lover and lives with him in the English countryside—much as Carpenter did. Both *Maurice* and Carpenter's *Homogenic Love* (1895) convey the same message—that homosexuality can bridge class divisions. ("His body had overlept class, and that night it yearned to feel corduroys" is the sort of thing Forster wrote in an early version of *Maurice*.)[69] C. R. Ashbee endorsed Carpenter's "homogenic love—fellowship—as the basis, or at least one of the motors of social reconstruction."[70] That faith was shared by two other friends of Carpenter's, Lowes Dickinson and Laurence Housman, and by a school of pedophilic "Uranian" poets that flourished in the Edwardian period.[71] G. E. Moore was not homosexual (excepting a single undergraduate infatuation), but his two most important teachers (Lowes Dickinson and J. M. E. McTaggart) were, as were several of his fellow Apostles. Two of them, Lytton Strachey and John Maynard Keynes, interpreted the human-relations philosophy of *Principia Ethica* as a endorsement of what they called the "higher sodomy," an idealized platonic homosexuality that became a favorite topic of conversation among the Apostles. In fact, *Principia Ethica* nowhere condoned homosexuality, but (as Paul Levy notes) Moore never objected to that reading of his book.[72]

The higher sodomy was one more variety of Edwardian surrogate religion. It was the displaced spirituality one finds in the sexual treatises of Edward Carpenter (who had served as a curate under F. D. Maurice before leaving the church in 1874), in the verse of Uranian poets like "Baron Corvo" and John Gambril Nicholson, and in Forrest Reid's Pan-fantasy *The Garden God* (1905). To the idyllic male bathing party in chapter 12 of *A Room with a View*, E. M. Forster brought that touch of spilt religion: "It had been a call to the blood and to the relaxed will, a passing benediction whose influence did not pass, a holiness, a spell, a momentary chalice for youth."

Each in His Prison

This idealized homoeroticism, as Paul Fussell has shown, would be a pervasive literary theme during the First World War.[73] In fact, in a paradoxical way, the whole Edwardian creed of fellowship received a tremendous boost from the war, at least in the early stages of the conflict. During the first months of combat, there was perhaps more social solidarity in Britain than at any other point in her history, not excluding the "finest hour" of the next war. George Dangerfield has dramatically described how Liberals, Tories, socialists, striking workers, militant suffragettes, Irish Nationalists, Ulster Unionists—all the warring parties that had been tearing Edwardian society apart among them—suddenly closed ranks at the declaration of war and channeled their political passions into the crusade against Germany.[74] There were, of course, some pacifists who opposed the war from the start, but what is remarkable is the much larger body of intellectuals who believed that the conflict was propelling Britain and the world toward the dream of an organic society. On 1 September 1914 Edward Carpenter, while acknowledging that the war was a catastrophe, hailed the "extraordinary and astounding development of solidarity and enthusiasm among the more pacific peoples of Western Europe." He predicted that the hostilities would bring about a socialist federation of Western Europe and realize his lifelong "ideal of a generous Common Life."[75] Gilbert Murray, who had been a pro-Boer and a stern critic of the foreign policy of Sir Edward Grey, became a supporter of the war after witnessing millions of people making heroic sacrifices for the sake of a common effort. It incensed Murray that Germany had violated her treaties guaranteeing the neutrality of Belgium, for that was a repudiation of the principle of fellowship, which T. H. Green had identified as the basis of human society. "There must be some elementary sense of relationship, of mutual duty, some elementary instinct of public right," Murray protested, "at least the elementary understanding that if a man pledges his word, he should keep it."[76]

For a time, it appeared that the war might realize the guild socialist ideal of a corporate society of worker-run industries. In return for maintaining production and preventing strikes, labor leaders were brought into the government, and trade unionists were allowed some control over manpower policy. In 1917 a government committee headed by J. H. Whitley, a Liberal M.P. and cotton spinner, proposed a system of permanent labor-management councils to negotiate industrial problems. The impact of the Whitley Councils was very limited, but Liberals like J. L. Hammond and A. G. Gardiner hailed them as a major step toward cooperative government of industry.[77] Guild socialists like G. D. H. Cole rejected the "joint control" of the Whitley Councils for total workers' control, but the very existence of the councils, together with growing labor demands for a voice in management, convinced Cole that the guild millennium was at hand. He published *Self-Government in Industry*, his first book on guild socialism, in the summer of 1917.[78]

By promoting close military cooperation among the dominions, the war also seemed to bring the dream of imperial union closer to reality. As early as November 1914, Lionel Curtis (of the Round Table) was discussing the possibility of a world state with C. R. Ashbee, and Ashbee was looking forward to a postwar "United States of Europe."[79] In 1916 Curtis published *The Problem of the Commonwealth*, where for the first time he explicitly proposed the creation of an imperial parliament empowered to tax the dominions. Meanwhile, the Round Table was advocating a postwar league of nations, as well as a trustee system to prepare former German and Turkish colonies for self-government.[80]

The League of Nations was conceived by its supporters as a first attempt to draw all humanity into an organic political community, perhaps leading, in the distant future, to a world government. The movement to establish the League, which began to coalesce in the first months of the war, attracted a large body of liberal and socialist intellectuals. In the autumn of 1914 Lowes Dickinson and Lord Bryce organized a Liberal study group on international organization, which included J. A. Hobson, Graham Wallas, and Arthur Ponsonby. In January 1915 the Fabians set up their own study group, directed by Leonard Woolf. The League movement was backed by the Union of Democratic Control, an antiwar group favoring open diplomacy and a negotiated peace, as well as by H. G. Wells, Arnold Bennett, William Archer, Sir Oliver Lodge, W. R. Inge, Bishop Gore, William Temple, and Randall Davidson, the archbishop of Canterbury. The League continued to command broad public support in Britain until at least 1931, and liberal academics like Lowes Dickinson and Gilbert Murray became deeply involved in its work.[81]

For the Round Table, however, *The Problem of the Commonwealth* proved to be a fatal mistake. It alienated supporters in the dominions, who were jealous of their independence and not willing to surrender any real power to a London-based parliament. The war, far from unifying the Empire, finally established the complete sovereignty and autonomy of the dominions, and the Round Table campaign for imperial union was exhausted by 1921.[82] The guild socialists continued to gain strength for a few years after the peace, chiefly in the construction industry, where a number of worker-run firms were set up to build homes subsidized by the Addison Housing Act of 1919. But the postwar recession and the repeal of the Addison Act in 1922 bankrupted the building guilds, and the guild socialist movement disintegrated by 1923.[83]

The wartime spirit of national solidarity ended with the so-called Khaki Election of December 1918, which degenerated into an orgy of intraparty squabbles, class hatred, and hysterical abuse of supposed pro-Germans and Bolsheviks in Parliament. Four years of trench warfare would have probably sufficed to wreck the Edwardian vision of fellowship, and they were followed by another interval of revolution and intermittent warfare throughout the European continent. There was civil war in Ireland and a wave of labor unrest in Britain, while the Versailles Conference succeeded only in confirming German hatred of the Allies and dividing the Allies against themselves. In the postwar world, the dream of an organic society would give way to increasing hostility between class and class, generation and generation, nation and nation, governors and governed.[84]

Amidst these hatreds, John Maynard Keynes still endeavored to uphold the ideals of *Principia Ethica* and apply them to the practical problem of settling the war. As a delegate to the peace negotiations, he drew on his faith in personal relations to break a frustrating deadlock. The talks had stalled over the Allied blockade of Germany, which was still in force several months after the armistice. There was real starvation throughout Central and Eastern Europe, but food shipments were being held up by distrust, stubbornness, and diplomatic evasion on both sides. Among the German delegates Keynes was able to pick out only one sincere face—that of Dr. Carl Melchior, a Hamburg banker. Keynes strained diplomatic protocol by arranging a private meeting with Melchior, in the hope they they might together attain G. E. Moore's ideal of discussing "the truth and the reality like sane and sensible persons." The two of them actually achieved a momentary flash of Moorean intimacy —"in a sort of way," Keynes later recalled, "I was in love with him." After some difficult diplomatic maneuvering and another private meeting with Melchior, the impasse was broken and food supplies began to move.[85]

Keynes's habit of thinking in terms of human relations is manifest in *The Economic Consequences of the Peace* (1919), his influential diatribe against the Versailles Treaty. The experience of working at the peace conference, Keynes wrote, transformed him from an "Englishman" into a "European"; it made him see the economic and cultural ties that united the continental nations.

> Europe is solid with herself. France, Germany, Italy, Austria, and Holland, Russia and Roumania and Poland, throb together, and their structure and civilisation are essentially one. They flourished together, they have rocked together in a war . . . , and they may fall together. In this lies the destructive significance of the Peace of Paris. If the European civil war is to end with France and Italy abusing their momentary victorious power to destroy Germany and Austria-Hungary now prostrate, they invite their own destruction also, being so deeply and inextricably intertwined with their victims by hidden psychic and economic bonds.[86]

In imposing a "Carthaginian peace" on Germany and demanding reparations she could not possibly afford to pay, the men of Versailles assumed that they could rebuild France by impoverishing her neighbor. Keynes thought otherwise: Moore's doctrine of organic unities had taught him that relations between human beings could enrich both parties, and he seems to have transferred this principle to his economics. He placed great emphasis on "the economic interdependence of Germany and her neighbours'': she was a major trading partner of every considerable European nation, and if her economy was crippled, she would drag the rest of the continent down with her. The result would be worldwide depression—and worse.

> If this view of nations and of their relation to one another is adopted by the democracies of Western Europe, and is financed by the United States, heaven help us all. If we aim deliberately at the impoverishment of Central Europe, vengeance, I dare predict, will not limp. Nothing can then delay for very long that final civil war between the forces of reaction and the despairing convulsions of revolution, before which the horrors of the late German war will fade into nothing, and which will destroy, whoever is victor, the civilisation and the progress of our generation. Even though the result disappoint us, must we not base our actions on better expectations, and believe that the prosperity and happiness of one country promotes that of others, that the solidarity of man is not a fiction, and that nations can still afford to treat other nations as fellow-creatures?[87]

The war and its aftermath convinced E. M. Forster, for one, that personal intimacy could not resolve international hostilities. In 1912 he began work on a novel to be entitled *Arctic Summer*, in which he planned, according to his usual formula, to oppose and reconcile two antithetical characters, in this case a Quaker social reformer and a combat-hungry army officer. But before Forster could work out the customary rapprochement, the war rendered the novel obsolete. It exploded the ideals of both characters and devastated Forster's faith in the power or even the possibility of intimate relations between individuals. "I am losing all sense of duty towards this world of blood stained fools," he told Lowes Dickinson in April 1916; "don't even bother to tell myself that creation and personal relations are arguably duties."[88] Forster never completed *Arctic Summer*. In the postwar world, he later wrote, the two half-heroes of the novel could never have found any common ground, except perhaps "as companions in defeat. But such an ending doesn't interest me."[89] Forster's next and last novel, *A Passage to India* (1924), ends with a rupture—Aziz and Fielding, India and England, cannot connect, at least not in the foreseeable future. The war had been followed by a surge of nationalist unrest in several British colonies; the authorities had responded with arbitrary repression and had victimized some of Forster's Oriental friends and lovers. Forster, much embittered, told one of those friends that before the war, when he began *A Passage to India*, "I thought of it as a little bridge of sympathy between East and West, but this conception has had to go, my sense of truth forbids anything so comfortable. I think that most Indians, like most English people, are shits, and I am not interested whether they sympathize with one another or not."[90]

D. H. Lawrence was equally caustic in *Aaron's Rod* (1922):

> The ideal of love, the ideal that it is better to give than to receive, the ideal of liberty, the ideal of the brotherhood of man, the ideal of the sanctity of human life, the ideal of what we call goodness, charity, benevolence, public spiritedness, the ideal of sacrifice for a cause, the ideal of unity and unanimity—all the lot—all the whole beehive of ideals—has all got the modern bee-disease, and gone putrid, stinking.[91]

And in the same year Virginia Woolf arrived, more delicately, at the same conclusion: "I am doubtful whether people, the best disposed towards each other, are capable of more than an intermittent signal as they forge past."[92]

Aldous Huxley initially viewed the world war as a force for human solidarity. "This war impresses on me more than ever the fact that friendship, love, whatever you like to call it is the only reality," he wrote in October 1915.[93] His postwar novels, however, hold out little hope of personal intimacy: men and women copulate freely but never connect. Huxley documented the loneliness of promiscuity in *Antic Hay*, where Myra Viveash wishes that people would conduct themselves like trains on parallel tracks, traveling together for brief intervals but never touching, always ready to pull away from each other the moment the conversation begins to pall.[94]

Early in the war, T. S. Eliot had sought an answer to the problem of human connection in the philosophy of F. H. Bradley, the dean of the British Idealists. Bradley refuted solipsism by arguing that the apparent separateness of human minds is an illusion, that all individuals, and in fact all reality, are abstracted from an Absolute that contains no real divisions. From 1914 to 1916 Eliot wrote a doctoral thesis on Bradley's philosophy, but in *The Waste Land* he offered a very different metaphysic.

> I have heard the key
> Turn in the door once and turn once only
> We think of the key, each in his prison
> Thinking of the key, each confirms a prison
> Only at nightfall, aethereal rumours
> Revive for a moment a broken Coriolanus.[95]

In a footnote to that passage, Eliot quoted from Bradley's *Appearance and Reality* (1893).

> My external sensations are no less private to myself than are my thoughts or my feelings. In either case my experience falls within my own circle, a circle closed on the outside; and, with all its elements alike, every sphere is opaque to the others which surround it. . . . In brief, regarded as an existence which appears in a soul, the whole world for each is peculiar and private to that soul.[96]

This quotation was taken out of context—Bradley was repudiating this sort of solipsism, not defending it—but it seems to describe Eliot's philosophical position in 1922.[97]

The war, of course, did not obliterate all traces of faith in human relations: intellectual movements of this scale do not disappear without leaving some residue behind them. "Only connect," according to Goronwy Rees, continued to be a popular Cambridge and Bloomsbury catchphrase after 1918: "It could be said that those two words, so seductive in their simplicity, so misleading in their ambiguity, had more influence in shaping the emotional attitudes of the English governing class between the two world wars than any other single phrase in the English language." What the war did effectively scotch was the notion that personal relations would solve all social conflicts. "Only connect" became, as Paul Fussell has suggested, a fervent but impotent protest against a world where nothing seemed to connect.[98] One might love love for its own sake but never again as a philosophical and political panacea, at least not until the Beatles.

Like Edwardian secular religion, the cult of personal relations presumed the reconcilability of everyone and everything. As such, it was a generous faith, but it could also be naive and wishful, and it was a bit too comfortable to be true. It demanded, admirably, a personal commitment to the poor, and for a time it did bring the ideal of One Nation—and, beyond that, One World—a bit closer to reality. Given more time, it might have done more to allay the chronic British disease of class hostility. The apostles of personal relations generally assumed that they would have all the time in the world to do their work—a long "Arctic summer" of endless sunlight, as E. M. Forster had it—and there lay their tragic flaw. They could not conceive of the holocaust that would explode their cherished ideal. As late as 1911 L. T. Hobhouse was still proclaiming that "the world is rapidly becoming one," that Britain and

Germany would soon abandon their arms race and compete instead in building universities and polytechnics.[99] One Edwardian who knew better was Charles Masterman. More clear-sighted and (hence) gloomier than most of his contemporaries, he warned in 1909 that the problem of human brotherhood might not work itself out as neatly as a Forster novel.

> With the vertical division between nation and nation armed to the teeth, and the horizontal division between rich and poor which has become a cosmopolitan fissure, the future of progress is still doubtful and precarious. . . . The wise man will still go softly all his days; working always for greater economic equality on the one hand, for understanding between estranged peoples on the other; apprehending always how slight an effort of stupidity or violence could strike a death-blow to twentieth-century civilisation.[100]

3. The Meanings of Life

In 1912 T. E. Hulme noted that British intelligentsia had become fixated on a new catchword. Once, he wrote, all intellectual life revolved around the word *God*, and then "for a hundred years it was Reason, and now," he complained, "all the best people take off their hats and lower their voices when they speak of Life."[1]

There was, in fact, a curious, often monotonous Edwardian obsession with that simple word. D. H. Lawrence reverentially invoked it literally hundreds of times in *The Rainbow* (1915).[2] As a popular literary cliché, it had a far-ranging influence on Edwardian thought, though it is a difficult term to define: with different writers, *life* took on a variety of significant meanings and implications. It could mean the surrogate religion of vitalism, the worship of the life process as a spiritual force. It could specifically mean the creation of new life, an erotic impulse breaking out of Victorian constraints and sometimes worshipped as a religion in itself. Life could also be a mysterious spiritual quality that endowed human beings with identity, consciousness, a moral sense, and free will—a vital spark very like the Christian concept of the soul. If man has no soul, wrote Joseph Conrad, then it is his "more intense life [that] makes his death more touching than the death of a tree" (*Jim* 223). The cult of Life represented as well a reaction against the late Victorian cults of Art and Decadence, and as such it had a remarkable impact on the form, theory, and thrust of English literature. In its most general sense, Life represented a demand for individual freedom and self-realization, a vague but fervent rallying cry for the poets, social rebels, and emancipated women who were fighting their way out of the drawing rooms of Edwardian England.

The Way of All Flesh

Vitalism never attracted a significant following among the Victorians. According to the *Oxford English Dictionary*, the expression *Life Force* did not even appear in English until 1896.[3] A few isolated vitalist philosophers, like James Hinton and Samuel Butler, preached from the fringes of the Victorian intellectual community, but they were generally dismissed as cranks by respectable opinion. The critical response to the work of Samuel Butler is, in fact, a good measure of intellectual attitudes toward vitalism, and it reveals a dramatic change of mood following Butler's death in 1902.

Butler anticipated, by a full generation, the thinking of an entire school of Edwardian intellectuals when he invented a surrogate religion of vitalism. The son of an Anglican minister and the grandson of a bishop, Butler abandoned Christianity for Darwinism in the 1860s, but he later experienced a more profound loss of faith in scientific materialism. In *Life and Habit* (1877) he argued that unconscious habits, acquired in the practical business of living, are more reliable guides to truth than empirical science. Butler turned against Darwin's theory of evolution, condemning it as a "mindless, mechanical, materialistic view of nature" that ignored the role of volition and intelligence in biological change. Drawing on the speculations of Jean-Baptiste de Lamarck, Butler contended that living beings could evolve through acts of will. The giraffe (the animal inevitably enlisted to make this point) did not develop his long neck through the blind process of natural selection; rather, he deliberately stretched his neck to eat succulent treetop leaves and passed this acquired characteristic on to his offspring. The impetus behind evolution was provided not by changes in the environment, as Darwin had claimed, but by the conscious action of life.

By 1879 Butler was beginning to perceive life as a sort of deity in itself. If, as materialist scientists claimed, protoplasm was the necessary basis of all life, "then," Butler reasoned, "this unity in the substance vivifying all, both animals and plants, must be held as uniting them into a single corporation or body. . . . This," he later recalled, "came practically to saying that protoplasm was God Almighty, who, of all the forms open to Him, had chosen this singularly unattractive one as the channel through which to make Himself manifest in the flesh by taking our nature upon Him, and animating us with His own spirit."[4] Butler believed that the common traits shared by all living beings were evidence of a common ancestor, which he identified as God. It was a finite, self-evolving God, uniting matter and spirit, immanent in all life, a God who was nothing more or less than life itself. All living organisms, Butler concluded, are parts of a great whole, "one soul and one body, one God and one Life."[5]

Butler recognized that he was "addressing the next generation rather than his own."[6] Victorian critics either ridiculed or ignored his books, and none of them, except *Erewhon*, was a commercial success in Butler's lifetime. *The Way of All Flesh*, written at intervals between 1873 and 1885, was posthumously published in 1903. Initially it aroused little interest, but within a year it had provoked an enthusiastic (though slightly delayed) critical response. According to Leonard Woolf, it was read worshipfully by his friends at Cambridge.[7] Suddenly there was tremendous public interest in Butler: for several months in 1903 the most frequently requested book at the London Library was *Erewhon*.[8] Butler's philosophy was popularized in 1904 by the publication of Bernard Shaw's *Man and Superman* and an article by Desmond MacCarthy in the *Independent Review*. There followed an admiring critique by R. A. Clutton-Brock in the *Times Literary Supplement* (1908) and adulatory studies by Gilbert Cannan (1915) and John Harris (1916). From 1908 until at least 1920 a new edition of *The Way of All Flesh* appeared every year, without exception.[9] In 1908 the first of the annual Erewhon Dinners was held to honor Butler's memory; the last dinner, in 1914, was attended by 160 cultural celebrities. When *The Note-Books of Samuel Butler* were published in 1912, they received nearly unanimous praise from the leading literary reviews. The list of novelists influenced by Butler is impressive: E. M. Forster, James Joyce, D. H. Lawrence, Arnold Bennett, Ford Madox Ford, H. G. Wells, May Sinclair, Somerset Maugham, and Robert Graves, the last of whom read Butler in school in 1913.

L. E. Holt, who surveyed Edwardian criticism of Butler, found that he was read not so much as an Oedipal rebel against the fathers of Victorian England, but as a champion of vitalism and the power of the will: "Butler was admired because he satisfied the need which people felt for a less mechanistic and intellectually determined view of life than that of the Victorian era."[10] Sydney Olivier and Graham Wallas praised him for saving their souls from Charles Darwin,[11] and Forster learned from him the "profound truth" that instinct is a better guide to right conduct than logic or ideals.[12] As a prophet of Edwardian vitalism, Butler was far more influential among British authors than Henri Bergson, whose *Creative Evolution* was not published in England until 1910.

Bernard Shaw in particular owed, and gratefully acknowledged, an intellectual debt to Butler. In 1874, as a Dublin adolescent, Shaw promised himself that he would one day found a new religion.[13] In his first novel, *Immaturity* (1879), he depicted himself as a strict rationalist despising all forms of theology. But this was a purely negative creed—all Shaw's hero can do is shake his head at the world[14]—and the very title of the book suggests that the author knew this would not be the end point of his religious development. Shaw had praised Darwin for refuting Genesis, but later he came to see that natural selection implied a denial of morality, will, consciousness, and divine purpose in the universe.

> There is a hideous fatalism about it, a ghastly and damnable reduction of beauty and intelligence, of strength and purpose, of honor and aspiration, to such casually picturesque changes as an avalanche may make in a mountain landscape, or a railway accident in a human figure. To call this Natural Selection is a blasphemy, possible to many for whom Nature is nothing but a casual aggregation of inert and dead matter, but eternally impossible to the spirits and souls of the righteous. If it be no blasphemy, but a truth of science, then the stars of heaven, the showers and the dew, the winter and the summer, the fire and heat, the mountains and hills, may no longer be called to exalt the Lord with us by praise; their work is to modify all things by blindly starving and murdering everything that is not lucky enough to survive in the universal struggle for hogwash.[15]

In 1887 Shaw read Butler's *Luck or Cunning?*, and by 1895 he had resolved "to write a big book of devotion for modern people, bringing all the truths latent in the old religious dogmas into contact with real life—a gospel of Shawianity, in fact."[16] That book would be *Man and Superman*, which propounded a new paratheology of the "Life Force." This was Shaw's understudy for God, a Universal Will working everywhere "to achieve higher and higher organization and completer self-consciousness," raising the entire biological universe, with inexorable Fabian gradualness, to divine perfection.

> Life is a force which has made innumerable experiments in organizing itself; . . . the mammoth and the man, the mouse and the megatherium, the flies and the fleas and the Fathers of the Church, are all more or less successful attempts to build up that raw force into higher and higher individuals, the ideal individual being omnipotent, omniscient, infallible, and withal completely, unilludedly self-conscious: in short, a god.[17]

Shaw outlined this theology in 1906 before the Guild of St. Matthew, headed by his Fabian colleague Stewart Headlam. Although the bishop of London compelled Headlam to repudiate Shaw's remarks publicly, it was clear that the socialist cleric was very much in accord with them. Another Fabian minister, the Congregationalist R. J. Campbell, who had no hierarchy to which to answer, asserted that Shaw had, by a circuitous route, arrived at the fundamental truths of Christianity. Shaw returned the compliment by declaring that Campbell's "New Theology" had made Christ credible by portraying him as an agent of the Life Force.[18] Vitalism, in fact, led Shaw halfway back to Christianity. In *The Perfect Wagnerite* (1898) he concluded (as Butler had) that organized Christianity was a flawed approximation of the true gospel of Life. In Shaw's hands, the Ring Cycle became a vitalist allegory, with Erda playing the role of "the First Mother of Life."

> The mysterious thing we call life organizes itself into all living shapes, bird, beast, beetle and fish, rising to the human marvel in cunning dwarfs and in laborious muscular giants, capable, these last, of . . . patient manual drudgery in the service of higher powers. And these higher powers are called into existence by the same self-organization of life still more wonderfully into rare persons capable of thought, whose aims extend far beyond the satisfaction of their bodily appetites and personal affections, since they perceive that it is only by the establishment of a social order founded on common bonds of moral faith that the world can rise from mere savagery.[19]

Shaw made the gods of Valhalla represent the elders of the Church, who know full well that the true faith is Life. But the "stupid giants" (the proletarian masses) cannot possibly comprehend the fluid, evolving theology of Life worship, so the gods are forced to freeze that anarchic religion into the easily grasped dogmas and commandments of Catholicism. But, Shaw warns, "however carefully these laws are framed to represent the highest thoughts of the framers at the moment of their promulgation, before a day has elapsed that thought has grown and widened by the ceaseless evolution of life; and lo! yesterday's law already fallen out with today's thought." The Life Force refuses to be bound by the straightjacket of Church dogma, and it spawns a hero to destroy that dogma—Siegfried, in whom the repressed vitalist impulse at the heart of Christianity becomes "effective will and life."[20] In his preface to *Androcles and the Lion* (1912) Shaw insisted that Jesus was a vitalist: "He declared that the reality behind the popular belief in God was a creative spirit in ourselves called by him the Heavenly Father and by us Evolution, Élan Vital, Life Force and other names." What Shaw objected to in Victorian Christianity was the idea of a transcendent, personal deity forever tinkering with the universe, and he applauded Darwin for making "short work of the theologians who conceived God as a magnate keeping men and angels as Lord Rothschild keeps buffaloes and emus at Tring." At the same time, he emphasized that "the efforts of Natural Selectionists . . . to reduce evolution to mere automatism have not touched the doctrine of Jesus," who was,

> as we now see, a first-rate biologist. It took a century and a half of evolutionary preachers, from Buffon and Goethe to Butler and Bergson, to convince us that we and our father are one; that as the kingdom of heaven is within us we need not rush about looking for it and crying Lo here! and Lo there!; that God is not a picture of a pompous person in white robes in the family bible, but a spirit; that it is through this spirit that we evolve towards greater abundance of life; that we are the lamps in which the light of the world burns: that, in short, we are gods though we die like men. All that is today sound biology.[21]

It was, in fact, anything but sound biology, even by Edwardian standards. Some scholars have speculated that Edwardian vitalism had its roots in contemporary discoveries in biology, specifically in the genetic studies of August Weismann and (in England) William Bateson,[22] but the work of these men actually militated against the idea of a Life Force. Weismann demonstrated the impossibility of inheriting acquired characteristics and thus brought the wrath of Bernard Shaw down upon his head.[23] Bateson was a partisan of Mendelian genetics, which held that heredity was determined not by Lamarckian striving but by the random recombination of dominant and recessive traits. Shaw liked to talk as if the vitalists had thoroughly discredited Darwinism, but the fact is that Edwardian research in biology provided no hard support for vitalism. In 1905 William Bateson declared that Butler's theories could "only be defended on grounds which to the biologist are mystical and unconvincing"; and as for the Life Force, "not one scrap of tangible evidence was ever produced pointing to the existence of any such 'force.' "[24]

It is revealing that, on this point, Edwardian men of letters were so much at odds with professional biologists. As Bateson complained in 1907, "the transmission of acquired characters," though "with singular unanimity abandoned" by scientists, was "a preconception still almost universal among the laity." The fact that so many educated people could embrace the gospel of Samuel Butler when science was driving new nails into its coffin seems to indicate that they desperately wanted to believe in it. They needed a God of sorts, and the temptation to believe overrode scientific caution. Even Bateson felt that temptation: he admired Butler and readily acknowledged that he had made a strong case against Darwin. "Those who desire to see how strong it is should turn to . . . *Life and Habit*," Bateson advised his readers, "and even if in reading they reiterate to themselves that no experimental evidence exists in support of the propositions advanced, the misgiving that none the less they may be true is likely to remain."[25] Patrick Geddes and J. Arthur Thomson, two academic biologists who wrote for a popular audience, were clearly drawn to a belief in "a creative agent, a striving will, a changeful Proteus, selecting its environment, adjusting itself to it, self-differentiating and self-adaptive—Life dominating nature, master of its fate." Their scientific consciences did not permit them to endorse vitalism, but they would not entirely let go of it.

> Despite the fact that as yet no vitalist writer has succeeded in making himself and his nomenclature really intelligible to any other, and that the frequent gibes at vitalist metaphysics and mysticism remain largely justified, we confess that the modern movement of vitalism has our increasing sympathy. It affects our evolutionism to the extent at least that we feel compelled to recognize the persistence of some originative impetus within the organism, which expresses itself in variation and mutation, and in all kinds of creative effort and endeavour.[26]

The fact that vitalism made such remarkable headway in the face of all experimental evidence underscores that recurrent weakness in Edwardian thought—wishful thinking. Most of the best minds of this period were prone to settle into exceedingly comfortable philosophies—to believe, for instance, that the conflict between religion and science could be worked out in a tidy synthesis. The Life Force was one such synthesis, preached by its apostles as a secular theology consistent with evolutionary science. In reality, it was a thoroughly unscientific religion: there was no more experimental evidence for the existence of the Life Force than there was for Jehovah. The Edwardian vitalists, far from making religion reasonable, simply abandoned one blind faith for another with far less grandeur, no tradition, and not much of a congregation.

The Sacrament of Sexuality

In one of its several variations, vitalism could take the form of a religion of sexuality. Here *life* was a euphemism for a mysterious procreative force—"the life that went on beneath the eyes and the mouth and the chin," as Virginia Woolf wrote (*Voyage* 315). This was yet another Edwardian attempt at a reconciling faith: by transmuting Christianity into a sanctified eroticism, it resolved the conflict between free sexual expression and religious morality.

According to Bernard Shaw, erotic desire was created by the Life Force as an incentive for bringing forth new life, a spell that works its magic whenever it perceives the "possibility of . . . fecundity." In *Man and Superman* it ensnares a helpless Don Juan: "Whilst I was in the act of framing my excuse to the lady, Life seized me and threw me into her arms as a sailor throws a scrap of fish into the mouth of a seabird." When there is the possibility of breeding superior life, of advancing the progress of Creative Evolution, then the lure of the Life Force assumes a religious intensity, as Doña Ana discovers: "(*Crossing herself devoutly*) I believe in the Life to Come. (*Crying to the universe*) A father! a father for the Superman!"[27]

John Tanner has the misfortune to be that potential father, and he is consequently dragged kicking and screaming into marriage with Ann Whitefield. "The trap," he discovers too late, "was laid from the beginning . . . by the Life Force."[28] It should be stressed that erotic love (which Shaw thought vastly overrated) was not the Life Force itself but the bait used by the Life Force to work its ends. "Life," Shaw pontificated, is "the highest good"; love is "only the universal delight that bribes all living things to travail with renewed life."[29]

In George Moore's novel *The Lake*, the sexuality of Nature is worshipped as the "Providence" that governs human fate.[30] *The Lake* is the story of Father Oliver Gogarty, a righteous but troubled Catholic priest in rural Ireland, who has driven an independent-minded schoolmistress named Rose Leicester from his parish for conceiving an illegitimate child. When a fellow priest reports that Rose is doing well in London and urges Father Gogarty to be more tolerant, the good priest looks around at the lush Irish countryside, teeming with "a phantom life," and receives a revelation of cosmic unity: "He and the trees were one, for there is but one life, one mother, one elemental substance out of which all has come. . . . Only in union is there happiness, and for many weary months he had been isolated, thrown out; but to-day he had been drafted suddenly into the general life, he had become again part of the general harmony, and that was why he was so happy."[31]

In the woods he perceives that "life is orientated like a temple; there are in every existence days when life streams down the nave, striking the forehead of the God" (*Lake* 56). Eventually he admits that he persecuted Rose, not out of a thirst for righteousness, but out of "sensual jealousy." He learns to love her as a wonderfully "primitive woman" who is "moved merely by impulses." "You dared to stretch out both hands to life and grasp it," he writes to her; "you accepted the spontaneous natural living wisdom of your instincts." "Woman is life," he concludes, and that is why the Church fears her and tries to shackle her (*Lake* 230, 256–257, 266–69). He therefore abandons Catholicism for a religion of Nature impervious to the assaults of science and biblical criticism. "My quest is life," he declares, by which he means self-realization: "the personal life—that intimate exaltation that comes to him who has striven to be himself, and nothing but himself." In Life the priest discovers his true soul—not the soul of Christian theology but a secular soul that is in no way distinct from the body. Father Gogarty has chosen the right vocation, only the wrong sect, and when he escapes the Church by pretending to have drowned in that mystic lake, Moore describes it as a second baptism that will "lead him even to a new faith" (*Lake* 301–4). (As an acolyte of the flesh, Father Oliver Gogarty was modeled after Oliver St. John Gogarty, though the latter was far less sanctimonious and much more of a ribald.)[32]

James Joyce ridiculed *The Lake* when it first appeared, but he later echoed Father Gogarty's Life worship in *A Portrait of the Artist as a Young Man*.[33] Stephen Dedalus, like Moore's priest, struggles with terrifying sexual anxieties and religious doubts until he rejects the Catholic priesthood for a new faith.

> This was the call of life to his soul not the dull gross voice of the world of duties and despair, not the inhuman voice that had called him to the pale service of the altar. . . . What were they now but cerements shaken from the body of death—the fear he had walked in night and day, the incertitude that had ringed him round, the shame that had abased him within and without—cerements, the linens of the grave?
>
> His soul had risen from the grave of boyhood, spurning her graveclothes. Yes! Yes! Yes! He would create proudly out of the freedom and power of his soul, as the great artificer whose name he bore, a living thing, new and soaring and beautiful, impalpable, imperishable.
>
> . . . A new wild life was singing in his veins. . . . He was . . . happy and near to the wild heart of life.[34]

Stephen is converted while watching his friends bathe in the Liffey, echoing the secular baptism that initiates Moore's Father Gogarty into the religion of Life: "His soul was all dewy wet. . . . He lay still, as if his soul lay amid cool waters. . . . A spirit filled him, pure as the purest water, sweet as dew. . . . His soul was waking slowly. . . . In a dream or vision he had known the ecstasy of seraphic life" (*Portrait* 217).

Much of the baptism imagery in *A Portrait of the Artist* is plainly sexual: "Her nakedness yielded to him, radiant, warm, odorous and lavish-limbed, enfolded him like a shining cloud, enfolded him like water with a liquid life" (*Portrait* 223). Immediately after his conversion, Stephen encounters a girl wading near the Liffey with her skirts drawn up above her thighs. "—Heavenly God! cried Stephen's soul, in an outburst of profane joy," for he has reconciled spirituality and profanity, religion and sexuality, in the worship of life.

> His cheeks were aflame; his body was aglow; his limbs were trembling. On and on and on and on he strode, far out over the sands, singing wildly to the sea, crying to greet the advent of the life that had cried to him.
>
> Her image had passed into his soul for ever and no word had broken the holy silence of his ecstasy. Her eyes had called to him and his soul had leaped at the call. To live, to err, to fall, to triumph, to recreate life out of life! A wild angel had appeared to him, the angel of mortal youth and beauty, an envoy from the fair courts of life, to throw open before him in an instant of ecstasy the gates of all the ways of error and glory. On and on and on and on! (*Portrait* 171–72)

Far from losing his soul through sin, Stephen discovers that his "soul had begun to live" only "when he had first sinned" (*Portrait* 222). In *A Portrait of the Artist*, as in *The Lake*, there is no conflict between sin and salvation. The body is a secular soul saved through the pursuit of "life," which for Stephen means freedom—spiritual, intellectual, artistic, and sexual freedom. Joyce was forever proclaiming his faith in his own soul, to which he dedicated his first major literary effort, an Ibsenish play that he later destroyed. "I want to achieve myself" was the credo of his new religion as he explained it to Lady Gregory in 1902: "All things are inconstant except the faith in the soul [and] I have found no man yet with a faith like mine."[35]

The gradual translation of Christianity into a sexual cult of Life can be tracked in the early letters of D. H. Lawrence. The consolation of religion, the assurance that "the great procession is marching, on the whole, in the right direction," was something vitally important to Lawrence.[36] Shortly after entering University College, Nottingham, in September 1906, he began to be troubled by religious doubts, which he discussed with the Reverend Robert Reid, a local minister who was a friend of his mother's. He told Rev. Reid that he had "been brought up to believe in the absolute necessity for a sudden spiritual conversion; I believed for many years that the Holy Ghost descended and took conscious possession of the 'elect'—the converted one; I thought all conversions were, to a greater or less degree, like that of Paul's. Naturally I yearned for the same, something the same."[37]

But the conversion would not come. Having studied T. H. Huxley, Darwin, Spencer, the biblical critic Ernest Renan, and the secularist writings of J. M. Robertson and Robert Blatchford, Lawrence felt his faith slipping away from him. He read R. J. Campbell's book *The New Theology* (1907), but Lawrence found this Modernist tract too close to agnosticism to be spiritually satisfying. Campbell did, however, convince him that religion could not be founded on the supernatural, and Lawrence began to turn in the direction of natural religion.[38] Here an important influence was a teacher at Nottingham, Ernest Alfred Smith. He taught, significantly, biology; he was also an amateur theologian, very liberal and advanced in his views, who later became a Unitarian minister. Under his tutelage, Lawrence won a distinction in botany, and he later thanked Smith for pointing him toward a new faith: "Life seems to me barbarous, recklessly wasteful and destructive, often hideous and dreadful; but, on the whole, beautiful. . . . I owe you a debt. You were my first live teacher of philosophy."[39]

In December 1907 Lawrence told Rev. Reid that he could no longer believe in the Christian idea of conversion: "I believe that a man is converted when first he hears the low, vast murmur of life, of human life, troubling his hitherto unconscious self."[40] Thereafter, he repeatedly affirmed that he worshipped not God but "life"[41]—a word Lawrence would use interchangeably with *soul* and *self*.[42] He rejected Jehovah as

> the Jew's idea of God—not ours. Christ was infinitely good, but mortal as we. There still remains a God, but not a personal God: a vast shimmering impulse which wavers onwards towards some end, I don't know what— taking no regard of the little individual, but taking regard for humanity. When we die, like raindrops falling back again into the sea, we fall back into the big, shimmering sea of unorganised life which we call God.[43]

Although Lawrence repudiated Christianity as such, his respect for the religious emotion behind Christianity was enhanced. In 1911 he told Rev. Reid that "I often turn . . . back into the Bible, and am ashamed of my old insolence."[44] Like George Emerson in *A Room with a View*, Will Brangwen in *The Rainbow* may not believe in miracles as literal historical events, but he does feel "in his blood and bones" that they express vital religious impulses. "His life was formed in these unquestioned concepts," and to limit belief to dry facts would be "death" (*Rainbow* 160–61). Will is "transported" by Lincoln Cathedral not as a monument to Christianity (he realizes that the building has "a false front") but as a temple of "life." It is "the perfect womb," a "she" charged with "fecundity," "a great, involved seed, whereof the flower would be radiant life inconceivable." The "clinching and mating of arches, the leap and thrust of the stone," rising to "the meeting, the clasp, the close embrace, the neutrality, the perfect, swooning consummation, the timeless ecstasy"—these form a "rainbow" in which "all was contained in oneness." Later, Will is reminded by nature—by the sound of thrushes and the sight of dandelions—that the Church falls short of this vitalist ideal, that there is still a great deal of "life outside the Church." But, like Bernard Shaw and Samuel Butler's Ernest Pontifex, Will continues to support the Church out of respect for the Life Force that Christianity imperfectly represents (*Rainbow* 188–94).

In 1908 Lawrence arrived at the conviction that love is "the fundamental vibration of the life force," resonating to "the great harmonies" of sexuality and "what we will call religious feeling (read it widely)."[45] A lovers' kiss sets up a "connection between the vigorous flow of two lives. Like a positive electricity, a current of creative life runs through two persons, and they are instinct with the same life force—the same vitality—the same I know not what." This "life-current . . . changes them forever"—and there Lawrence found that sudden spiritual conversion for which he had been taught as a boy to prepare. Sexuality provided his epiphany: "Somehow," he wrote, "I think we come into knowledge (unconscious) of the most vital parts of the cosmos through touching things."[46] Lawrence often described the sex act in terms of being "born again": it left one "newly created, as after a gestation, a new birth, in the womb of darkness" (*Rainbow* 38).

In Life worship Lawrence reconciled the "Sunday world" of religion with the "weekday world" of secular reality. When Ursula Brangwen tries to make her religious "vision . . . translate itself into weekday terms," she develops a distinctly erotic "passion" for Jesus (*Rainbow* 266–71). But she learns that Christianity is too "passive," too repressive to be transformed into a phallic cult of life. Its ceremonies have ossified into stale "mechanical action," and it is too much concerned with death. "The Resurrection," Lawrence proclaims,

> is to life, not to death. Shall I not see those who have risen again walk here among men perfect in body and spirit, whole and glad in the flesh, living in the flesh, loving in the flesh, begetting children in the flesh, arrived at last to wholeness, perfect without scar or blemish, healthy without fear of ill-health? Is this not the period of manhood and of joy and fulfilment, after the Resurrection? Who shall be shadowed by Death and the Cross, being risen, and who shall fear the mystic, perfect flesh that belongs to heaven? . . . Is the flesh which was crucified become as poison to the crowds in the street, or is it as a strong gladness and hope to them, as the first flower blossoming out of the earth's humus? (*Rainbow* 264–65).

In Lawrence's religion the Resurrection is literal rebirth, the creation of new life perceivable in "the swelling and heaving contour of the new generation." This reconciliation of the worldly and the otherworldly is perfectly symbolized in the rainbow, an arch between heaven and earth. Lawrence may have borrowed that image from W. H. Hudson, who used it for the same purpose in *Idle Days in Patagonia* (1893); and in *Howards End* as well E. M. Forster invoked "the rainbow bridge that should connect the prose in us with the passion."[47] That symbol, of course, is ultimately drawn from the story of Noah, and Lawrence quotes at length from this section of the Bible, underscoring the divine injunction to "be fruitful and multiply and replenish the earth" (*Rainbow* 305–7, 466–67).

Lawrence's cult of Life was bound up with feelings of great ambivalence and wariness toward women. At times he worshipped the female as the source of all life, but she could also be the possessive, consuming "Magna Mater, . . . the awful, arrogant queen of life, as if she were a queen bee on whom all the rest depended." Because she had brought man into the world she might claim, "with horrible, insidious arrogance and female tyranny, her own again, claiming back the man she had borne in suffering." Lawrence therefore commonly associated women with decadence and death. In *Women in Love* (practically completed by 1916) Diana Crich drowns her lover in a stream that Birkin has just finished denouncing as a "dark river of dissolution . . . of corruption," breeding "fleurs de mal." For Lawrence, Aphrodite symbolized "the flowering mystery of the death-process"; she is the child of "universal dissolution," born whenever "the stream of synthetic creation lapses."[48] His first two novels, *The White Peacock* (1911) and *The Tres-passer* (1912), had both centered on a stock figure of the Decadent literature of the nineties—the man-devouring vampire-woman who possesses and destroys a weak-willed, epicene male.

Lawrence's portrait of the female as the deadlier of the species was largely rooted in his relationship with his parents. His mother was a former schoolteacher—well-read, acutely intellectual, intimidatingly civilized, interested in religion and public affairs, and an amateur poet. Lawrence, struggling to break a consuming attachment to her, apparently came to view the things she represented—culture, Christianity, and the intellect—as repressive and antilife, as so many female tricks designed to tame the male and destroy the vitality in him. Lawrence's father, on the other hand, was a barely literate mine worker, temperamental and brutal, always at loggerheads with his cultivated wife. But he had a remarkable knowledge of and rapport with nature, and he left his son with the conviction that the male must fight free of the social controls ostensibly imposed by women.[49]

For men and women, then, it is "a fight to the death between them—or to new life." In *Women in Love* the only alternative to protracted war between the sexes is an equal relation in which both freely express their vitality—"an equilibrium, a pure balance of two single beings:—as the stars balance each other." Each partner must be whole and individual: "The man is pure man, the woman pure woman, they are perfectly polarised . . . each constituting the freedom of the other, balancing each other like two poles of one force." Both must cast off their social selves and respond only to the impulses of the blood, "responsible for nothing, asked for nothing, giving nothing, only each taking according to the primal desire." When Ursula presents Birkin with a flower—a fragment of life—they tap into "the source of the deepest life-force" and finally achieve, in sexual union, what Lawrence calls "star-equilibrium." This is a religious consummation: Birkin and Ursula pass a church immediately afterward, and she recalls the passage from the Bible "where the sons of God saw the daughters of men, that they were fair." Lawrence also echoes here the Edwardian religion of personal relations, proclaiming a cosmic harmony that follows from human harmony: "The world is only held together by the mystic conjunction, the ultimate unison between people—a bond."[50]

Two other notable Edwardian sexual prophets transformed Christianity into a cult of Life—Havelock Ellis and Edward Carpenter. Ellis was descended from a long line of clergymen, and he had planned to take orders himself until, at the age of sixteen, he was weaned away from Christianity by Shelley, Renan, Darwin, and Swinburne. In materialism, however, Ellis discovered only "a blank and empty desert," an "alien universe of whirling machinery." He searched for some way of reconciling science and religion: for a time he was enthusiastic about Robert Chambers's *Vestiges of the Natural History of Creation* (1844), which offered a theory of biological evolution compatible with Christianity.[51]

In 1878 Ellis became a schoolteacher in a small town in the Australian bush, where he suffered terrible loneliness. His spiritual hunger translated itself into a longing for an ideal woman. He rediscovered the Bible and read it with pleasure, although he now considered it a work of literature rather than a holy book. He also read *Life in Nature* by James Hinton, an obscure vitalist mystic. One afternoon, inspired by "the vast and sunny expanse of Nature," Ellis experienced what he called, "in the precise and full sense of the word, a revelation." He had been torn between "the hopeless discrepancy of two different conceptions of the universe," the spiritual and the materialistic. But Hinton argued that all so-called dead matter was in fact imbued with "life," and thus he persuaded Ellis that "these two conflicting attitudes are really but harmonious though different aspects of the same unity." After this "conversion," as he called it, Ellis saw "the real harmony between Mysticism and Science." He insisted that "a fundamental antagonism of the two . . . is not to be thought of; it is unthinkable, even absurd."[52]

As a sexual libertarian, Hinton eliminated another antagonism that had troubled Ellis—the conflict between sexuality and "purity." "The opposites are reconciled," Ellis declared in 1881, and four years later he resolved "to follow the true law of life" rather than "the numberless rigid and arbitrary laws of men."[53] As early as 1884 Ellis recognized that he had fallen into the habit of using "the physical . . . as a symbol of the spiritual" in his writings: "I cannot feel anything at all about physical sexual feeling except as a 'sacrament'—the outward and visible sign of an inward and spiritual grace." His later investigations of sexual behavior consequently reflected a reconciling impulse "to gather up

. . . into one expression the poetry and the prose of life," to impart a religious aura to the erotic. In volume 1 (1900) of his *Studies in the Psychology of Sex*, he discussed at length the "close affinity between the sexual and the religious emotions," noting the "sexual and orgiastic" nature of some primitive religious ceremonies. There were armies of Victorian men and especially women who sublimated their sexual urges into ecstatic spirituality; Ellis and Lawrence reversed that transformation, venting religious emotion in a sacramental sexuality. "For," Ellis wrote in his autobiography, "I have always instinctively desired to spiritualise the things that have been counted low and material, if not disgusting; and where others have seen all things secular, I have seen all things sacred."[54]

Christianity was transmuted into a religion of homosexuality by Edward Carpenter, a friend of Ellis's. In his autobiography, Carpenter remembered wandering about the Cambridge University gardens, filled with an inexplicable "kind of longing . . . —something partly sexual, partly religious . . . ; but anyhow it was something that brooded about and enveloped my life, and makes those hours still stand out for me as the most pregnant of my then existence." He wrote undergraduate poems that cried out for "Life—true life that cannot cease," and he called upon God to reveal the "strange mystery" of "deep-fountained life."[55] In the poetry of Walt Whitman, Carpenter found not only an implied vindication of homosexuality but also a new religion of nature: "I began in fact to realize that, above all else, I had come into contact with a great Man; not great thoughts, theories, views of life, but a great Individuality, a great Life." Christianity, Carpenter concluded, would eventually evolve into a "New Paganism" based on free sexual expression and "a concrete appreciation of the value and beauty of actual life."[56] Emile Delavenay argues that the Life cult of Edward Carpenter directly inspired D. H. Lawrence, who knew several followers of Carpenter and may have read some of his works.[57] It seems more likely, however, that Lawrence, Carpenter, and Ellis arrived at similar conclusions simply because they confronted similar problems—a combination of spiritual and sexual anxieties led all three of them to a surrogate religion of sexuality.

The principal deity of this religion was Pan, the premoral nature god who incarnated the Edwardian Id. In Lawrence's *White Peacock*, Pan appears in Maurice Greiffenhagen's painting "An Idyll" carrying off a swooning aesthetic damozel. George and Lettie are at once aroused and embarrassed by the picture, and they carefully talk around the erotic aspects of it until "it was a torture to each of them to look thus nakedly at the other."[58] Later, disgusted with civilization, Lawrence would search for Pan among the Indians of New Mexico. He believed that Christianity would have been much improved if only Jesus had been a bit more like Pan,[59] whereas Havelock Ellis felt that the two deities were "one at heart."[60] In one of E. M. Forster's earliest tales, "The Story of a Panic" (1902), a dull little English boy, traveling with a tourist party in Italy, is possessed by the horned god and explodes in abandonment. Forster was indignant when one reader detected hints of buggery and bestiality in the story, but later he recognized that this interpretation had been entirely correct: he remembered feeling a distinctly sexual excitement while writing those parts of the story where "something was up."[61] Another "worshipper of the god Pan" was Arnold Bennett's Daniel Povey, the confectioner and sexual libertine of *The Old Wives' Tale* (1908). His more repressed cousin Samuel would sometimes "gaze downwards at the faint patch of flour on Daniel's right leg"—a nice seminal image—"and conceive that life was, and must always be, life."[62]

Some Edwardians were prepared to applaud any woman who brought forth new life, even if she violated the sanctities of matrimony. H. G. Wells aroused a storm of protest with *Ann Veronica* (1909), in which the heroine runs off with a married college instructor. Wells wrote the novel while conceiving an irregular issue with Amber Reeves: "We . . . were both inordinately greedy of life," he later explained.[63] At least Wells had the decency to marry Ann Veronica and her lover before they began having children, but other authors were more daring. In *The Blue Lagoon* (1908)—which is alluded to in *Ann Veronica*—H. de Vere Stacpoole stranded two first cousins on a desert island, where they bear an illegitimate (not to mention incestuous) child. Both Wells and Stacpoole sanitized their novels with pontifications about life welling up from the subconscious and seeking renewal.[64] There was also Rose Leicester in *The Lake*, Marion Yates in Harley Granville Barker's drama *The Madras House* (1910), and Helen Schlegel in *Howards End*, as well as the title character in Bernard Shaw's suppressed play *Mrs. Warren's Profession* (1894)—all of them bear children out of wedlock. Victorian literary conventions dictated that the unwed mother had to pay for her sins through suicide, ostracism, or some other punishment; but these Edwardian heroines, significantly, all prosper in spite of their transgressions.

This new tolerance was partly a response to the fact that the British birth rate fell sharply between 1900 and 1914—a ten percent drop overall and considerably more among the affluent and educated classes. That decline was widely perceived as yet another sign of national decadence, and it aroused great public concern. Sidney Webb wrote a Fabian tract on the problem in 1907, and a National Birth-Rate Commission was set up, with government sanction, in 1913.[65] The falling birth rate is explicitly called to Leonard Bast's attention early in *Howards End*, well before he impregnates Helen Schlegel.[66] H. G. Wells broadly underscored the fact that the three principal women of *Tono-Bungay* (1909) have no children: "What hope is there for a people whose women become fruitless?"[67] In *The Madras House* Granville Barker marched six unwed and childless sisters onstage to make the same point.

Stillbirth is a preoccupation in the early works of W. Somerset Maugham—*Liza of Lambeth* (1897), *A Man of Honour* (1903), and *Mrs. Craddock* (1904). But *Of Human Bondage* (1915) introduces the lusty character of Athelny, who has cast off respectability and sired nine strapping "bastards." Maugham's mother had died after giving birth to a stillborn son, but Maugham went on to train in obstetrics. He delivered several dozen babies as a medical student, and he conceived his first child—out of wedlock—at about the same time he wrote *Of Human Bondage*.[68]

"The day is coming when great nations will find their numbers dwindling from census to census," warns Don Juan in *Man and Superman*. The world, he predicts, will only be repopulated by allowing "the Force of Life" free rein, without regard to the marriage bond. His descendant, John Tanner, indignantly defends Violet Robinson for realizing "her highest purpose and greatest function—to increase, multiply, and replenish the earth," at least until he makes the mortifying discovery that she is (contrary to what he had innocently assumed) married.[69]

The Captain of My Soul

Machinery and *materialism* were unspeakable words to Edwardian vitalists. For them, Life was a way of repudiating the determinism of mechanistic science and affirming belief in free will. They repeatedly (and unfairly) denounced the nineteenth-century science of Herbert Spencer,

Charles Darwin, John Tyndall, and T. H. Huxley as mere "mechanical aptitude," which "in itself could never furnish any guide to life" and "never taught the art of living," according to Havelock Ellis.[70] Victorian materialists, complained T. E. Hulme, conceived of the universe as a frictionless billiard table on which particles ricocheted off one another according to fixed Newtonian laws—a system without purpose, unity, intelligence, or freedom. Everything was predetermined: as Laplace once concluded, we could in theory predict the future, given a large enough calculator, if we knew the exact mass, velocity, and position of every particle in the system at any one moment.

Hulme suggested, however, that if one of those billiard balls was gifted with what he called life, it would be capable of spontaneous action and could throw off all of Laplace's calculations. It could begin rolling of its own volition and thus introduce new energy onto the billiard table: that would abrogate Newton's laws of inertia, as well as that cornerstone of Victorian physics, the law of conservation of energy.[71] Scientists like William McDougall and Sir Oliver Lodge noted this contradiction between Newton's laws and vitalism and tried to discover some way of resolving it.[72] Arthur Balfour suggested to Lodge that the conflict might be worked out by defining *life* as "the power of directing and transforming energy without the employment of stresses," though he could not explain how any force could accomplish such a trick.[73] Lodge finally concluded "that Life introduces something incalculable and purposeful amid the laws of physics." It was a "supernatural, *i.e.*, literally superphysical" force, above the laws of science. "The vagaries of a fire or a cyclone could all be predicted by Laplace's Calculator," Lodge declared, "but no mathematician could calculate the orbit of a common house-fly," and the physicist J. H. Poynting wrote in much the same vein.[74]

Materialist science had predicted that "entropy" would inevitably dissipate all the energy in the universe, but F. W. H. Myers suggested that "life" was a form of "transcendental energy" capable of "entrophy," or the creation of new energy, "which out of Chaos shapes Cosmos & order of Nature." According to Myers, each individual soul, as well as the aggregate "World-Soul" that he called "God," was charged with "life" and could therefore counter the forces of "death & dissolution" in the universe.[75] As leading members of the Society for Psychical Research, Myers, Lodge, Balfour, and McDougall discovered in "life" what the SPR had always searched for—a surrogate human soul, a spark that would make man something more than clockwork.

In 1913 T. E. Hulme used the *élan vital* of Henri Bergson, "that stream of impulse which constitutes life," to deny the "mechanism and fatalism" of Herbert Spencer. Hulme contended that every human being is composed of two selves—a "superficial self," which thinks in purely rational terms and functions according to the laws of materialist science, and a "fundamental self," which is capable of making intuitive, heuristic mental leaps for which materialism cannot account. On the level of the material self, all things are predetermined, but the fundamental self is a "living" self, and "in life," Hulme wrote, "you do appear to get continuous evolution and creation," as well as an element of freedom.[76] Bernard Shaw's Life Force possessed free will—and yet, since it was certain of final triumph, it also made for that happy Fabian fatalism summed up in Sidney Webb's phrase "the inevitability of gradualness." That, according to Shaw, was why Wagner described his vitalist hero Siegfried "as the Freewiller of Necessity, thereby beyond measure exasperating Englishmen with a congenital incapacity for metaphysics."[77]

That allowance for freedom attracted Shaw's friend Sydney Olivier to the voluntarist evolution of Samuel Butler. Olivier, like most leading Fabians, rejected Marxian determinism: socialism would be brought about not by inexorable economic forces but by the concerted ethical will of individuals, namely the Fabians. For Olivier, socialism was a means of enhancing individual freedom, of creating the economic security needed "to live the largest and freest life permitted by the physical environment."[78] As a member of the SPR, Olivier believed in an immortal vitalist soul "not subject to or dependent upon heredity or the laws of animal life; it is our authority for revolt against the dogmatic fatalisms of hereditarians, Determinists, Eugenists; it is essentially individual, personal, free; and . . . that in which it lives can preserve it and its own proper body to everlasting life."[79]

With his faith in individuality, Olivier constantly found himself pitted against institutions, and he always took the side of the people who wanted to shake things up. Convinced that the Fabian Society had become "ossified," he backed H. G. Wells in his 1906 attempt to take control of the group and transform it into a revolutionary political party. As a colonial administrator, Olivier pressed forward his idiosyncratic policies without regard for regulations or tradition, oblivious to the wishes of the planters and the natives. He dismissed the Colonial Office as a bureaucratic "engine" that impeded his personal freedom, and he bitterly opposed the Boer War. Bernard Shaw assured him that small nations like the Boer republics would inevitably be absorbed into larger political units, but this sort of argument enraged Olivier, who hated the very word *fatalistic*. The war, he told Shaw, had been caused not by some irresistible force of social evolution but by Lord Milner and his pigheadedness. History was made by individuals—nothing was automatic—and the Fabians had to resist the imperialist "machine."[80] A recent study of the Society for Psychical Research indicates that it attracted antiorganization men of Olivier's type. They were eccentrics who kicked out against bureaucracies and searched for a "secular soul" for much the same reason—they had a highly developed sense of individuality, and they refused to be cogs in any administrative or cosmic machine.[81]

Victorian psychology had been dominated by movements that discouraged belief in free will. According to the associationist psychology of Herbert Spencer, human thought was mostly a matter of receiving impressions from the environment, associating impressions that were related in terms of time or space or appearance, and responding to outside stimuli. Henry Maudsley and the physiological psychologists, on the other hand, found the roots of behavior in the structure of the brain and nervous system. Either way, man was mainly a machine, able to seek his own nourishment, happiness, and self-preservation, but having little or no spontaneous initiative of his own. Between 1830 and 1880 research in the area of reflex action appeared to confirm that all psychology could be reduced to a simple machinery of stimulus and response. Charles Darwin would reinforce that mechanistic approach to behavior by pointing out the role of instinct in the struggle for survival. The highwater mark of robot psychology came in 1874, when T. H. Huxley caused a sensation with his address to the British Association "Of the Hypothesis That All Animals Are Automata."[82]

Toward the end of the century, a number of social scientists recoiled from this sort of fatalism. F. W. H. Myers tried to formulate a psychology of will, as did L. T. Hobhouse, who performed experiments on higher animals to prove that "self-conscious effort" and intelligence were more important to survival than instinct. Even Huxley took a step back from his position of 1874: in his 1893 Romanes Lecture "Evolution and Ethics," he allowed that man might not be a helpless prisoner of his environment, that he could work with the forces of nature and mold society according to his will.[83]

Much of the credit for turning British psychology in this direction belongs to James Ward, who developed a vitalist psychology out of an attempt to reconcile science and religion. He came from a strict Nonconformist home and trained to be a Congregational minister, but his studies in natural science undermined his faith. Desperately he searched for some way of framing "an apology for Christianity . . . that shall rest on first principles." In the early 1870s he determined "to resolve the present general laws of Physics into a higher—in short what might be called cosmology philosophically considered. . . . Shall I after all turn to science . . . and unlike other inquirers proclaim Nature as a Revelation of God, and by living a Christian life though retired shew that Science and Faith can go together?"[84]

At Cambridge, Ward studied under a man who was also searching for a synthesis of science and faith—Henry Sidgwick—and took up psychology. In this field Ward achieved distinction as a Trinity College lecturer, but he still felt keenly the loss of religion. Social morality, he warned in 1878, would collapse "without religious aspirations and the old feelings of awe and mystery that Nature inspired in the best minds. . . . These springs of higher life must revive again or the beggarly elements will starve us back into savages."[85] Man still needed something like a soul to ensure his good behavior, but it would have to be a secular soul, credible in the light of contemporary science.

The ninth edition of the *Encyclopaedia Britannica* (1886) was the first to devote an article to psychology, and it was contributed by James Ward. That essay caused a great commotion in professional circles, and it set the dominant tone for British psychology for the next generation. Ward bluntly attacked the associationists and physiologists for reducing man to an automaton, capable only of responding to his environment. This, as he later put it, was worse than "a psychology without a soul," it was "a psychology without even consciousness."[86] Account had to be taken of an autonomous human will, of a "pure Ego or Subject." In his definitive work, *Psychological Principles* (1918), Ward declared that psychology had to deal with not only passive cognition, "but also, and above all, conative activity or behaviour." It had to study the individual from "the standpoint of conscious Life—or more fully the standpoint of the living subject in intercourse with his special environment."[87] Behavior was not entirely controlled by conditioning; some human activity sprang from an emotional, nonrational "Ego" struggling for "self-realization."[88] As a believer in the will and an Idealist philosopher, Ward repudiated laissez-faire economics and insisted that man could reshape his social environment through welfare legislation.[89] Human beings were not the prisoners of natural laws, Ward proclaimed: "There are no laws antecedent to the active individuals who compose the world, no laws determining *them*, unless we call their own nature a law."

The ego was Ward's replacement for the soul, a semispiritual force forever seeking "more and fuller life" for the individual.[90] Only Life, according to Ward, could account for the fact of progress and evolution: "Mechanism can always, life and experience can never, be made to move backwards: for the one composition and dissolution are altogether on a par, in that they entail no change of either mass or energy; for the other there is the vital difference of value between organization and disorganization, sense and nonsense." Mechanism is the source of all decadence whereas life constantly works against decadence: "The steady downward trend, the katabolic, levelling tendencies attributed to unchecked mechanism we find not merely suspended but reversed wherever there is life and mind." Ward suggested that life was exempt from the law of conservation of energy—it might manufacture new energy and roll back entropy.

As a creative evolutionist, Ward attacked Darwin's mechanistic evolution as a contradiction in terms. A machine cannot truly evolve, Ward reasoned, it can only change according to a predetermined pattern, like the face of a clock. There is no genuine novelty in this, no clear break with the past. That can only result from the "creative synthesis" produced by life.[91] (T. E. Hulme, incidentally, used the same logic to defend Henri Bergson and attack materialism.)[92]

At the same time, a parallel revolt against fatalism was breaking out in literature. Among the late Victorians, Thomas Hardy, George Gissing, and George Moore had populated their novels with prisoners of circumstance, who are shaped largely by their heredity and their environment. "Change the surroundings in which a man lives, and, in two or three generations you will have changed his physical constitution, his habits of life, and a goodly number of his ideas"—so reads the prefatory epigram to Moore's *A Mummer's Wife* (1885). Moore and Gissing experimented with English versions of French Naturalism, which applied the determinism of science to literature. Nothing could be further from a celebration of life than Hardy's *Jude the Obscure* (1895), in which Jude's son dies miserably, anticipating "the coming universal wish not to live."[93] In his 1890 essay "The Critic as Artist," Oscar Wilde used fatalism to defend the idle "contemplative life" of the aesthete. "By revealing to us the absolute mechanism of all action," Wilde wrote, the science of heredity had demonstrated that the true end of life is "not *doing* but *being*."[94]

"In our modern mythology," wrote May Sinclair in 1897, "Custom, Circumstance, and Heredity are the three Fates that weave the web of human life."[95] Her choice of the word *mythology*, however, indicates that she herself did not subscribe to this creed, and her 1919 novel *Mary Olivier* was actually an explicit attack on the determinism of Spencer and Maudsley. Around 1895 the tide had turned against fatalism in English literature. The clear message of George Bernard Shaw, H. G. Wells, D. H. Lawrence, E. M. Forster, G. K. Chesterton, J. M. Barrie, Harley Granville Barker, John Galsworthy, Rudyard Kipling, and James Joyce is that the individual can resist, struggle, and prevail. The fatalism of George Moore's early work gave way to the optimism of *The Lake*, in which Rose Leicester and Father Gogarty, far from being products of their environment, revolt against their milieu and break free of it. Joseph Conrad was much less of an optimist than any of the above, but even Lord Jim and Lena succeed, in the end, in taking control of their destinies, though they accept death in doing so. When Jim faces the wrath of the natives of Patusan, he is not cravenly submitting to fate. He is asserting "his exalted egoism," attempting "to prove his power . . . and conquer the fatal destiny itself"—and it is precisely Jim's "intensity of life" that drives him to defy that destiny (*Jim* chaps. 21, 45).

The cutting edge of this reaction against fatalism was provided by W. E. Henley, an editor and an admirer of Conrad and one of the most influential literary midwives of his day. Crippled by tubercular arthritis, Henley aggressively affirmed his optimism and love of life. His 1875 poem "Invictus" ("I am the master of my fate;/I am the captain of my soul") was reverentially quoted by H. G. Wells, J. M. Barrie, and D. H. Lawrence.[96] As editor of the *National Observer* (1889–1894) and the *New Review* (1894–1897), Henley had a great impact on several of the leading authors of Edwardian England. He slashed away at "degenerate" aesthetes and decadents, gloated over the downfall of Oscar Wilde, and championed youth and vitality in literature. Henley's vitality often manifested itself in saber-rattling imperialism (one of his followers was Rudyard Kipling), but his magazines were also read by good anti-imperialist Liberals like C. F. G. Masterman.[97] "What a feast of good things was represented by the old *National Observer!*" wrote Masterman. It may have been reactionary in its politics, "but it was alive, fervent," and Henley was without doubt one of the most "original and formative minds in English letters."[98]

One example of Henley's voluntarist influence is *The Time Machine* (1895), which he both encouraged H. G. Wells to write and serialized in the *New Review*. In its original form, *The Time Machine* was dismally fatalistic. The future is already *there*, completely plotted out, and it promises nothing but universal entropy and the decay of civilization. But Henley persuaded Wells to add a postscript in which the narrator, having seen the inevitable, simply refuses to accept it: "I, for my own part, cannot think that these latter days of weak experiment, fragmentary theory, and mutual discord are indeed man's culminating time! . . . If that is so, it remains for us to live as though it were not so."[99] Wells went on to become a vociferous exponent of the power of the will.

> If the world does not please you, *you can change it*. Determine to alter it at any price, and you can change it altogether. You may change it to something sinister and angry, to something appalling, but it may be you will change it to something brighter, something more agreeable, and at the worst something much more interesting. There is only one sort of man who is absolutely to blame for his own misery, and that is the man who finds life dull and dreary. There are no circumstances in the world that determined action cannot alter, unless, perhaps, they are the walls of a prison cell, and even those will dissolve and change, I am told, into the infirmary compartment, at any rate, for the man who can fast with resolution.[100]

Until 1895 Henry James generally allowed his heroes and heroines limited freedom of will. "You wanted to look at life for yourself," Ralph Touchett tells Isabel Archer in *The Portrait of a Lady* (1881), "but you were not allowed; you were punished for your wish. You were ground in the very mill of the conventional!"[101] Even Isabel, however, manages to preserve "the attitude of a woman who had her life to live. . . . Deep in her soul—deeper than any appetite for renunciation— was the sense that life would be her business for a long time to come."[102] And after the *Guy Domville* disaster, there would be still more room for life and initiative in James's fiction. The title character of *What Maisie Knew* (1897), serialized in Henley's *New Review*, is an acquiescent passenger in the novel until the very end, allowing herself to be handed from parent to parent to stepparent. Then, in the final pages, she takes control of the story, refusing to be separated from her nurse unless her guardians end their immoral liaison. Maisie's sudden assertion of will arises out of a basic animal reflex, and her admiring stepfather can find only one word to describe it: "I think I've produced life. I don't know what to call it—I have n't even known how decently to deal with it, to approach it; but whatever it is, it's the most beautiful thing I've ever met—it's exquisite, it's sacred."[103] Granted, Strether assures us in *The Ambassadors* that there is no such thing as free will, that "the affair of life [is] at the best a tin mould . . . into which, a helpless jelly, one's consciousness is poured. . . . Still," he affirms, "one has the illusion of freedom," and one should follow that illusion. "Live!" he urges Little Bilham. "Live all you can; it's a mistake not to. It does n't so much matter what you do in particular, so long as you have your life" (*Ambass.* 21:217–18).

Literary historians have noted that the Edwardian cult of Life gave rise to the "open-ended" novel—a novel (to give the simplest definition) that ends before the story ends, leaving the impression that the plot extends beyond the final page.[104] Joseph Conrad pointed out that Henry James created this effect by concluding his novels with renunciations (such as Strether's renunciation of Mrs. Newsome and Miss Gostrey) that left the original conflicts unresolved.

> It is obvious that a solution by rejection must always present a certain lack of finality, especially startling when contrasted with the usual methods of solution by rewards and punishments, by crowned love, by fortune, by a broken leg or a sudden death. Why the reading public which, as a body, has never laid upon a story-teller the command to be an artist, should demand from him this sham of Divine Omnipotence, is utterly incomprehensible. . . . One is never set at rest by Mr. Henry James's novels. His books end as an episode in life ends. You remain with the sense of the life still going on; and even the subtle presence of the dead is felt in that silence that comes upon the artist-creation when the last word has been read. It is eminently satisfying, but it is not final.[105]

Life, in other words, is not divided into discrete novel-length segments, with clear beginnings and neat resolutions. It is a continuous stream that never comes to a full stop and never works out every problem. James knew that the end of a novel is an artificial frame imposed on the unending flow of life: "Really, universally, relations stop nowhere, and the exquisite problem of the artist is eternally but to draw, by a geometry of his own, the circle within which they shall happily *appear* to do so."[106] Virginia Woolf could have brought *The Voyage Out* to a close with Rachel's death, but she wrote two additional chapters to allow the other characters to resume the business of living. "What I wanted to do," she explained to Lytton Strachey, "was to give the feeling of a vast tumult of life, as various and disorderly as possible, which should be cut short for a moment by the death, and go on again."[107] H. G. Wells, whom Virginia Woolf disdained as a hopelessly crude artist, described his *Tono-Bungay* in very similar terms—"a miscellaneous tasting of life," a sprawling collection of "unmanageable realities"[108]—and *Tono-Bungay* has the same open-ended structure as *The Voyage Out*. Rather than conclude with the spectacular crash of the Ponderevo patent-medicine empire, Wells adds another chapter, in which George Ponderevo designs a swift destroyer and embarks on his own voyage out. That ending followed logically from Wells's faith in the will. Because the individual can always change the course of destiny, no conclusion can be final: "We are all things that make and pass, striving upon a hidden mission, out to the open sea."[109]

E. M. Forster seconded Wells on that point. "After all, why has a novel to be planned?" he asked. "Cannot it grow? Why need it close, as a play closes? Cannot it open out?" The novel should be like a symphony, harmonious yet free, expanding in all directions and never entirely finished. "When the symphony is over we feel that the notes and the tunes composing it have been liberated, they have found in the rhythm of the whole their individual freedom," Forster wrote in *Aspects of the Novel* (1927). "Cannot the novel be like that?"[110] Regarding the Victorian convention of ending a novel with a marriage, Forster objected not to the marriage but to the ending: "Artists now realize that marriage, the old full stop, is not an end at all.[111] There is life after matrimony, which is why Forster hazarded to put a marriage smack in the middle of *Howards End.*

Life led D. H. Lawrence directly to the open-ended story. His first novel, *The White Peacock*, is steeped in the dismal fatalism of Decadent literature. George is Lettie's powerless victim, unable to extricate himself from her toils, and the whole story is predicated on the assumption that "we can't help ourselves, we're all chessmen."[112] *The Trespasser*, however, uses a similar plot to convey the opposite message: Siegmund is also destroyed by a woman, but he clearly could have saved himself and only failed to do so through lack of will. "After all, if you're alive you've got to live," a friend asserts at the beginning of the novel, "there's no such thing as passive existence."[113] *Sons and Lovers* (1913), Lawrence's third novel, was the first to have an open ending. Paul Morel, after mercifully hastening his mother's death and losing both of the women he loves, sinks into suicidal misery, but in the last brief paragraph the novel abruptly changes course—Paul steels himself, sets his face toward the city, and resolves to press on with life. The same sudden shift to affirmation occurs in the concluding pages of *The Rainbow* and the final sentence of *Women in Love.*

These last-minute changes of key reflect Lawrence's faith in the possibilities of life, a faith that grew out of his own personal tragedies and triumphs. Lawrence wrote most of *Sons and Lovers* after his mother's death in December 1910, a loss that plunged him for a time into a morose fatalism. "Life is a strange, inflexible, dreadful thing which turns us slowly in its lathe," he wrote in March 1911. "The thing is not to resist too strenuously this graving tool."[114] But before he completed the book, he escaped to the continent with Frieda Walkley, a daring dash for freedom that convinced him of the potency of the will. "Life *can* be great—quite god-like," he now affirmed. "It *can* be so. God be thanked I have proved it."[115] "*Do* it," he urged his friends. "Now decide to live."[116] He condemned "this giving in before you start, that pervades all Conrad and such folks—The Writer among the Ruins. I can't forgive Conrad for being so sad and for giving in."[117]

The individual cannot be limited by anything, not by convention, not by fate, not by a stifling marriage, and certainly not by the fact that the novelist has to wind up his story somewhere. The novel, then, must end by affirming the potentiality of life. *The Rainbow* concludes with the promise of "a new germination" and "a new growth," promising as well another novel to follow it. Likewise, "Welcome, O life!" at the close of *A Portrait of the Artist as a Young Man* signals that there will be more to the story of Stephen Dedalus. The Lawrentian individual is an "allotropic" creature, always becoming, without clear limits, and consequently the Lawrentian novel must also spill over its boundaries. "Life, the ever-present, knows no finality, no finished crystallization. . . . There must be mutation, swifter than irridescence, haste, not rest, come-and-go, not fixity, inconclusiveness, immediacy, the quality of life itself, without denouement or close."[118]

William C. Frierson identified a whole school of Edwardian "life-novels," each chronicling the struggle of the individual to master his fate. *The Way of All Flesh* was the seminal work in this subgenre, in which Frierson included *Sons and Lovers, A Portrait of the Artist*, Hugh Walpole's *Fortitude* (1914), Compton Mackenzie's *Sinister Street* (1914), and Somerset Maugham's *Of Human Bondage*.[119] (Wells's *Tono-Bungay* certainly belongs on this list as well.) In 1916 Arthur Waugh celebrated these novels as a revolt against all forms of nineteenth-century fatalism.

> Victorian realism . . . was a realism hedged in and limited by convention. Certain elementary laws of life were taken for granted; certain moral and spiritual restrictions accepted. . . . There succeeded the rather anaemic, drab, and squalid realism of George Gissing and Mr. George Moore, where incident was piled upon incident with the scrupulous exactness of an inventory, and life emerged from the picture, where its outline could be discerned at all, as a perpetual struggle against an overpowering and soul-sapping array of circumstance. . . . Its interest was almost exclusively confined to the effect of a man's surroundings upon his life and character. . . . And here, once more, the conventional standards were regarded as being so far binding upon the individual, that his failure to conform to them implied an almost inevitable failure to survive in the struggle for existence.

That dismal realism had been superseded by an Edwardian "New Realism," which proclaimed that "life is full of adventure and recompense." Of course, life could also be a succession of disappointments and frustrations: the New Realists did not fall into an optimistic fatalism that ignored unpleasant facts or assumed the inevitability of human progress. But they affirmed that "the soul of man," by sheer effort of will, could prevail against any material handicap or social restriction. In an almost religious sense, Waugh concluded, the New Realism transcended

> the conventional realism of conditions and environment; its interest is not in the material convenience or inconvenience of life, but the spiritual achievement of man, and his ultimate realisation of his soul's possibilities. For the artist of the new realism the Kingdom of Heaven lies within the soul of man; for the realist of the last generation, it was almost invariably sought from without, in the individual's relation with the rest of the world.[120]

Art for Life's Sake

The concept of Life was at the root of another celebrated innovation in the art of the novel: the stream of consciousness. William James had invented the term in 1890, and at the time he had suggested another possible name for the same process: one could just as easily "call it the stream . . . of conscious life."[121] The materialist psychology of Locke and Spencer, as James later noted, treated ideas as discrete "elementary psychic particles or atoms of 'mind-stuff,' . . . the bricks of which our mental architecture is built up."[122] That conception of the mind fitted the old technique of telling a story in distinct, logically ordered frames. Vitalism, however, suggested a continuous flow of mental processes. The pioneers of the stream of consciousness, like Henri Bergson and James Joyce, also happened to be apostles of Life. "There are *no* clearly outlined and separated states . . . of mind," wrote T. E. Hulme in his defense of Bergson; "each state fades away into and interpenetrates the next state" in an endless "stream of impulse which constitutes life."[123] In the words of Edouard Dujardin, from whom Joyce borrowed the technique, the stream-of-consciousness method recorded "la vie intérieur."[124]

Ultimately, the origins of the interior monologue can be traced back to a religious vacuum. Having lost faith in the Christian soul, Joyce and Hulme were able to find a secular soul in the current of conscious life. The novelist Dorothy Richardson, like her heroine Miriam Henderson, was a deeply skeptical woman with strong religious impulses, and her novel cycle *Pilgrimage* (as the title suggests) chronicles a spiritual quest. She was attracted to John Bunyan's *Pilgrim's Progress* and particularly to the Quaker doctrine of the "inner light," the idea of faith in the "single human soul." She wrote *Pointed Roofs* (1915), the first installment of *Pilgrimage*, in a converted chapel. Telling her story from the individual "center of being," she converted the inner light to an inner monologue.[125] Using that method, Miss Richardson could focus on the soul of a heroine and depict "life streaming out behind her, spreading and shining and rippling, herself the radiant point of that wonderful life."[126] "The only satisfactory definition of a man's consciousness is his life," she wrote in 1933. "And this, superficially regarded, does seem to exhibit a sort of stream-line."[127]

In the April 1918 *Egoist*, May Sinclair hailed this new type of novel in which "nothing happens. It is just life going on and on."[128] A reader of Samuel Butler, Miss Sinclair would use a similar technique in her novel *Mary Olivier* (1919). Virginia Woolf read Richardson and Joyce, and she may well have picked up some Bergsonian philosophy from her sister-in-law Karin Stephen, who published a treatise on Bergson in 1922. But the dissemination of the interior monologue cannot be explained entirely by tracking down influences. As far back as *The Voyage Out*, Mrs.

Woolf had been concerned with "the vast tumult of life," and the idea of Life itself made her receptive to the new technique. "All the real part of your life has a real dream in it," Dorothy Richardson had written in *The Tunnel* (1919), and when you follow that stream of consciousness "you are really following your life." Mrs. Woolf immediately grasped that specific passage and Richardson's method, "plaiting incessantly the many-coloured and innumerable threads of life." That often-quoted passage from Woolf's essay "Modern Fiction" (1919) has to be read in that context: "Life is not a series of gig-lamps symmetrically arranged; life is a luminous halo, a semi-transparent envelope surrounding us from the beginning of consciousness to the end."[129]

"Life" had one other important effect on Edwardian art: it directly clashed with late Victorian Aestheticism. Oscar Wilde had always regarded "life—poor, probable, uninteresting human life"—as a tedious thing, at least until it had been transformed into art. "Life and Nature may sometimes be used as part of Art's rough material," he conceded, "but before they are of any real service to Art they must be translated into artistic conventions."[130] Wilde particularly disliked the unpredictability of life—which, according to the old saw, is what happens when you are planning something else. For Wilde, controllability was one of the great virtues of art: the artist entirely determines what goes into it, and the aesthete can sample it at will, savoring an appropriate book or painting whenever he wants to experience a given emotion. "There is no passion that we cannot feel, no pleasure that we may not gratify, and we can choose the time of our initiation and the time of our freedom also," Wilde wrote in an 1890 essay. "Life," on the other hand, "is a thing narrowed by circumstances, incoherent in its utterance, and without that fine correspondence of form and spirit which is the only thing that can satisfy the artistic and critical temperament."[131]

At the beginning of *The Ambassadors*, Strether is very much an aesthete in this mold, thoroughly in control of a tasteful and predictable existence. He is sent to Paris to see to it that Chad Newsome is "protected . . . from life" by returning him to Massachusetts, settling him into a respectable marriage and business career, and in general shielding him from the unanticipated. But Strether himself comes smack up against the unexpected when he finds Chad inexplicably and profoundly matured—"a miracle almost monstrous"—and he discovers that he likes this element of unpredictability. He gropes for a word to describe it: it is "the fate that waits for one, the dark doom that rides, . . . the uncanny. . . . Call it then life . . . call it poor dear old life simply that springs the surprise" (*Ambass.* 21:167-68).

Strether still tends to treat life as a work of art. He embarks on a rail excursion to the French countryside to take in the landscape as he would a painting. At one small rural depot he finds it: everything falls "into a composition, full of felicity," all neatly enclosed within an imaginary "oblong gilt frame." He feels that he has stepped into a Maupassant story, and he enjoys watching life as a "picture," a "play," "a scene and a stage." His day has all the controlled perfection of art: events are "not only inevitable, but so much more nearly natural and right . . . that they were . . . easier, pleasanter to put up with." But then life intrudes "like some unprovoked harsh note." Chad and his mistress make an awkward and unforeseen entrance into the picture, breaking the composition and smashing the frame (*Ambass.* 22:245–66).

James realized that art needs the shock of unpredictable reality. Literature, he asserted in *The Golden Bowl*, must have "arrests and surprises, emotions alike of disappointment and elation." It must, in short, be "a *living* affair."[132] But James, like Wilde, could not use life in its raw form. It had to be softened, arranged, edited, and highlighted by art before it was of any use to the novelist: "Art *makes* life, makes interest, makes importance."

Here James was fighting a strong Edwardian current. In a March 1914 article in the *Times Literary Supplement*, he complained that the "younger generation" of English novelists—Arnold Bennett, Gilbert Cannan, Compton Mackenzie, Hugh Walpole, and H. G. Wells—were sacrificing form to realism and vitality. Each of their works, he acknowledged, was an authentic "expression of life," full of revealing details, "saturated" with atmosphere and energy, but to what purpose? "Where is the interest itself, where and what is its centre and how are we to measure it in relation to *that*?" James was a good friend of Wells's, and he complimented him on writing novels "more convulsed with life and more brimming with blood than any it is given me nowadays to meet." But to Mrs. Humphry Ward, James confided that he was distressed by Wells's crudeness, by "the co-existence of so much talent with so little art, so much life with (so to speak) so little living!"[133] In *Tono-Bungay*, Wells had conceded that

my ideas of a novel all through are comprehensive rather than austere. . . . I'll own that here, with the pen already started, I realise what a fermenting mass of things learned and emotions experienced and theories formed I've got to deal with, and how, in a sense, hopeless my book must be from the very outset. I suppose what I'm really trying to render is nothing more nor less than Life—as one man has found it . . . without having any of the discipline to refrain and omit that I suppose the regular novel-writer acquires. . . . I fail to see how I can be other than a lax, undisciplined storyteller. I must sprawl and flounder, comment and theorise, if I am to get the thing out I have in mind. And it isn't a constructed tale I have to tell but unmanageable realities.[134]

James's critique, however, enraged Wells, and in his 1914 novel *Boon* he inserted a rather vicious attack on Jamesian fiction.

If the novel is to follow life it must be various and discursive. Life is diversity and entertainment, not completeness and satisfaction. All actions are half-hearted, shot delightfully with wandering thoughts—about something else. All true stories are a felt of irrelevances. But James sets out to make his novels with the presupposition that they can be made continuously relevant. And perceiving the discordant things, he tries to get rid of them. He sets himself to pick the straws out of the hair of Life before he paints her. But without the straws she is no longer the mad woman we love.[135]

Bernard Shaw contrasted aesthetes unfavorably with his vitalist heroes—Praed and Vivie in *Mrs. Warren's Profession*, Apollodorus and Caesar in *Caesar and Cleopatra* (1898), and Octavius and Tanner (not to mention the Devil and Don Juan) in *Man and Superman*. *Candida* (1896) ends with Marchbanks, the poet, repudiating the lower pleasures of art ("life is nobler than that") to serve the Universal Will ("I am impatient to do what must be done").[136] Heaven in *Man and Superman* is an austere place, the home of the rigorous vitalist, whereas Hell is a gaudy aesthetic paradise of perpetual concerts ("music is the brandy of the damned"). "The poetic temperament's a very nice temperament, very amiable, very harmless and poetic, I daresay," remarks Ann Whitefield, "but it's an old maid's temperament." "Barren," Tanner acknowledges. "The Life Force passes it by."[137] In *Women in Love*, Lawrence said the same of the aesthetic "half men" who frequent the Pompadour Cafe and titter over Birkin's vitalist sermons.[138]

E. M. Forster, in his lifelong quest for reconciliation, was able to fuse vitality and aesthetics in *A Room with a View*. A view, after all, suggests both art and life: it is beautiful and framed but also expansive, open-ended, and real. The decadent aestheticism of Cecil Vyse is the product

of a stuffy drawing room, "with no view" (*Room* 165–66). Forster preferred the primitive vitality of early Italian art: "One doesn't come to
Italy for niceness, one comes for life" (*Room* 33). At first Lucy Honeychurch is careful to keep her art and her life separate, playing the piano
with a passion she excludes from the rest of her existence. She is "not
wonderful as far as life goes," a friend observes, but eventually "the
water-tight compartments in her will break down, and the music and
life will mingle. Then we shall have her heroically good, heroically
bad—too heroic, perhaps, to be good or bad" (*Room* 52–55, 67–68,
144–45). Lucy's meticulously planned art tour (like Lambert Strether's)
is upset by an unexpected eruption of life, when she and George witness
that murder in the streets. The shock comes as a revelation to George ("I
shall want to live, I say"), and it forces Lucy to accept "the most price-
less of all possessions—her own soul" (*Room* 171–72). Cecil had always
treated Lucy "as a work of art," but Italy teaches her to let her temper
rip with a healthy disregard for aesthetics. "Rant is a sign of vitality,"
Forster assures us; "it mars the beautiful creature, but shows that she is
alive." When Lucy breaks her engagement with Cecil, she is thoroughly
transformed: "From a Leonardo she had become a living woman, with
mysteries and forces of her own, with qualities that even eluded art"
(*Room* 155, 165–66, 261).

Of course, Forster, Lawrence, and Shaw were not hostile to art as
such; but they insisted that art was more than idle appreciation. The
artist had to be a vitalist as well, like Paul Morel in *Sons and Lovers* or
Louis Dubedat in Shaw's play *The Doctor's Dilemma* (1906). This vision of
art was popularized in Somerset Maugham's *Of Human Bondage*, in
which Philip Carey successively rejects the Church of England, French
Impressionism, aestheticism, and decadence, all for the same failing:
"He had always had a passion for life, and the idealism he had come
across seemed to him for the most part a cowardly shrinking from it.
. . . Philip clamoured for life as it stood; sordidness, vice, deformity,
did not offend him; he declared that he wanted man in his nakedness."
Convinced that "life was to be lived rather than portrayed," Philip
works as an intern in a charity hospital ("It was life"), but he finally
discovers a vital flame in the paintings of Goya.

> [It] was something better than . . . realism. . . ; but certainly it was not
> the bloodless idealism which stepped aside from life in weakness; it was too
> strong; it was virile; it accepted life in all its vivacity, ugliness and beauty,

squalor and heroism; it was realism still; but it was realism carried to some higher pitch, in which facts were transformed by the more vivid light in which they were seen. . . . He was always seeking for a meaning in life, and here it seemed to him that a meaning was offered. . . . He seemed to see that a man need not leave his life to chance, but that his will was powerful; . . . that the inward life might be as manifold, as varied, as rich with experience, as the life of one who conquered realms and explored unknown lands.[139]

This vitality found expression in the work of Augustus John, the recognized leader of the avant-garde in Edwardian art. John was married to Ida Nettleship, a niece of James Hinton who was devoted to vitalist religion ("God is the spirit of Life and we are full of that spirit . . ."). John never worked out his life aesthetic on paper: clearly it was something too protean, too impulsive to be killed and mounted in a treatise. It is defined only in his slashing, mobile style of painting. The lustiness of his art offended the aesthete in Henry James—"John paints human beings as if they were animals"—but Laurence Binyon recognized this quality as a great strength.

> Somehow everything lives. Even the paint, rudely dashed on the canvas, seems to be rebelling into beauties of its own. . . . A tall woman leaning on a staff; a little boy in scarlet on a cliff-edge against a blue sea; a woman carrying bundles of lavender: the description of these says nothing, but they themselves seem creatures of the infancy of the world, aboriginals of the earth, with an animal dignity and strangeness, swift of gesture, beautifully poised. That is the secret of Mr. John's power. . . . There is a jet of elemental energy, something powerful and unaccountable, like life itself.

Like James Joyce, John described artistic creation as an act of "parturition" and brought a sacramental carnality to his portraits of women. Mothers and babies were John's favorite subjects, and he sired a legendary number of children, most of them out of wedlock.[140] Indeed, Holbrook Jackson reported, among Edwardian artists in general, *Art for Art's Sake* had been supplanted by *Art for Life's Sake*.[141]

Life for Life's Sake

The title of Richard Aldington's autobiography, *Life for Life's Sake*, might have been an even better way to express that ideal. For Edwardian bohemians, life meant freedom for the individual, freedom from convention and security, freedom to do and see—freedom, simply, to experience life. Aldington himself turned his back on a respectable career to become a poor poet in the service of "my lady Life," who embodied "everything that has made life valuable—freedom of living, thinking, and utterance; the exercise of a natural aptitude or talent, disinterested friendship, passionate love, travel, the arts, idleness."[142]

Significantly, Aldington did not include happiness in that definition. Life, in this sense, was a repudiation of hedonism and Victorian utilitarianism. The adventure of living was valuable for its own sake, not because it necessarily made for personal felicity. As Gilbert Murray argued, "Utility," "Happiness," and "Pleasure" were vague expressions, and they put "too much stress on the future result to be obtained, whereas the truth is that The End of Life is in the Processes of Life."[143] "Damn your happiness!" spits Paul Morel on behalf of D. H. Lawrence. "So long as life's full, it doesn't matter whether it's happy or not."[144] In *The Rainbow* Anton Skrebensky devotes himself to that utilitarian ideal, "the good of the greatest number," and in doing so he is reduced to "a sort of nullity," robbed of "his own instrinsic life" and "the vital fulfilment of his soul" (*Rainbow* 308–10). In *Man and Superman* John Tanner is terrified by the prospect of "a lifetime of happiness! No man alive could bear it: it would be hell on earth."[145] Don Juan's Hell is, in fact, a utilitarian utopia, "the home . . . of the seekers for happiness," whereas Heaven is the kingdom of "Life,"[146] "and courage," Shaw wrote elsewhere, "consists in the readiness to sacrifice happiness for an intenser quality of life."[147]

George Dangerfield characterizes the concurrent movement for women's rights as a "drive toward life,"[148] but Edwardian feminists were in fact divided on this point. Some, like Dorothy Richardson, did indeed see emancipated women voyaging "out into life, scored and scarred, but alive and changeable, able to become quite new," rejecting domestic security for individual and sexual freedom.[149] But the Women's Social and Political Union, the most militant of the suffrage organizations, was single-mindedly devoted to winning, not life, but the vote, and the two objectives sometimes conflicted. Life-worshipping feminists were searching, like Ursula Brangwen, for some "strange, passionate knowledge of religion and living far transcending the limits of the automatic system that contained the vote" (*Rainbow* 383-84).

Dora Marsden was a WSPU member who had served time in jail for the cause of suffragism, but in 1911 she and Harriet Shaw Weaver launched the *Freewoman*, a weekly magazine that dismissed votes for women as an "empty concept" and campaigned "not for the advancement of Woman, but for the empowering of individuals, men and women." The feminist polemics of the *Freewoman* were gradually subsumed in a more general call for personal liberation. Accordingly, at the end of 1913, the magazine was rechristened the *Egoist*, and it went on to serialize James Joyce's paean to life and self, *A Portrait of the Artist as a Young Man*. There was not much room for self-realization in the WSPU, which, under the frankly dictatorial rule of Emmeline and Christabel Pankhurst, subjected its members to quasi-military discipline. Christabel Pankhurst had no use for anarchic talk of free love: her 1913 tract *The Great Scourge* claimed (absurdly) that the vast majority of men were infected with venereal disease, and she assured readers that, for women, the sex act was usually dangerous or distasteful. Dora Marsden promptly attacked *The Great Scourge* as spinsterish and backward looking. Chastity, she asserted, was a symptom of "weak vitality," an affliction worse than any social disease.

> It is more important to heighten vitality than to combat disease: which as a matter of fact can only be overcome by increased vitality, and there is more danger to "health" to be awaited from the misery of renunciation and the dull heats of virginity than from the ills of syphilis and gonorrhoea. . . . In disease life is afflicted, but it is petrified by dulness. . . . The seeking after the "vicious" is a small ineffectual wriggle which life makes to escape the boredom of the "pure."[150]

Rebecca West, Dora Marsden's young literary discovery, also repudiated the Pankhurst line as inimical to life. In the spring of 1913 she fell in love with H. G. Wells; when her first overtures to him were rebuffed, she left for Spain in a rage, lecturing her fellow passengers on the necessity of women's suffrage. The rough sensuality of Spain, however, convinced her "that the mere framework of life is so imperishable and delicious that with all else lost it is worth living for," and she took up the worship of "refreshing flesh and blood." Now she rejected the political fervor of the militant suffragettes as self-destructive, "a treachery against the orderly procession of generation after generation, which we call life." She went as far as to compare the WSPU to a lynch mob in the southern United States. In October Wells suggested that she publish her collected articles under the title *The Taste of Life*; shortly thereafter they became lovers. By December 1913 Miss West declared herself "purged of political passion" and dedicated to "self-realisation whether it leads to death or gaiety."[151]

In *Ann Veronica*, written some time before he met Rebecca West, H. G. Wells preached much the same moral. The heroine, who talks endlessly of her hunger for "Life,"[152] leaves her stuffy suburban home and her dictatorial father to make a career for herself in London. She participates in a suffragette raid on Parliament, but she finds the militants too antimale and eventually elopes with her college tutor. He teaches biology (of course), and with him she learns that the "Life" she is seeking is more than "rebellion": it is above all the "eternal Bios," the breeding instinct.[153] *Ann Veronica* scored a *succès de scandale* among the emancipated young women of 1909, like the Bloomsbury artist Dora Carrington.[154] Although it was based on another of Wells's extramarital affairs, it closely parallels the early life and intellectual development of Rebecca West, who bore an illegitimate child fathered by Wells.

"It's life that matters, nothing but life—the process of discovering— the everlasting and perpetual process, not the discovery itself at all."[155] That was the teleology of Virginia Woolf, whose novels always depict political feminists as somehow deficient in "life." Evelyn Murgatroyd, in *The Voyage Out*, is an arrogant and patronizing do-gooder, so wrapped up in politics that she is incapable of personal intimacy—a mortal sin in Bloomsbury. She is "tormented by the little spark of life in her which was always trying to work through to other people, and was always being rebuffed" (*Voyage* 251). In *Night and Day* there is Mary Dachet, who "had renounced something, and was now . . . not quite 'in the running' for life" (*Night* 265). Virginia Woolf's heroines discover life not in politics but in personal relations—Rachel Vinrace with Hirst and Hewet, from whom "all life seemed to radiate" (*Voyage* 175), and Katherine Hilbery with Ralph Denham, who is a veritable "source of life" (*Night* 503-5). Mary Dachet finds politics deadly because it splits humanity into parties whereas she looks for a "vision . . . of harmony" among individuals: "She could not see the world divided into separate compartments of good and bad people, any more than she could believe so implicitly in the rightness of her own thought as to wish to bring the population of the British Isles into agreement with it." Fixated on the vote, Virginia Woolf's suffragettes are isolated, one-sided "shadow people, flitting in and out of the ranks of the living—eccentrics, undeveloped human beings, from whose substance some essential part had been cut away" (*Night* chap. 20). Richard Dalloway, the benign Conservative politician of *The Voyage Out*, is a far more attractive character because he perceives an intangible spirit—"something alive"—that binds all humanity in an organic Moorean relationship. The fact that he opposes women's suffrage does not make him unlikable in the eyes of Rachel Vinrace or Mrs. Woolf. The vote does not mean much to Rachel, who is more interested in her piano and her personal relationships (*Voyage* 64–68, 213).

This is not to imply that any of these authors objected to enfranchising women. Virginia Woolf addressed envelopes for an adult suffrage group, and D. H. Lawrence proclaimed that "the woman-suffragists . . . are certainly the bravest, and, in the old sense, most heroic party amongst us." The Life worshippers insisted, however, that emancipation meant more than a ballot paper: it meant complete freedom of the spirit. Suffragism, Lawrence wrote, was all very "worthy and admirable," but women really ought to fight, not for participation in government, but for freedom from government—"then the woman's movement would be a living human movement."[156]

A Rendezvous with Death

The darkest irony of the Edwardian Life worshippers is that so many of them found their holy grail in the First World War. One of the legacies of that conflict would be an obsession with death and decadence in postwar English literature, but these themes predominated only after the July 1916 disaster at the Somme. In the initial public enthusiasm that greeted the declaration of war, in the patriotic demonstrations and the rush to the recruiting stations, many onlookers perceived a wonderful outburst of vital energy. For C. R. Ashbee, the war was an epic adventure that would "intensify life" for hordes of tired clerks and shop boys, now transformed into jaunty soldiers.[157] Edward Carpenter affirmed that,

> terrible as war is, and terrible the apparent folly of mankind which allows it to continue, still it is to my mind obvious that those engaged in it could not give their lives, as they so constantly do, not only with conscious devotion to some high purpose, but even with an instinctive exaltation and savage joy in the very act of death, if they were not impelled to do so by the insurgence of a greater life within—a life within each one more vivid and even more tremendous than that which he throws away.[158]

"I think Life's FAR more romantic than any books," Rupert Brooke wrote home from the navy, three months before he died.[159] Other young war poets, like the American Alan Seeger, "drained deeper the deep cup of life" as they prepared for their "Rendezvous with Death."[160] Julian Grenfell (died of wounds, 30 April 1915) proclaimed that

>   . . . life is colour and warmth and light,
>   And a striving evermore for these;
>   And he is dead who will not fight;
>   And he who dies fighting has increase.
>
> The fighting man shall from the sun
>   Take warmth, and life from the glowing earth;
> Speed with the light-foot winds to run,
>   And with the trees to newer birth.[161]

Francis Ledwidge (killed in Flanders, 31 July 1917) recalled that

> When I was young I had a care
> Lest I should cheat me of my share
> Of that which makes it sweet to strive
> For life. . . .

But now he had discovered life in death.

> A keen-edged sword, a soldier's heart,
> Is greater than a poet's art.
> And greater than a poet's fame
> A little grave that has no name.[162]

Robert Graves too "found/Beauty in Death,/In dead men, breath."[163] Life and death are often treated as one in wartime poetry, with voices like Yeats's Irish airman pursuing "this life, this death."[164] That was the inevitable end of the Edwardian cult of Life. The word had always implied adventure, intense and passionate experience, and in 1914 the greatest adventure of all was to die fighting for England.

Even before the war, T. E. Hulme had shifted from Bergsonian vitalism to classical conservative values, orthodox religion, and original sin. He came to regard "Life" as so much humanitarian cant, and he increasingly viewed man as a depraved creature who could only attain nobility through strict social discipline. The war offered him an escape from life, and he enlisted to fight in France, where he was killed in 1917. Reporting from the front for the *New Age*, Hulme protested that all rationalist, humanist, and progressive ideologies are corrupt because their "fundamental values are *Life* and *Personality*, and everything has reference to that." He now believed in a military ethic of courage, obedience, and self-sacrifice, a "more heroic or tragic system of values. Values are not relative only to life. In a sense it may be called *irrational* if . . . those values are rational which can be reasonably based on *life*. It is generally associated with a more pessimistic conception of the nature of man."[165]

Bernard Shaw's *Heartbreak House* (written 1913–1917) reveals a badly shaken faith in vitalism. Captain Shotover still preaches that gospel ("At your age I looked for hardship, danger, horror, and death, that I might feel the life in me more intensely"), but the people of Heartbreak House are idle, drifting, and aging. *Man and Superman* repudiated happiness for life; now creeping senility is submerging Shotover in "the accursed happiness I have dreaded all my life long: the happiness that comes as life goes, the happiness of yielding and dreaming instead of resisting and doing, the sweetness of the fruit that is going rotten."[166] Something has gone strangely wrong with the Life Force. Don Juan assured us that "Life cannot will its own extinction,"[167] but the Heartbreak people are in the thrall of a death wish: in the midst of a German air raid, they turn on every light in the house to attract the zeppelins. (Shaw had actually witnessed this suicidal behavior in London air raids—people commandeering taxis and demanding to be taken to where the bombs were falling—and he was shocked to find himself "hoping next night that there would be another raid.")[168] Shaw's vitalist polemics after *Heartbreak House* grew tired and cranky. His only answer to the problems of the postwar world was to suggest, in *Back to Methuselah* (1920), that human life expectancy be extended to three hundred years. He was exasperatingly unhelpful when it came to explaining how this change would be effected. Apparently he thought the life span could be stretched by a act of creative evolution, like the neck of Lamarck's giraffe.

After the war, the Life religion of D. H. Lawrence also went sour, becoming the basis of a cult of dictatorship. "A circuit of vitalism . . . flows between master and man and forms a very precious nourishment to each, and keeps both in a state of subtle, quivering vital equilibrium. Deny it as you like," he wrote in 1923, but any other system of government is "anti-life."[169] Lawrence's postwar vitalist tracts were testy, sputtering, and almost incoherent. In *Psychoanalysis and the Unconscious*

(1921) and *Fantasia of the Unconscious* (1922) he spun out occult theories about some visceral "life-knowledge" supposedly contained in the solar plexus and the lumbar ganglia.[170] Aldous Huxley had wicked fun with that in *Antic Hay* (1923), where it became the theme of an ad campaign for trousers with air-cushioned seats.

> We could put in a lot about the dark powerful sense-life, sex-life, instinct-life which is controlled by the lumbar ganglion. How important it is that it shouldn't be damaged. That already our modern conditions of civilisation tend to unduly develop the intellect and the thoracic ganglia controlling the higher emotions. That we're wearing out, growing feeble, losing our balance in consequence. And that the only cure—if we are to continue our present mode of civilized life—is to be found in Gumbril's Patent Small Clothes.[171]

Casimir Lypiatt, the failed artist in *Antic Hay*, rails endlessly about getting life into his art, and that, Huxley writes, "was precisely why his paintings were so bad— . . . there was no life in them."[172] Huxley later came to admire Lawrence and put his Life gospel into the mouths of Mark Rampion (*Point Counter Point*) and the Savage (*Brave New World*), but they are voices in the wilderness, disregarded by society at large. All their talk of Life ends in suicide—contemplated by Lypiatt, witnessed by Rampion, committed by the Savage. The Savage, interestingly, is defeated by a system of psychological conditioning that programs human beings like machines. Perhaps Huxley's grandfather had been right after all: perhaps man was an automaton. The voluntarist psychology of James Ward went out of vogue after the war, supplanted by Freudianism, which allowed far less power to the will, and by a new form of robot psychology known as Behaviorism.

In the novels of Huxley and Evelyn Waugh, in T. S. Eliot's poetry, and among the brilliant young beasts chronicled by Martin Green in *Children of the Sun*, decay and death were now the central preoccupations. It became fashionable to depict modern mass man as a walking corpse: "A crowd flowed over London Bridge, so many,/I had not thought death had undone so many."[173] Virginia Woolf had once been keenly interested in Life, but in 1927 she no longer knew what the word meant: "What is this 'Life' that keeps cropping up so mysteriously and so complacently in books about fiction?"[174]

Well she might ask. Often Life was only a vacant cliché, the Edwardian equivalent of *je ne sais quoi*, an imposing word to toss out when one was at a loss for words. At the end of the seventeen volumes of *Life and Labour of the People in London*, when Charles Booth should be offering some concrete solution to the problem of poverty, it is aggravating to find a lot of meaningless talk about the need for "more vigorous life in every direction: social, educational, industrial, political, and religious." But this much can be said for Life: whatever it meant, it always implied progress, movement, and creation. The apostles of Life relished newness: "A running stream is always wholesome," Booth asserted, "a stagnant pool, the danger."[175] R. C. K. Ensor recalls that the young people of his generation, who grew up in the Edwardian years, "felt themselves at the beginning, not at the end, of an age."[176] As a way of expressing the thrill of entering into "an epoch of expansion," *Life* was a convenient shorthand.

4. The Efficiency Men

The vast majority of King Edward's subjects were governed by Lord Curzon, viceroy of India from 1899 to 1905. "If I were asked to sum up my work in a single word," Curzon remarked on leaving office, "I would say 'Efficiency.' That has been our gospel, the keynote of our administration."[1] Efficiency was, in fact, one of the great shibboleths of the Edwardian period. Along with its antonyms *waste* and *muddle*, it pervaded discussions of imperial policy, industrial organization, social legislation, personal hygiene, and religion. It was a favorite byword of army and navy reformers, technical educators, scientific researchers, and eugenicists. With some writers, it even had an influence on literary style.

Cheapness had been the guiding passion of Victorian political economy, but the Edwardian fetish of efficiency was something very different. Efficiency weighed costs against benefits, including the social costs and benefits of a given policy. The partisans of efficiency naturally tried to achieve their goals as economically as possible, but they were willing to fund costly welfare programs, which would not have been considered a generation before, because they realized that poverty was far more expensive. "We pay for it in infantile deaths," railed Philip Snowden, "in the crippled and damaged bodies of the children who survive, in the inadequate return we get from the expenditure on education, in the creation of unemployables, in sickness and loss of work, in consumption and other diseases, in pauperism, in the cost of public and charitable institutions for the support of the sick, the poor, and the insane, and in the incalculable loss of industrial and mental efficiency."[2]

Britain, once the world's first commercial power, was being overtaken by the United States and Germany, and this relative decline was widely attributed to the wretchedness of the working classes: people without adequate housing, food, sanitation, medical care, and technical education were bound to be unproductive workers. Urban poverty was also blamed for Britain's mediocre performance in the Boer War: army officers estimated that something over half of all volunteers were physically unfit for military service. In response, a vocal school of "social imperialists" argued that a rickety, stunted slum population could not provide the "efficient" soldiery needed to meet the growing military threat of Germany, and they advocated welfare legislation as a means of making the British people fit to defend their empire.

Shaken by the Boer War, the Edwardian colonial service concentrated on improving the management of its vast territories rather than on further expansion. In India Lord Curzon worked long hours to promote industry, reform the police, and modernize the railway network. (His efforts to streamline Indian administration had one disastrous consequence, however: in 1905 he partitioned the province of Bengal, cutting across ethnic and religious lines, and provoked five years of Bengali protests and violence.)[3] The German menace, meanwhile, prompted radical reforms in the British armed forces. Sir John Fisher, first lord of the Admiralty from 1904 to 1910, ruthlessly scrapped obsolete warships and built the Dreadnought class of battleships. R. B. Haldane, who headed the War Office from 1905, created an Expeditionary Force of six divisions and a Territorial Reserve Army for home defense.[4]

Historians generally describe the Edwardian cult of Efficiency in these terms: as a simple reaction to the German military challenge, to setbacks in the Boer War, and to growing world economic competition.[5] But this alone is not an adequate explanation: it fails to account for the fact that, at this time, there was an equally vigorous "national efficiency" movement in the United States, promoted by Theodore Roosevelt, Woodrow Wilson, Herbert Hoover, Louis D. Brandeis, and the *New Republic* under Herbert Croly and Walter Lippmann.[6] If efficiency was a response to imperial decline, why did it also obsess turn-of-the-century Americans, who were celebrating their effortless victory over Spain, discovering the thrill of global power, and outproducing every other nation on earth? What induced Britain and the United States to embrace the gospel of Efficiency at the same point in history?

The New Class

The common stimulus was the emergence of a new class of white-collar workers, who were the political base of the national efficiency movement. They followed not the old respected callings of law, medicine, and divinity but professions that were just beginning to establish themselves as recognized professions—science, engineering, teaching, journalism, government service, public health and welfare, sociology, and business administration. They were, in short, social and technical engineers, and they tried to impress efficiency, the engineering ethic, on Edwardian society.

Not until the end of the nineteenth century did British and American white-collar workers have the numbers, the organization, and the professional standing to campaign effectively for national efficiency. W.J. Reader has described the process by which ill-paid, low-status occupational groups in Victorian Britain evolved into respectable professions. The usual pattern was a rapid expansion of membership followed by the foundation of professional organizations and journals, the replacement of apprenticeships with formal education and certification, and the granting of royal charters or some other form of state recognition.[7] Around 1900 a host of white-collar occupations underwent this process of maturation. Once organized, the new professionals were able to expose waste in their respective fields of work, and they set out to persuade the government that national efficiency could be maximized by "experts"—that is, themselves.

In Victorian Britain these new professionals had been paid meager salaries and relegated to a doubtful place in the class hierarchy. The efficiency movement was their way of securing better professional training, higher pay, administrative power, and subsidies for their research. Certainly, British setbacks in both international trade and the Boer War figured heavily in the propaganda for national efficiency. But often these issues were convenient arguing points fronting for a more basic concern on the part of the new professionals—their own position in British society. They had been talking about efficiency well before the Boer War, when British industrial might was still unchallenged. In the afterglow of the Great Exhibition of 1851, Lyon Playfair and several other scientists warned that Britain would lose her commercial supremacy unless she devoted more resources to technical research and education. In 1887 T. H. Huxley declared that "we are entering, indeed we have already entered, upon the most serious struggle for existence to which this country was ever committed. The latter years of the century promise to see us in an industrial war of far more serious import than the military wars of its opening years." These worries were sincere enough, but they also reflected some anxiety to improve the miserable pay, social status, and education of Victorian scientists. "A man who chooses a life of science chooses not a life of poverty, but, so far as I can see a life of *nothing*," Huxley had earlier complained, and with good reason: in 1854 he was paid a paltry two hundred pounds a year to teach at the Government School of Mines. "Science in England is not a profession," the mathematician Charles Babbage protested in 1851; "its cultivators are scarcely recognised even as a class."

By the Edwardian period, however, the professionalization of the scientist was well under way. As late as 1881 professional scientists were a minority of Royal Society Fellows; by 1914 they outnumbered the gentleman amateurs by three or four to one, thanks to the development of electricity and other new technologies.[8] A host of technical societies and journals were founded and began to agitate for national efficiency.[9] In 1911 the British Engineers' Association was organized specifically to lobby for improved technical training. The Institution of Civil Engineers had existed in some form since 1818, but only around the turn of the century did it begin to set up professional standards and examinations, and in 1903 it founded a special committee on technical education. The Society of Telegraph Engineers and Electricians, reorganized on a broader basis as the Institution of Electrical Engineers in 1888, agitated to remove legislative obstructions to the development of the electric power industry.[10] In his speech "The Influence of Brain Power on History," Sir Norman Lockyer, the editor of *Nature*, urged the British Association to become a lobby for science. When it declined to do so, Lockyer organized his own British Science Guild in 1905. At the guild's first meeting, R. B. Haldane urged the creation of a permanent government advisory commission on applied science. The guild issued recommendations for improving productivity in agriculture, industry, energy, and the civil service; and Haldane conveyed that advice to the highest levels of government.[11]

Edwardian newspapers were filled with apprehensive reports on the challenge of American competition—on American achievements in engineering, toolmaking, labor-saving devices, mass transit, office equipment, scientific management, business education, marketing, cost accounting, military technology, electrification, mechanization, standardization, and trustification. British scientific workers capitalized on that issue to win some remarkable improvements in technical education.[12] Eleven technical colleges were founded between 1871 and 1902, all of which soon evolved into "red-brick" universities. The Normal School of Science was set up in 1881 under the direction of T. H. Huxley; in 1907 it was absorbed into the new Imperial College of Science and Technology. Between 1880 and 1900 for every bachelor of science honors degree granted by Oxford or Cambridge, four were awarded by the new provincial colleges and five by the University of London. For science students like H. G. Wells, Oliver Lodge, and Ernest Rutherford, these reforms opened up educational opportunities that had not existed a few years before, when Wells would have been doomed to spend his life working in a draper's establishment. Technical instruction on a more basic level was being provided by the polytechnics, which sprang up after 1880. Parliamentary acts in 1889 and 1890 enabled county councils to fund technical schools, and by 1895, 93 out of 129 local authorities were availing themselves of this option.

Victorian England left scientific research to the private sector, but when German steel and aniline dyes began to compete successfully with British products, British scientists were at last offered government subsidies. Responding to the inauguration of a German state research institute at Charlottenburg in 1895, Oliver Lodge, Norman Lockyer, Lord Rayleigh, Arthur Balfour, Lord Rosebery, R. B. Haldane, and Sidney Webb secured the foundation of a state-supported National Physical Laboratory in 1902. Following this action, the British government provided increased assistance to red-brick universities, supported aircraft development from 1909, and began to aid research in agriculture and fishing in 1910.[13] Politicians, Balfour declared, now had to take account of "the intimate relation between scientific discovery and industrial efficiency."[14]

Another group of white-collar workers—government employees— was also becoming an organized force for national efficiency. Between 1881 and 1911 the civil service, on both the local and national levels, expanded by about fifty percent each decade. Thanks to the Education Acts of 1870 and 1902, the ranks of the teaching profession also swelled, especially on the secondary level. Between 1870 and 1902, teachers, school administrators, librarians, customs and postal officials, and government workers all formed their own professional societies.[15] Several new engineering professions were called into existence by the growth of municipal services, including the Gas Engineers (organized 1863), the Institution of Municipal Engineers (1873), the Institute of Sanitary Engineers (1895), the Waterworks Institute (1896), and the Institution of Heating and Ventilation Engineers (1897).[16]

As government employees, these new professionals were naturally disposed to argue that national efficiency could be improved through government regulation and social services. It was their job and interest to expose social ills and to demand more power and personnel to cope with those evils. The Victorian state had made very limited efforts to improve working conditions and public health, but once it took the step of appointing a corps of inspectors, however few in number and restricted in power, it created a pressure group for state regulation. Armed with the authority of their offices, these inspectors would point out gaps in existing legislation, press the government to employ their talents as trained "experts," and secure better delivery of the public services they were trained to provide. Air pollution, for example, had been attacked by a parliamentary act as early as 1863. That legislation applied only to alkali works and authorized the appointment of only five poorly paid inspectors for the entire kingdom, but the investigations of those officials induced Parliament to broaden the scope of the law in 1874. In 1878 a royal commission, including four chemists, recommended still more regulations and more inspectors. Parliament complied in 1881, and in 1892 controls were extended to all chemical factories and some other industries.[17] Thus, by the end of the century, a tiny Victorian inspectorate had snowballed into a powerful body of state regulators engaged in an ongoing campaign for public health and efficiency. In this way, writes Oliver MacDonagh, a "new and more or less conscious Fabianism worked itself into modes of government which seems to us peculiarly modern."[18]

The Fabians

Fabianism is an appropriate word to use here, because the Fabian Society was in the forefront of the national efficiency movement, the growth of state social services, and the rise of the new administrative class. The Fabians believed that socialism would be brought about by a continuation of the process described above: white-collar administrators would progressively increase government regulation of the economy to the point where private industries were effectively or actually nationalized. The Local Government Acts of 1888 and 1894 gave municipal authorities broad powers to regulate and administer public services, and the early Fabians welcomed these measures as the opening wedge of collectivism. They concentrated their energies on winning election to the London County Council, which, they insisted, could run public transport and utilities more economically than the private sector. "Without efficient local machinery the replacement of private enterprise by State enterprise is out of the question," Bernard Shaw wrote in 1889, but he was confident that the act of 1888 provided "the machinery for socialism."[19] More radical socialists sneered at the "gas-and-water socialism" of the Fabians and demanded to know whether well-run municipal tramlines would mean true equality for the workers. The fact is that for the majority of Fabians efficiency took priority over equality, and proletarian democracy was less attractive than government by their own class of new professionals.

Some students of class would deny that white-collar workers constitute a "class" unto themselves, but the leading Fabians were acutely conscious of belonging to what they variously called the "salariat," the "*nouvelle couche sociale,*" the "professional proletariat," the "literary proletariat," the "black-coated proletariat," or simply a caste of "brain workers."[20] "The commercial clerk," wrote Bernard Shaw, "is a proletarian, and a very miserable proletarian" in the Marxian sense of the term.[21] He did not own the means of production and lived by selling his labor—"by the sweat of my brain," as Shaw put it.[22] Shaw had been converted to socialism by *Das Kapital,* but he criticized Marx's "lack of administrative experience" and rejected H. M. Hyndman's Social Democratic Federation, with its Marxist dogma and "manual-working" membership. He turned instead to "the newly founded Fabian Society, in which I recognized a more appropriate *milieu* as a body of educated middle-class intelligentsia: my own class in fact."[23] New professionals dominated the Fabian Society, making up about half the membership. Ramsay MacDonald, who began his career as secretary and journalist, wanted the socialist revolution to be a "revolution directed from the study; to be one, not of brutal need, but of intellectual development; to be, in fact, a revolution of the comparatively well-to-do."[24]

The Fabians generally favored a bureaucratic socialist state, ruled by the intellectual proletariat, as the most efficient form of government. Along with such conservative efficiency men as Lord Milner, William Cunningham, and Sir William Ashley, they rejected class conflict as wasteful and destructive. Sidney Webb held that strikes, though "sometimes necessary," were "equivalent in barbarism to civil war." Like any good engineer, the Fabians tried to make forces work together rather than in opposition. Hence they favored compromise, collective bargaining, and arbitration over "the crude and old-fashioned strike."[25] The

system in which "employer and employed stood in marked antagonism," wrote H. G. Wells, only encouraged the capitalist to keep his
laborers poor and ignorant whereas the workers were forced to protect
themselves by enforcing "elaborate rules for restricting hours of toil,
making its performance needlessly complex, and shirking with extreme
ingenuity and conscientiousness."[26]

Most Fabians believed that capitalists could be persuaded that certain
paternal welfare measures would make their industries more profitable,
a moral taught in Shaw's *Major Barbara*. Beatrice Webb was convinced
that her 1909 scheme for reforming the Poor Law would save so much
tax money, and so far improve the character and productivity of the
working classes, that all owners of capital and land would profit from
it.[27] Even G. D. H. Cole, who believed very strongly in class conflict as a
political weapon, argued for worker control of industry on grounds of
efficiency, insisting that laborers knew best how to increase productivity in their own work places. Cole predicted (accurately, it seems) that if
workers' demands for self-government were not answered, class hostilities would strangle the British economy "slowly and very uncomfort-
ably for all of us, and we shall see year by year not merely industry
growing inefficient, but everything growing more and more dirty and
uncomfortable and nasty and hopeless, and more like a story by H. G.
Wells."[28]

Many Fabians had been efficiency men before they became socialists.
The hero of Bernard Shaw's first novel, *Immaturity* (1879), endures a
miserable life as a clerk (as Shaw did for a time) until he wins power and
prestige through good management: he becomes a secretary to an inef-
fectual member of Parliament, sorts out his employer's muddled affairs,
and thus acquires considerable political influence. Shaw's next novel,
The Irrational Knot (1880), deals with a monomaniacally efficient engineer who invents an electric motor that generates "hardly any waste,"[29]
a character possibly modeled on the American technicians whom Shaw
met while working for the Edison Telephone Company.[30] Sidney Webb
devoted his entire life to the elimination of social friction: he was the
sort of consummate bureaucrat who could attend the Oberammergau
Passion Play and come away sympathizing with Pontius Pilate. "My
profession made me realise entirely his position," he wrote. "I should
have acted just as he did. . . . [Jesus] brought about his own death by
his contumacy."[31] Sydney Olivier was attracted to Fabian socialism primarily as a "means of organising production. There is now so much

waste," he complained in 1883, "so many fluctuations in employment of labour owing to there being no concert between employers, each trying to make his own fortune."[32]

When capitalists set out to make their businesses more efficient, most Fabians were happy to offer support and advice. In 1886 H. G. Wells had welcomed the growth of the "very efficient" chain stores that were bankrupting his father's tiny business. Later, in 1901, he scoffed at American socialists who talked of taking over the trusts, which Wells admired as "efficient machines of production and public service."[33] William Clarke and H. W. Macrosty viewed concentration of industry as a step in the direction of a socialist managerial state. "We positively like Monopoly, for it means economy and efficiency," proclaimed G. R. S. Taylor; "it is the Monopolist we dislike."[34] Other Fabians, like J. McKillop, praised the monopolist also, provided he was a "real business man, the best kind of 'practical' man," as opposed to a "mere financier."[35] Beatrice Webb dismissed William Jennings Bryan's antitrust speeches as "infantile" and favored a government of businessmen. Long before she became a socialist, she had passionately admired the entrepreneurial talents of her father and her one-time suitor, Joseph Chamberlain.[36] Her husband worked on government committees to plan agricultural settlements and emigration, the Territorial Army, the Census of Production, and technical education. All of this had little to do with economic equality, but it did enable British capitalism to operate more efficiently.

In 1894 the Fabian Society received the Henry Hutchinson bequest of ten thousand pounds, with instructions to spend it for "propaganda and other purposes." Sidney Webb saw to it that the money was used not to promote socialism but to found the London School of Economics, Britain's first training academy for brain workers. This was a watershed in the history of the Fabian Society, when it dropped all pretense of being a revolutionary organization and devoted its main energies to the education of an efficient administrative class. The Webbs, Graham Wallas (who taught political science at the LSE) and W. A. S. Hewins (the school's first director) all shared a common faith in government by a trained corps of civil servants. The LSE turned out a steady stream of welfare workers, social scientists, and leftist intellectuals, but it was also Britain's first true school of business, offering popular courses in railway management and insurance. The board of governors included Lord Rothschild and the directors of several railway companies, which encouraged their employees to attend the school by subsidizing their tuition.[37] Inasmuch as these wealthy trustees and the London County Council paid a large portion of the operating expenses of the school,[38] the Webbs were naturally anxious to conciliate them, even if it meant sacrificing socialism to efficiency. Beatrice urged Sidney, when he defended the LSE before the Technical Education Board of the LCC, to wind up

> by remarking that difference of opinion on social and economic questions was rapidly being merged into one cry for efficiency—that *we* were anxious for the efficiency of private enterprise (railway companies) and the Rothschilds were anxious for efficiency in municipal enterprise. That when we had by lectures and education made all officials efficient we might leave the future generations the task of deciding which form of organisation was *most* convenient.[39]

Shaw, Wells, and the Webbs believed that their politics of efficiency had reduced government to an objective science, and they regarded democracy as a nuisance apt to obstruct the work of intelligent social planners. "The modern democracy," Wells wrote in 1901, "conducts its affairs as though there was no such thing as special knowledge or practical education." It disregarded "the new mass of capable men, of which the engineers are typical, . . . the man who has concerned himself with the public health, with army organisation, with educational improvement, or with vital matters of transport and communication." Eventually, whipped up by politicians and the yellow press, the masses would stumble into a disastrous war. In the ensuing chaos the "scientifically trained middle class" would take power and become "*the* State, controlling and restricting very greatly" all other classes—a dictatorship of the intellectual proletariat.[40]

Besides a passing sympathy for big-city political machines ("which are at any rate efficient in what they set out to do") and an unbounded admiration for the tidy, theocratic municipality of Salt Lake City, the Webbs dismissed popular government in the United States as a hopeless muddle. According to Beatrice, the Americans desperately needed "an occasional Sidney Webb to invent ways of dodging their silly constitutions."[41] The Webbs accepted democracy only because they realized that an authoritarian government in England would face crippling opposition: "if [the state] does not carry with it in the popular mind the consciousness of consent, it will inevitably find itself restricted in its

operations, lacking in stability, and thus falling far short of efficiency."[42] They did not hide their admiration of the "technically efficient" country gentleman of the eighteenth century, "the benevolent
autocrat of the parish," devoted to maintaining order, "healing petty
differences and preventing vexatious prosecutions."[43]

For socialists, the Fabians could be strikingly hostile to the working
class, which (in their view) lacked the intelligence, training, and public
spirit to carry on efficient government. When H. G. Wells had Spade
House built for his family in 1900, he was appalled to find the laborers
sticking to old-fashioned methods and obstructive union rules, "doing
the minimum of work in the maximum of time." Wells warned that
trade unions would "stagnate" British industry.[44] He grew to fear and
distrust the Labour Party and its proletarian constituency—"hostile to
the higher education," "almost destitute of ideas," "far more ignorant
and incapable of management than a shareholders' meeting"—and by
1906 he was urging the Fabian Society to organize itself into a rival
middle-class socialist party.[45] Throughout his entire career as a writer,
from his first novel to the Attlee government, Bernard Shaw railed
against the tyranny of trade unions. He entirely approved of Wells's
projected party of the "professional proletariat," without which, Shaw
predicted,

> the costs of pensions and all other reforms extorted by Labor will be thrown
> on [our] rates & taxes. . . . Labor will join with Plutocracy to make us
> their common slaves. The Labor Electorate has no sense of the rights of Art,
> of Intellect, or even of business organization and finance. To them the em-
> ployer is a tyrant, a stockbroker a swindler who foments wars, a philosopher
> a fool, an artist a guy. We have spent 25 years in putting them in the way of
> their own salvation: now we must begin to look after our own.[46]

In 1897 the Webbs had praised trade unions as a managerial experiment, in "which the working man copes with the problem of combining
administrative efficiency with popular control." By 1913, however,
they had less confidence in organized labor and were frightened by
G. D. H. Cole's proposals for workers' control of industry. Even Cole
criticized the Labour Party for not appealing to the middle class, and he
pointedly included white-collar workers in his plans for work-place
democracy. Cole had rejected the syndicalist movement because it repudiated any alliance with the middle class. His guild socialism was
essentially a white-collar revision of syndicalism, in which mental and

manual workers would together seize control of the means of production. In 1920 he organized the National Federation of Professional Workers, arguing that the British economy had "to be drastically and fundamentally reorganised on a basis which will allow to the professional man, the man who has technical skill and ability, a far greater chance of making industry and the public services efficient than he was allowed under the old system."[47]

Until the First World War, issues of class and efficiency precluded a close alliance between the Fabian Society and labor leaders, who habitually used the word *intellectual* as a term of abuse. Labour M.P.s conducted their party as a pressure group for organized workers, and they did not care to be told that the special interests of trade unions were interfering with national efficiency.[48] Of the seven contributors to *Fabian Essays* (1889), only Hubert Bland called for a common front of intellectual and manual workers, and this attitude seems to have reflected Bland's failure to make a career for himself. He insisted that "keenness of competition, making it every year more obviously impossible for those who are born without capital ever to achieve it, will deprive the capitalist class of the support it receives from educated and cultivated but impecunious young men whose material interest must finally triumph over their class sympathies."[49] Most other leading Fabians, however, were upwardly mobile. Capitalism, far from impoverishing the intellectual, was opening new careers to him in literature and management. Ramsay MacDonald, Sydney Olivier, and Sidney Webb correctly foresaw a brilliant future for themselves in government. That social mobility naturally led the Fabians to reject proletarian revolution in favor of a bureaucratic state.[50] Of the seven Fabian essayists, five (Shaw, Olivier, Sidney Webb, Graham Wallas, and Annie Besant) argued for state socialism on the grounds that it would eliminate "waste" and promote "efficiency." Shaw, for instance, declared that the Post Office had "shewn the perfect efficiency of State enterprise when the officials are made responsible to the class interested in its success."[51]

A. M. McBriar has noted that the leaders of the rival Social Democratic Federation (H. M. Hyndman, William Morris, H. H. Champion) were mainly men of independent means, who could preach Marxist revolution with impunity. But the brain workers of the Fabian Society had their jobs to think of, and they could not antagonize their employers or their reading public by veering too far to the left. If for no other reason than that, they had to restrict themselves to a low-keyed advocacy of

gradual socialism based on the respectable argument of national efficiency.[52] The Fabians made efficiency their tactic as well as their objective: they declined to waste their energies on quixotic revolutionary
adventures. Gradualism, "permeation" of established political parties,
Shavian humor, a reputable public image, and the slogan "national efficiency" itself seemed to be the most efficient means of selling socialist
policies to a nation still frightened of the word *socialism*. The society
prudently avoided involvement with any other issue that might alienate
potential supporters, disclaiming any "distinctive opinions on the Marriage Question, Religion, Art, abstract Economics, or any other subject
other than its own special business of practical Democracy and Socialism."[53] As Shaw told the antiwar activist C. H. Norman:

> If you have a destination, you will not get to it if you stop to fight people on
> the way. You will have your hands full with the people who are *in* the way. I
> notice a disposition on your part to reproach me for not getting into trouble
> when I can possibly help it, and for not doing what everyone expects me to
> do in controversies; but I find my unavoidable troubles quite enough for me;
> and the expected blow is the one that gets countered.[54]

This was an essentially pugilistic strategy, striving for maximum impact with a minimum of risk. "Ease and strength, effort and weakness,
go together," Shaw wrote in *Cashel Byron's Profession* (1883), his celebration of the sport of prizefighting.[55] The very name and motto of the
Fabian Society recommended the economical use of limited strength:
"For the right moment you must wait, as Fabius did most patiently,
when warring against Hannibal, though many censured his delays; but
when the time comes you must strike hard, as Fabius did, or your wait-
ing will be in vain, and fruitless." What distinguished the Fabians from
other socialists was their overriding concern with the intelligent use of
force—which is itself a good definition of efficiency.

Social Imperialism

This preoccupation with efficiency led many Fabians to support an
institution that had heretofore been anathema to socialists—the British
Empire. It was, after all, a highly cost-effective unit of government.
With a small and well-trained civil service, it ruled over a quarter of the
world's population, maintained peace and free trade within its borders,
and introduced primitive societies to modern technology and adminis-

tration. Imperialism might be undemocratic, but the Fabians generally admired good government more than self-government.

The debacles of the Boer War had created a compelling case for social reform—good housing, public health measures, adequate education, clean air and water, and a living wage were all needed to provide healthy manpower for the armies and industries of the Empire. The social Darwinism of Herbert Spencer had emphasized competition among individuals, but for the Fabian social imperialist Karl Pearson, the crucial struggle for survival was "the struggle of tribe against tribe, of race against race." Britain could not win that battle by producing "a few prize cattle among innumerable lean kine," Pearson warned. Only socialism could maintain "a decently-bred and properly-fed herd." By attending to the welfare of her workers, by limiting internal competition, the British Empire could prevail in "extra-group" competition with other nations.[56] This was an argument for socialism that could and did appeal even to reactionaries. Lord Milner (the man largely responsible for the Boer War) and Beatrice Webb found a common ground here, and they complimented each other on the wisdom of their imperial collectivism.[57]

The Fabians had been united by their common opposition to Britain's imperial policies in Ireland and the Near East between 1876 and 1882, but at the end of the century they voted, 259 to 217, against taking a position on the Boer War. Bernard Shaw completely reversed his earlier attacks on Gladstone's Nile policy; in 1899 he scolded himself for not having "urged the miserable Little England Government to follow up their blow and make Gordon master of the Soudan." The Boer republics, Shaw reasoned, ought to be absorbed into a better-managed empire as a step in the direction of socialism and a world federation of nations: "I object to stray little states lying about in the way of great powers. I did not object to America assimilating Honolulu, nor to Germany assimilating Samoa. It is to me as if a trust had annexed a small shopkeeper: a capitalistic transaction, no doubt, but one making, like all advanced capitalism, for Socialism."[58]

In 1900 Shaw had the audacity to claim that the Fabians—by advocating "State Organization, Efficient Government, Industrial Civil Service, Regulation of all private enterprise in the common interest, and dissolution of Frontiers through international industrial organization" —had been responsible for converting England to imperialism.[59] That, of course, was ridiculous, but it is true that Shaw had already written several polemics on imperial efficiency. *Arms and the Man* (1894) introduced a new type of military hero to the stage: Captain Bluntschli, a dismayingly "efficient" mercenary fighting an imperial war, explicitly modeled on Sidney Webb.[60] *The Man of Destiny* (1896) is Shaw's tribute to the organizational genius of Napoleon. In *The Devil's Disciple* (1897) England loses an empire through the "jobbery and snobbery, incompetence and Red Tape" of her War Office;[61] and in *Caesar and Cleopatra* (1898) Rome wins an empire through the ruthless pragmatism of Julius Caesar. *Captain Brassbound's Conversion* (1899) contrasted two celebrated African explorers, Mary Kingsley and H. M. Stanley, and showed that her motherly affability was far more effective in winning native loyalty than his violence and bluster. Before the Boer War, then, before his tract *Fabianism and the Empire* (1900), Shaw had largely worked out his theory of social imperialism.

The Fabians had a model imperial administrator in the person of Sydney Olivier, who held a number of important posts in the Caribbean, including the governorship of Jamaica. He was skilled at balancing budgets and protecting colored laborers from exploitation, but he could be equally efficient in putting down native riots, and he cavalierly disregarded elected colonial councils when they became obstructive.[62] The Fabians approved of Olivier's autocratic administration because it avoided the squabbles of party politics. In *English Local Government* (1908) the Webbs stressed the inefficiency of an adversary two-party democracy, where the Opposition constantly frustrates the work of the Government.[63] H. G. Wells denounced the House of Commons as "the seat of party conflicts, a faction fight of initiated persons, that has long ceased to bear any relation to current social processes." He looked forward to "the suppression of the party machine . . . by capable operative and administrative men" who would build a federal empire of the English-speaking peoples.[64]

Between 1901 and 1903 Shaw and the Webbs tried to unite imperialist Liberals and reforming Conservatives in a "Party of National Efficiency." It was to include Haldane, Asquith, Sir Edward Grey, Balfour, and Joseph Chamberlain under the leadership of Lord Rosebery, who then appeared to be working up to a break with the pro-Boer wing of the Liberal Party. With such a broad base of support, opposed only by old-fashioned Radicals and Tories, this party would have a more or less permanent majority in Parliament and would speedily enact a program of social imperialism. In the September 1901 number of the *Nineteenth*

Century, Sidney Webb presented Rosebery with a platform that included reform of housing, the War Office, education (especially technical education), the Poor Law, labor legislation, and sanitary regulations. Rosebery, Haldane, Grey, and Asquith all admired Webb's article and Shaw's earlier *Fabianism and the Empire*; Haldane even proposed to find Webb a seat in Parliament. In his Chesterfield Speech of 16 December 1901, Rosebery outlined a program of social legislation designed to build an imperial race. Shortly thereafter, he repudiated the Liberal dogma of Irish Home Rule, and he made contact with such disaffected Conservatives as Winston Churchill, who wanted Rosebery to lead a centrist government.[65]

In his *Nineteenth Century* article, Webb had emphasized that this new party would need a circle of expert brain workers to map out policy. To fill this role he and his wife organized the Coefficients, a dinner and discussion club that met once a month beginning in November 1902. The group included as permanent members Haldane, Grey, H. G. Wells, and Bertrand Russell. There were also several military and naval experts (Carlyon Bellairs, Charles Repington, Julian Corbett, Leopold Amery, and the imperialist versifier Henry Newbolt), colonial officials (Lord Milner and William Pember Reeves), a pioneer in the study of geopolitics (Halford Mackinder), financiers (Sir Clinton Dawkins, who was also an experienced colonial administrator, and Sir Henry Birchenough, a South African tycoon), economists (W. A. S. Hewins and Theodore Morison), Tory journalists (J. L. Garvin and Leopold Maxse), and, appropriately, the biographers of Alexander Hamilton (F. S. Oliver) and Disraeli (W. P. Monypenny).[66] It is notable that the Webbs, who invited so many Conservatives into the Coefficients, neglected to include any welfare workers or professional social reformers, except for an occasional invitation sent to C. F. G. Masterman. As social imperialists, the Coefficients were more imperialist than social, a fact that made Wells and Russell feel quite isolated and uncomfortable at those monthly dinners.[67]

Then on 15 May 1903 Joseph Chamberlain announced his program for tariff reform. He advocated duties on food and manufactured goods imported from outside the British Empire, and he proposed to use the customs revenues to set up a system of old-age pensions. This was a classic piece of social imperialism, and as such it won the sympathy of Beatrice Webb, Bernard Shaw, L. S. Amery, and W. A. S. Hewins; but it effectively wrecked the Party of National Efficiency. The threat of taxes on imported food reunited the imperialist and anti-imperialist wings of the Liberal Party in defense of Free Trade, and the British party system returned to its traditional polarity. The Coefficients were deeply divided on imperial tariffs, and after a heated debate in May 1903 the group largely disintegrated, although meetings continued until 1908.[68]

In 1910 Liberal efforts to abolish the veto of the House of Lords produced a bitter parliamentary deadlock, and two ex-Coefficients, J. L. Garvin and F. S. Oliver, revived the idea of a grand coalition for national efficiency as a way of ending the impasse. This "Truce of God" particularly appealed to Lloyd George. "No party has a monopoly of able and efficient men," he declared, and the threat of foreign industrial competition made it necessary "to sink our differences and to unite in combined and sustained effort to reorganise the national life of our country in all its branches, so as to put us in a position where we need have no apprehension as to the future of the British Empire." He secretly asked Balfour to bring the Conservatives into a coalition government based on a program of social imperialism. In return for a compulsory national militia, a big navy, modernization of inland transport, and some tariffs, Lloyd George wanted reforms affecting "the health, the vitality, the efficiency, and the happiness" of the working masses, including improved housing and education, health and unemployment insurance, death benefits, reform of the Poor Law, and land redistribution. Balfour was tempted by the proposal, but he was tied to his Ulster Protestant allies, and he could not accept Lloyd George's demand for Irish Home Rule. The negotiations ended without result.[69]

The men of the Round Table had learned the virtues of imperial efficiency in South Africa, where they had worked to unify the railway network, government administration, and native labor policy. They were also influenced by F. S. Oliver and his biography of Alexander Hamilton, which had been written as a tract for imperial federalism. Much like the Fabians, the Round Table men were idealistic young brain workers who attempted to permeate and convert influential elites in Britain and the colonies. They warned of the military threat from Germany, and they condemned party politics as divisive. One of their number was Leopold Amery, who had been a Fabian at Oxford and a member of the Coefficients. In 1904 Amery had formed the Compatriots Club, a pressure group for imperial union and tariff reform, which was later headed by Lord Milner.[70]

Social imperialism, incidentally, did not necessarily mean white imperialism. One of Rudyard Kipling's heroes was Sir Purun Dass, K.C.I.E., an Indian statesman who moves effortlessly between his two roles as an efficient executive and a mystical hermit.[71] The emergence of Japan (Britain's ally since 1902) as an imperial power was hailed by Lord Rosebery, H. G. Wells, and Sidney and Beatrice Webb. The Webbs effusively complimented the "instructed and highly intelligent civil service" of Japan for its "standard of national efficiency," and for bringing roads, schools, and sound administration to Korea, which had become a Japanese possession in 1910. In the light of these achievements, the brutal repression of Japanese socialists and trade unions did not greatly distress the Webbs. Even the admirers of the Japanese, however, regarded them as exceptional among nonwhite peoples, most of whom, according to Wells and the Webbs, were hopelessly inefficient and doomed to extinction or colonization.[72]

Until 1916 Britain was the only major European power that did not require its citizens to perform some sort of military service. But a growing body of opinion held that imperial efficiency demanded a program of compulsory peacetime military training—if not actual conscription, as a royal commission recommended in 1904. According to Samuel Hynes, the advocates of a compulsory militia were mostly Tories: Lord Roberts led the campaign from his National Service League and the Lads' Rifle Brigade, and Lord Baden-Powell founded the Boy Scouts around 1907 as a paramilitary training organization.[73] Similar proposals, however, were also advanced by liberals and socialists. They argued that apart from its military benefits compulsory training would take the British laborer out of the slums, drill him in the open air, feed him well, teach him self-discipline and personal hygiene, and thus make him a more productive worker.

H. W. Nevinson, a radical journalist, had proposed universal military service on the German model back in the 1880s. The suggestion was generally condemned at the time, but Nevinson went on to drill a slum cadet corps for Toynbee Hall. Octavia Hill, the housing reformer, borrowed the idea for her Southwark Settlement, and by 1913 at least nine settlement houses sponsored some sort of drill team or scouting troop.[74] C. R. Ashbee spoke for many social reformers when in August 1901 he described the British worker as a stunted and undisciplined product "of artificial conditions in the great city, of civilization reacting unsoundly upon an already enfeebled constitution. Lack of sunshine, lack of colour, lack of green and the things that make for stamina; there we have it.

. . . And how to correct it?" That question was answered a few months later, when a former worker at Ashbee's Guild of Handicraft returned from the Boer War in splendid physical condition and started a shop discussion on the virtues of compulsory service. Ashbee had always opposed conscription,

> but when I look at the crowded streets, the bent shoulders, the broken lungs, notice the poor sight, the slouching gait, the slovenliness and vulgar truculence of the undergrown ill-bred mass of East London as it passes to and from its work, I begin to think differently, and that our parents were wrong, and the instinct of the boys right. They want drill, they must have it, there is little in the life of modern cities that supplies that want. . . . I think there is scarcely one of our . . . lads whom such an 18 months' rough, sturdy, and unquestioning discipline would not have improved and made more efficient generally for the work we want him to do.[75]

Among the Fabians, Robert Blatchford (a former sergeant in the 103d Dublin Fusileers) demanded peacetime conscription and military drill for schoolboys beginning at age ten. Bernard Shaw (in *Fabianism and the Empire*), Sidney and Beatrice Webb, Karl Pearson, and Hubert Bland all favored some type of compulsory military training.[76] H. G. Wells hailed the Boy Scout movement as a force for "social efficiency," as did left-wing Liberals like C. F. G. Masterman and J. L. Hammond.[77] Henry Arthur Jones wrote a short play, *Fall in Rookies* (1910), as propaganda for Lord Roberts's National Service League, which was also backed by Bishop Gore;[78] and Sir Oliver Lodge was willing to accept conscription as a means of combating juvenile delinquency.[79] In 1911 John Galsworthy enthusiastically outlined a proposal for "national open air training together with technical schooling in all the various crafts and occupations including agriculture, for six months in the year, of all boys between the ages of 14 and 17, (not debarred by physical or mental infirmity,) whose parents cannot satisfy the State that they are giving their sons an efficient secondary education under manifestly healthy conditions." The program, he predicted, would pay for itself several times over in increased labor productivity. Galsworthy brushed aside the argument that the system would restrict "the liberty of boys. What liberty have they in the present muddle? What liberty have boys of the more fortunate classes? Why should boys have liberty? This objection will only be that of the crank."[80]

The specter of an inefficient urban proletariat also lent support to another nostrum for imperial efficiency—eugenics, the selective breeding of human beings. Although the concept can be traced back to Plato, Francis Galton did not invent the term until 1883, and he only aroused serious public interest in his proposals after 1901, when he effectively capitalized on increasing popular concern with national efficiency. In 1907 a Eugenics Education Society was formed and attracted an eminently respectable membership, including J. A. Thomson (biologist), William McDougall and Cyril Burt (psychologists), Arthur Balfour, Havelock Ellis, Dean Inge, Edward Lyttelton (headmaster of Eton), William Joynson-Hicks, Neville Chamberlain, two sons of Charles Darwin, and many eminent geneticists and sociologists. Havelock Ellis tried to explain criminal behavior through heredity, and his interest in sexuality was partly rooted in eugenics—that is why he devoted the entire first section of his autobiography (about eighty pages) to his family tree.[81]

Geoffrey Searle describes eugenics as a movement of the "Radical Right," but it also had supporters on the left: Ellis, John Maynard Keynes, Goldsworthy Lowes Dickinson, Alfred Russel Wallace, R. J. Campbell, Harold Laski, J. B. S. Haldane, and A. R. Orage's *New Age*.[82] In *Man and Superman* Bernard Shaw insisted that real social progress would be impossible unless steps were taken to breed a new type of human being. Together with Graham Wallas, he criticized the London School Board for not allowing its schoolmistresses to marry, a policy that meant the effective "sterilization" of intellectually superior women.[83] Karl Pearson was the first professor of eugenics at the University of London, and his work interested Shaw, Wells, Cecil Chesterton, and the Webbs. (All of these Fabians, however, rejected the idea that poverty was caused by bad genes.)[84]

The first volumes of Charles Booth's *Life and Labour of the People in London*, published in 1889, convinced many readers that the subnormal population was multiplying too rapidly. Booth attributed most of the social ills of the slums not to the working class as a whole but to two subproletarian classes that together accounted for one out of every eight Londoners. "Class A" consisted of "occasional labourers, street-sellers, loafers, criminals, and semi-criminals," and Booth bluntly recommended that they be "harried out of existence" by (for example) condemning the tenements in which they lived. Just above them was a "Class B" of irregular laborers earning less than eighteen shillings a week. Booth found that "most of the work done by Class B is inefficiently done, both badly and slowly." These menials actually created poverty by underselling the labor of honest workers, and they were a tremendous drain on charities and social services. Poverty, Booth concluded, could only be ended by "the entire removal of this very poor class out of the daily struggle for existence," and that could only be effected by what he frankly called "State slavery." By forcing these derelicts to work in strictly regimented government labor colonies, the entire national economy would be made "more efficient."[85] Compulsory labor was endorsed by a number of sincere social reformers, including L. T. Hobhouse, Beatrice Webb, Winston Churchill, W. H. Beveridge, Herbert Samuel, and Canon Barnett. It was also incorporated into the unsuccessful Unemployed Workmen's Bills of 1907 and 1908, proposed by the Labour Party.[86]

Booth was not a eugenicist, and he assured his readers that this underclass was not breeding out of control, but Francis Galton nevertheless used Booth's findings in his eugenic propaganda. Disturbed by *Life and Labour*, young Liberals like Noel Buxton, Walter Hoare, and A. C. Pigou suggested the elimination of the "submerged tenth" through some sort of eugenic policy, although they shied away from specific proposals.[87] A Liberal government, under considerable pressure, passed the Mental Deficiency Act of 1913, which authorized the forcible segregation and institutionalization of the feeble-minded. The legislation was drafted by Winston Churchill, who suggested that X rays be used to sterilize mental defectives. In 1910 Bernard Shaw appalled even the Eugenics Education Society by recommending the gas chamber for social undesirables.[88] (He had made the same suggestion in *Major Barbara*, in which he defined those undesirables as habitual criminals and persons with private incomes.)[89] In *Anticipations* (1901) H. G. Wells wrote that his "New Republic" of brain workers would "favour the procreation of what is fine and efficient and beautiful in humanity—beautiful and strong bodies, clear and powerful minds, and a growing body of knowledge—and . . . check the procreation of base and servile types, of fear-driven and cowardly souls, of all that is mean and ugly and bestial in the souls, bodies, or habits of men." The method of eugenic control would be, simply, "death."

> The new ethics will hold life to be a privilege and a responsibility, not a sort of night refuge for base spirits out of the void; and the alternative in right conduct between living fully, beautifully, and efficiently will be to die. For a

multitude of contemptible and silly creatures, fear-driven and helpless and useless, unhappy or hatefully happy in the midst of squalid dishonour, feeble, ugly, inefficient, born of unrestrained lusts, and increasing and multiplying through sheer incontinence and stupidity, the men of the New Republic will have little pity and less benevolence.

Habitual criminals would be exterminated, and persons suffering from alcoholism or hereditary diseases would be prohibited from having children on pain of death.[90] Race, ostensibly, would not prejudice the eugenics of the New Republic: "Whatever men may come into its efficient citizenship it will let come—white, black, red, or brown; the efficiency will be the test." But Wells was convinced that most nonwhite peoples would not meet "the new needs of efficiency," and their fate was settled: "Well, the world is a world, and not a charitable institution, and I take it they will have to go. . . . So far as they fail to develop sane, vigorous, and distinctive personalities for the great world of the future, it is their portion to die out and disappear."[91]

Wells retreated a long way from this position in *Mankind in the Making* (1903), in which he acknowledged the difficulty of selecting qualities worth breeding. But he continued to hold that workers who could not raise their earnings above a given minimum wage should not be permitted to have children and that babies with serious genetic defects should be killed at birth.[92] Very few eugenists openly advocated the extermination of the subnormal, but the suggestion was sometimes made in private, even by Virginia Woolf.[93]

Measures to check inferior breeding were "negative eugenics"; "positive eugenics" aimed to encourage superior breeding and was far more acceptable to Edwardian public opinion. Beatrice Webb was very much interested in Mormon plural marriages as an experiment in "scientific breeding," and she regretted that the United States government had put a stop to it.[94] Harley Granville Barker, in his play *The Madras House*, protested that many healthy Englishwomen could not find husbands (as a result of emigration among young men) and half seriously suggested polygamy as a solution. Most leading Fabians and many eugenicists advocated the "Endowment of Motherhood," a state-funded child allowance generous enough to enable any woman, married or otherwise, to raise a brood of children for the Empire without depending on a man for economic support.[95] One small step in this direction was taken in Lloyd George's 1911 Insurance Act: a thirty-shilling maternity benefit.

With its emphasis on compulsory eugenics and military training, there was an illiberal aspect of the national efficiency movement to which even Liberals were not immune. Compared with the Fabians, however, Liberal intellectuals were more likely to temper efficiency with a concern for individual liberty. L. T. Hobhouse (unlike the Webbs) believed that personal freedom had an intrinsic moral value quite apart from its social utility. Together with G. K. Chesteron, Hilaire Belloc, Arthur Quiller-Couch, and the *Nation*, he sharply criticized the Mental Deficiency Bill.[96] Belloc satirized the notion of a coalition party of national efficiency in his novels *Mr. Clutterbuck's Election* (1908) and *Pongo and the Bull* (1910). British colonies and workhouses might be "clean, efficient, austere, intolerably just," wrote Charles Masterman, but they were still essentially prisons, incarcerating people who had every right to hate their jailers.[97] J. L. Hammond took direct aim at the social imperialists when he condemned, in 1903, the

> pseudo-scientific . . . arguments of men to whom all government is a function of police, and the life of a nation a mere symmetry of administrative excellence and precision. . . . Self-government is better than good government. It is the essence of the Liberal temperament that it believes a freedom which goes in rags to be preferable to all the gracious luxuries of slavery, and that it holds the varieties and discrepancies of civilisation to be better for mankind than a prim monotony of drilled perfection.[98]

When Conservatives agitated for a larger fleet, radical M.P.s led by Sir John Brunner and Murray MacDonald turned the efficiency argument against them, contending that greater naval expenditures would depress the national economy: "Our Army and Navy may be in numbers and material equipment overwhelmingly strong; but if that strength is purchased at the cost of the development and efficiency of the people, it will prove but a weak defense in the day of trial."[99]

This was the running theme of New Liberal polemics like *The Heart of the Empire* (1901) and *England: A Nation* (1904): only temperance, proper housing and education, untaxed food, and a living wage could produce an efficient workforce.[100] Seebohm Rowntree, in his 1901 volume *Poverty: A Study of Town Life*, defined the "poverty line" as the minimum income required to maintain "a state of bare physical efficiency."[101] After Rowntree and Booth revealed that about thirty percent of the British people fell below this line, the New Liberals vociferously protested the "waste" of poverty, drink, arms expenditures, luxurious private consumption, child mortality, and "inefficient" sweated labor.[102] For H. W. Nevinson *waste* meant

> the multitudes of boys and girls who never get a chance of fulfilling their inborn capacities. . . . That a nature capable of high development should be precluded by poverty from all development is the deepest of personal and national disasters. . . . Physical waste is bad enough—the waste of strength and health that could easily be retained by fresh air, open spaces, and decent food. . . . This physical waste has already created such a broad distinction that foreigners coming among us detect two species of the English people. But the mental waste is worse.[103]

In *Imperialism: A Study* (1902) J. A. Hobson blasted the social imperialism of Karl Pearson. Colonial expansion did not promote "social efficiency," wrote Hobson; it was merely a means of protecting overseas markets and investments.[104] The British Empire was the result of maldistribution of wealth, "an acute form of economic waste": the rich were sinking surplus capital into the colonies while "hungry mouths, ill-clad backs, ill-furnished houses indicate countless unsatisfied material wants among our own population." If British industry needed markets, new customers could be created at home by redistributing income to Rowntree's "inefficient fourth," thus increasing the purchasing power of the poor. Then "there would be no need for pushful Imperialism, and the cause of social reform would have won its greatest victory."[105]

The defenders of social imperialism were mainly brain workers. Benjamin Kidd, who popularized the ideology in his book *Social Evolution* (1894), was a minor civil servant, and Karl Pearson had taught as a professor of applied mathematics and mechanics. The tariff reformer William Ashley was a professor of commerce at the University of Birmingham; he was also one of the first academics to recognize "the increased importance of the managing director" in mature capitalism.[106] Clifford Sharp, who edited the *New Statesman* for the Webbs, was an engineer by training, and Leonard Woolf recalled that he brought "to human relations and politics . . . the attitude of the engineer, of a sanitary inspector or super-plumber," as well as an enthusiasm for "collectivism and drainage—material or spiritual."[107]

White-collar workers dominated the Eugenics Education Society, which judged that class superior to all other classes. Edwardian eugenicists generally argued that laborers were genetically incapable of being anything more than laborers and that the rich, protected from the struggle for existence by their rents and dividends, were growing soft and degenerate. The brain worker, who had struggled up the ladder of professional success and competitive examination, was the highest product of human development: salary, not wealth, was the measure of social efficiency. Eugenicists often protested that the government, by taxing the middle class to provide social services for the poor, was depressing the white-collar birth rate and encouraging the multiplication of the subnormal. In his 1909 "People's Budget," Lloyd George introduced an income tax deduction of £10 (raised to £20 in 1914) for every child under sixteen. This measure was effectively targeted at the middle class (those who earned between £160 and £500 a year), and as such it was applauded by Karl Pearson, Sidney and Beatrice Webb, and the Eugenics Education Society.[108]

The Boer War had exposed incompetence throughout the administrative structure of the state, and postwar reforms enhanced the authority of brain workers in the armed forces. R. B. Haldane created an Army General Staff, and under Admiral Fisher naval engineers for the first time enjoyed the same privileges, promotional opportunities, and basic training as other officers.[109] "Science offers the soldier transport that he does not use, maps that he does not use, entrenching devices, road-making devices, balloons and flying scouts, portable foods, security from disease," complained H. G. Wells. "Muddle is the enemy," he asserted, and out of that muddle "a new sort of soldier will emerge, a sober, considerate, engineering man."[110]

Rudyard Kipling drew his colonial heroes from that same class—engineers and middle-level administrators. Bernard Shaw was convinced that brain workers would rise above pointless provincial squabbles and bind nations into larger and more rational imperial units. In *John Bull's Other Island* an Irish engineer tells his English partner that Irish separatism violates the most basic ethic of their profession.

> Whatever else metallurgical chemistry may be, it's not national. It's international. And my business and yours as civil engineers is to join countries, not to separate them. The one real political conviction that our business has rubbed into us is that frontiers are hindrances and flags confounded nuisances. [I don't want] to make St. George's Channel a frontier and hoist a green flag on College Green; . . . I want to bring Galway within 3 hours of Colchester and 24 of New York. I want Ireland to be the brains and imagination of a big Commonwealth, not a Robinson Crusoe island.[111]

In that context, "Efficiency" was another way of saying "Only connect"—and there lay the fundamental weakness of the idea. It rested on that congenial Edwardian assumption that all conflicts were reconcilable. Every quarrel between individuals, businesses, classes, and nations could be settled by managerial referees for the benefit of all. In the Marxian scheme of things, one class can prosper only by "expropriating" the other, but the efficiency movement promised that production and distribution could be reorganized to provide more for everyone. That is why the Fabians rejected revolution for education and research: if efficiency benefited all, if it challenged no vested interests (except those of a few middlemen, idlers, and repair workers), then it could be brought about by simple persuasion. The Marxist critic Christopher Caudwell came down hard on H. G. Wells for assuming that socialism would be realized merely by showing people that it was a better system.[112] One does not have to be a Marxist to see that the efficiency men greatly underestimated the power of class interest, not to mention the force of tradition, nationalism, moral sentiment, and human evil. They approached each problem in an engineering spirit, and they saw no reason why laymen would not accept the most rational solution—once it had been clearly explained to them, of course.

How to Live on Twenty-four Hours a Day

Efficiency was more than a political program. For its most devoted partisans, it was a means of organizing daily life, and it accounts for the impressive productivity of some Edwardian authors. Charles Booth managed to write his multivolume *Life and Labour* by scheduling his work very methodically and cutting to a minimum the time he allowed for eating and sleeping.[113] Bernard Shaw and Gilbert Murray abstained from alcohol and animal food not only for humanitarian or puritanical reasons but also to perserve their physical energies and mental clarity.[114] Beatrice Webb saved time by studiously neglecting her toilette, and she dampened down distracting sexual urges by strict dieting.[115] H. G. Wells preferred to control his sexual impulses by freely gratifying them—"frankly on Pauline lines, wine for the stomach's sake, and it is better to marry than to burn, a concession to the flesh necessary to secure efficiency." He insisted, however, that the leaders of his projected utopias deny themselves stimulants, theatergoing, most forms of recreation, and (four nights out of every five) sexual relations.[116]

Personal efficiency was a necessity of life for brain workers. Often beginning their careers on the margin of poverty, they could only hope to scramble up the economic ladder through prodigies of work and self-discipline. As a pupil-teacher, Wells lived according to a timetable that allowed absolutely no leisure or diversions except for hour-long walks taken at a pace of no less than four miles per hour. It was a killing routine, but Wells knew that the only alternative was a life as a draper's assistant: "I was making my desperate get-away from the shop and the street."[117] As a journeyman author, Wells had to calculate the money he could earn for every hour of writing, only taking on jobs that yielded the greatest return. Thus he built up the amazing creative speed that later enabled him to churn out two or more books a year.[118]

In the midnineties, Bernard Shaw advised a young journalist to "make the attainment of EFFICIENCY your sole object for the next fifteen years." By "EFFICIENCY" Shaw meant learning how to write, how to get published, how to use free libraries, how to speak in public, and how to live on fifty pounds a year—the same formula that Shaw had used to achieve literary success. Shaw also suggested working for the Fabians as a means of sharpening one's mental skills; he frankly admitted that he had used the society "as an instrument for increasing [my] own efficiency."[119]

Arnold Bennett made an extraordinarily lucrative career for himself by dint of hard work, careful planning, and writing for the market. He shared his knowledge in books with titles like *Mental Efficiency* (1912) and *How to Live on Twenty-four Hours a Day* (1912). These guides were aimed at the ambitious office workers who took courses in "Brain Power" at the Pelman Institute, the sort of people who were the target of this 1901 advertising slogan for Grape-Nuts cereal: "Brain Workers require special food."[120]

Edwardian social reformers often pursued the goal of personal efficiency for the sake of economic justice. Put simply, they believed that no one should take out of the community more than he put in and that everyone should receive an income equal in value to the goods and services he produced. Bernard Shaw proposed in *Major Barbara* that

> the daily ceremony of dividing the wealth of the country among its inhabitants shall be so conducted that no crumb shall, save as a criminal's ration, go

to any able-bodied adults who are not producing by their personal exertions not only a full equivalent for what they take, but a surplus sufficient to provide for their superannuation and pay back the debt due for their nurture.[121]

The New Liberals were thinking along similar lines, defining any income that did not contribute to social efficiency as an "unearned increment." "Economic justice is to render . . . to each individual . . . engaged in the performance of useful service . . . the amount necessary to stimulate and maintain the efficient exercise of that useful function," wrote L. T. Hobhouse in his essay *Liberalism* (1911).[122] C. P. Trevelyan denounced the lavish consumption of the upper classes on the grounds "that all expenditure must be made to make us efficient for our chosen service, and that all above that is a source of subtle degradation, of blunting our realization of the real facts."[123] The playwright Henry Arthur Jones tried to express in equations what he called "The Great Law of Waste": "How much of that man's energy and time goes to feed or clothe me and give me power to write a play—how much is my play worth as a service to humanity."[124] "Efficiency . . . is a form of altruism," Bertrand Russell told Gilbert Murray, "and however narrow the specialist becomes, we ought to pardon him if he does good work."[125]

"Unless each individual does work equal in utility to the utility of the commodities he consumes," wrote Sidney Webb in 1887, "he is a dead loss to the world. The lives of the workers would be happier if he did not exist." From this principle Webb concluded that "the maximum justifiable expenditure for anybody is the amount which keeps him in the fullest working efficiency. . . . This would include however his *mental* needs, as for instance, some art and relaxation, as being necessary to the fullest efficiency of life."[126] This meant that Beatrice Webb could spend money on Morris wallpapers without feeling too much guilt as she was able to work better in artistic surroundings.[127]

Sidney Webb derived his economics of efficiency partly from the American liberal economist F. A. Walker, who in 1887 defended capitalists' profits as a legitimate fee for the use of their entrepreneurial and managerial skills—a "rent of ability," as he called it. Webb immediately countered that many capitalists were idle shareholders who performed no administrative work whatsoever. All skilled manual and brain workers, Webb argued, were entitled to a "rent of ability," but only those capitalists who were genuine managers could claim a share of it.[128] Here again there was a bias toward the intellectual proletariat, which was presumed to be the most productive class and therefore entitled to generous remuneration. Charles Booth, who was very much a managerial capitalist, held that most wealth was created by "head labour," without which undirected manual workers could do very little useful work. He therefore concluded that "low as its pay is, mere labour has, on the score of production, little if any claim to anything more."[129] S. G. Hobson favored pay differentials for engineers, "the aristocrats of labor,"[130] and Sidney Webb believed that administrative workers should be rewarded with "a living wage at their customary standard of comfort," as well as permanent tenure.[131] H. G. Wells proposed to abolish inherited wealth by confiscatory death duties, but he was quite willing to allow enterprising individuals to build up large private fortunes: he wanted to reward the efficient without creating an unproductive *rentier* class.[132] Of the leading Fabians, only Shaw, in 1910, advocated absolute equality of income.[133] Even he, in the 1930s, endorsed the large pay differentials granted to Stalin's white-collar workers, on the grounds that "first-class brain work or authoritative direction" was impossible without providing "the refinements and comparative seclusion and distinction which are necessary to such persons."[134]

Explain, Simplify, Clarify

The drive for efficiency spilled over into literature, where it promoted directness, clarity, and economy, often at the expense of other aesthetic values. There were attempts to rationalize English orthography: Robert Bridges (named poet laureate in 1913) and Bernard Shaw agitated for a phonetic alphabet and corresponded on the subject.[135] In 1908 the Simplified Spelling Society was founded: Gilbert Murray, William Archer, the philologist F. J. Furnivall, H. G. Wells, and Lord Bryce served as officers. The propaganda of the society emphasized that rational spelling would speed the acceptance of English as a universal language, whch in itself would be a tremendous contribution to world efficiency. Shaw used the same argument to dismiss the Gaelic Revival: why should the Irish resuscitate a dying tongue spoken nowhere else in the world when they already had a language shared with half the human race?[136] Wells noted that "the wider the area a periodical or book serves the bigger, more attractive, and better it can be made for the same money," and he looked forward to the day when "inconvenient" local dialects would die out and give way to a few international languages.[137]

According to Richard Ellmann, the Edwardians wrote more tightly than the Victorians: "Their sentences grew more vigorous and concentrated."[138] Certainly the taut prose of Shaw, Wells, Kipling, and Bennett contrasts sharply with the ornate, decorated language of Dickens, George Eliot, Arnold, Pater, and Wilde. In fact, English novels generally became more concise at the end of the nineteenth century, if only because the three-volume novel, which dominated Victorian fiction and demanded outrageous padding, suddenly became extinct after 1895.[139] At the same time, the New Journalism of George Newnes and Alfred Harmsworth encouraged terse, vigorous writing in popular newspapers and magazines. "Explain, Simplify, Clarify" was Harmsworth's formula.

The challenge of American efficiency was felt in literature as well as in industry. Writers from across the Atlantic were now asserting the virtues of simple, direct United States English. Ezra Pound arrived in London in 1908 and, with A. R. Orage, compaigned in the *New Age* for basic language in prose and poetry. Pound regarded the writer as an "engineer" whose artistic mission was to "gather the latent energy of Nature and focus it on a certain resistance."[140] He persuaded William Butler Yeats to abandon the loose, aesthetic style of his early poetry and taught him to make every word tell. Richard Ellmann notices the improvement: Yeats's later "verse is more spare, the images are exactly delimited by the words, every shadow is removed."[141] The weaving, leisurely fiction of Henry James was criticized by a chorus of American intellectuals, including his brother William ("Say it *out*, for God's sake and have done with it") and Woodrow Wilson.[142]

The directness and "intellectual energy" of H. G. Wells were generously praised and even envied by Henry James—"I who was accursedly born to touch nothing save to complicate it."[143] For his part, Wells worried whether James was efficiently reaching his readers: "How much will they get out of what you have got in?"[144] Wells produced some modest but honest attempts at literary artistry—*Love and Mr. Lewisham* (1899), *Kipps* (1905), *Tono-Bungay* (1909), and *The History of Mr. Polly* (1910)—but thereafter he allowed himself to be diverted to propaganda. Attacked on all sides for his extramarital affairs and his advocacy of sexual freedom, frustrated in his efforts to take over the Fabian Society, he began to churn out fictional tracts, "scamping" each book in order to get on to the next.

James tried to warn Wells away from "the loose, the improvised, the cheap and the easy." He singled out a passage in *Marriage* (1912), where a couple fall in love after talking for three hours, and the novel never hints at what they said to each other. This, James admonished, was an impermissible short cut: Wells obviously had not bothered to think out the conversation. In fact, the characters in the novel hardly converse at all; they only propound Wellsian schemes for social efficiency.[145] Wells was chastened ("My art is abortion—on the shelves of my study stand a little vain-gloriously—thirty-odd premature births"), and he promised to take more trouble with his writing in the future.[146]

That was in September 1913; the following March James published his misgivings about Wells in the *Times Literary Supplement*. Wells responded with his vindictive novel *Boon*, which lampooned Jamesian style as a tangle of qualifications, digressions, adverbial shadings, subordinate clauses, and subsubordinate clauses. Wells compared James to "a magnificent but painful hippopotamus resolved at any cost, even at the cost of its dignity, upon picking up a pea which has got into a corner of its den." Why couldn't James be more direct, more pragmatic, more like his "incomparable" brother William? Literature should be "something that pierces always down towards the core of things, something that carries and changes all the activities of the race. . . . First the end must be judged—and then if you like talk of how it is done. Get there as splendidly as possible. But get there."[147]

Boon is not really a novel at all; it is only the outline of a novel, with a few brief scenes fleshed in. Wells never developed the book beyond the talking stage, but he was willing to rush it out to his public in that skeletal form. In his quest for maximum impact and output, Wells stripped fiction down to a blueprint for social reorganization. Plot, description, and character delineation were all jettisoned, leaving, in *The Undying Fire* (1919), nothing but lectures and expository dialogue. To James Joyce, Wells was willing to concede that *Finnegans Wake* was "a considerable thing. . . . But I don't think it gets anywhere." Wells was striving for "increase of power and range by economy and concentration of effort," and for that he needed "language and statement as simple and clear as possible."[148]

That aesthetic imparted a sterile, machine-tooled quality to Wells's novels and to the plays of his Fabian colleague Harley Granville Barker. As both a playwright and a director, Barker let nothing go to waste; he made every line and gesture push the story forward or underscore some unifying theme. His 1912 productions of *Twelfth Night* and *A Winter's Tale* were landmarks in theater history. Barker did away with the elaborately realistic sets of Victorian Shakespeare productions and substituted a spare, geometrical décor. He drilled his actors to deliver their lines with perfect diction, great energy, and stupendous speed—so fast, in fact, that he was able to present Shakespeare practically uncut, an unheard-of feat in his day. John Masefield was dazzled by Barker's engineering: "What I admire so much in your work is its fineness and precision, it is like fine metal-work, all certain and strong and lithe, all the unnecessary cut away."[149] These same qualities, however, made Barker's own plays dismally one dimensional and propagandistic. They relentlessly bludgeoned the audience with a single message, allowing no diversions, no art for its own sake; and not one of Barker's works is a living theater piece today.

Artists accounted for only 2.5 to 4.5 percent of the Fabian membership. Other Fabians tended to treat art and literature as propaganda or sociological documents. In 1907 Holbrook Jackson and A. R. Orage organized a Fabian Arts Group, but it soon drifted over to the guild socialists, who were much more hospitable to the arts and crafts. Eric Gill complained that "the Fabian Society looks at things too much from the point of view of the managing director," and he left the organization in 1911. Legend has it that A. J. Penty quit the Fabians when he learned that the Webbs had selected a design for the London School of Economics solely because it offered a maximum of floor space. That story may well be apocryphal, but it is certainly true that Penty reviled Sidney Webb's tracts on national efficiency.[150]

If efficiency was the credo of the brain worker, it was the bane of most Edwardian artists. G. K. Chesterton (who studied at the Slade) regularly ridiculed the concept, and Max Beerbohm conjured up a nightmare future of simplified spelling and "very-well-cared-for" utopians, each with a state identification number, each sprayed regularly with carbolic acid.[151] Writers who thought of themselves as artists, who had never been brain workers—like Henry James, W. B. Yeats, and James Joyce—were no more sympathetic. The young aesthetes of the Bloomsbury Group, and Virginia Woolf especially, disdained the utilitarian politics of the Webbs. Beatrice Webb returned their scorn in kind, denouncing *Principia Ethica* (quite inaccurately) as "a metaphysical justification for doing what you like and what other people disapprove of!" and "a denial . . . of the scientific method."[152] E. M. Forster briefly took an interest in "economic trend, efficiency," and tried to meet its apostles halfway in *Howards End* (1910).[153] But the character of Henry Wilcox only illustrates the poverty of "sound business methods" —the advice he gives is simply wrong and, for the poor clerk who follows it, terribly costly—and Forster had earlier satirized Wellsian technocracy in his short story "The Machine Stops" (1908).

Most of the Bloomsbury people could afford to sneer at efficiency: they had private incomes that elevated them above the ranks of the brain workers. Leonard Woolf, however, was one member of the group who had no money to speak of, and he knew from an early age that "my future depended upon my brain." After coming down from Cambridge in 1904, he became a colonial administrator in Ceylon. He quickly developed "a passion for efficiency"—answering letters the day they were received, taking an accurate census, cutting costs in the government salt concession, improving peasant cultivation, and controlling cattle diseases. By 1912 he decided that, rather than "make my District or Province the most efficient, the most prosperous in Asia," he preferred to marry Virginia Stephen and become a writer.[154] But even after his return to England, Woolf did work for the Webbs on the subject of international government. He also contributed articles to Clifford Sharp's *New Statesman*, including a guardedly favorable piece on scientific factory management.[155]

The artistic resistance to efficiency extended to English architects, who produced no functional architecture comparable to the work of Louis Sullivan and Frank Lloyd Wright. In Britain there were only a few tentative experiments in this direction, such as C. F. A. Voysey's Sanderson Wallpaper Factory in Chiswick (1902–1903) and John Burnet's Kodak Building in Kingsway (1910–1911). There was no interest in exposed steel, which in any case was prohibited by London building codes. This backwardness may have been connected to the fact that turn-of-the-century architects revolted against the process of professionalization that white-collar workers were eagerly pushing forward in their own occupations. In *Architecture, a Profession or an Art* (1892) Norman Shaw, Edward Prior, W. R. Lethaby, and other prominent architects argued forcefully for the latter alternative. This resistance delayed the adoption of a uniform system of training and examination. Most Edwardian architects were trained in apprenticeships, in which they studied architectural history rather than the use of steel, glass, and reinforced concrete, so that even those few who wanted to experiment with streamlined styles of building (like Lethaby) lacked the necessary technical skills. Edwardian architecture was consequently a medley of backward-looking styles: quaint rustic cottages, overdecorated baroque public buildings, late Gothic and Byzantine churches, Georgian townhouses, lavish beaux-arts clubs and hotels. *Efficiency* is the last word they bring to mind.[156]

Archdeacon into Inspector

In some of its manifestations, the national efficiency movement took the form of a surrogate theology. Sir Francis Galton frankly preached eugenics as "a new religion," "an orthodox religious tenet of the future," "a 'Jehad,' or Holy War,"[157] and W. A. S. Hewins acknowledged that his faith in imperial efficiency was a substitute for the Roman Catholic faith in which he had been raised.[158] Once, the moral and intellectual leadership of the nation had rested with the clergy: now that role was being taken over by new professions in science and social service. Ministers of religion, who concerned themselves with ultimate values, were increasingly outnumbered by managers and technicians, who tended to judge things by practical results. There was, consequently, a change in the basic direction of British intellectual discourse, a shift of emphasis from ends to means, from teleological thinking to instrumental thinking, from morality to problem solving.

In the course of Victoria's reign, public school graduates had turned from careers in the church to the new professions. At Winchester, for example, twenty-three students out of sixty in the class of 1836 had taken orders while five entered the civil service and one went into business. Only four of eighty-three graduates of 1893 were ministers, but eight were civil servants, nine were businessmen, and several entered professions that had not even appeared on the 1836 register, including six engineers, two journalists, and three accountants.[159] In the book industry, toward the end of the century, religious publishing was declining while categories reflecting the interests of the new professions were expanding at an explosive rate. In 1893 the *Publishers' Circular* determined that social and economic science accounted for only 1.3 percent of all book titles. The editors lumped natural science together with "Illustrated Works and Arts," which added up to 1.9 percent. By 1913 sociology alone accounted for 7.4 percent of all titles (more than religion) while science and technology totaled 11.5 percent. Richard Altick has determined that British authors who came to literature from other occupations between 1800 and 1870 were most often clergymen and only rarely teachers; by the period 1900–1935, these two professions had reversed positions.[160]

Some Edwardians, like C. F. G. Masterman, looked hopefully to the "intellectual proletariat" to provide the ethical vision once provided by ministers of religion.[161] The Fabians in particular wanted to assume the role of a white-collar clerisy. "Theatre is a social service," declared Granville Barker, and he tried to elevate the status of the performing artist by agitating for an actors' trade union and a national theater.[162] Barker's 1907 play *Waste* proposed to disestablish the Church of England and use its endowment to train a quasi-religious order of intellectuals consecrated to the cause of education. Thus Barker effected the "disappearance of . . . the Archdeacon into the Inspector." He also specified a raise in salary for these white-collar friars, who would follow no dogma other than "efficiency"—that was Barker's "prose for God." For all his efficiency, the hero of the play rather carelessly impregnates a married woman, and when the scandal wrecks his disestablishment bill, he tries to revive sympathy for the measure by committing suicide. It strikes him as the only efficient thing to do in the circumstances: "God is infinitely economical and wastes perhaps less of the power in us after our death than men do while we live."[163]

H. G. Wells built a substitute religion of his own around a priesthood of engineers. At an early age he repudiated hellfire Christianity as a "lie,"[164] but eventually, when he studied under T. H. Huxley at the Normal School of Science, Wells discovered that science could lead to conclusions as terrifying as the sternest theology. Long before Freud, Darwin had uncovered the beast in man. He had shown that humanity was only a few million years removed from the apes, and some Victorians concluded that man might someday slough off civilization and revert to his origins. "I know of no study which is so utterly saddening as that of the evolution of humanity," Huxley lamented, and he warned that the evolutionary process could reverse itself at any moment. The specter of regressive evolution horrified Wells, and he worked it into every one of his early novels—the simian Morlocks in *The Time Machine* (1895), the half-humans of *The Island of Dr. Moreau* (1896), the "paeleolithic" killer of *The Invisible Man* (1897), and the squidlike man-eating Martians of *The War of the Worlds* (1898).[165]

To preserve the forward momentum of human progress, Wells looked to a technocratic elite he called the "New Republicans." As defined in *Anticipations* (1901), this class took in all "the unorganized myriads that one can cover by the phrase 'mechanics and engineers,' if one uses it in its widest possible sense," including even bicycle mechanics. In Edwardian England these "efficients" had to endure "poverty and popular neglect," but they were evolving from self-taught "irregulars" into educated technicians possessing "a common fund of intellectual training" and "a common class-consciousness." Because society needed their skills, these specialists would inevitably become the ruling class. Once in power, they would promote scientific progress, continually improve social efficiency, and ensure, through a code of strict eugenic controls, that mankind would never revert to its animal origins. In doing that, Wells emphasized, the New Republicans would be fulfilling a spiritual mission.

> Now quite inevitably these men will be religious men. *Being themselves, as by the nature of the forces that have selected them they certainly will be, men of will and purpose, they will be disposed to find, and consequently they will find, an effect of purpose in the totality of things.* Either one must believe the Universe to be one and systematic, and held together by some omnipresent quality, or one must believe it to be a casual aggregation, an incoherent accumulation with no unity whatsoever outside the unity of the personality regarding it. All science and most modern religious systems presuppose the former; and to believe the former is, to any one not too anxious to quibble, to believe in God.[166]

As a scientist, Wells was horrified by the possibility that scientific progress would someday come to an end: human beings might eventually solve every material problem and settle into lotus-eating sloth, like the Eloi in *The Time Machine*. He therefore invented a God who was nothing more than a force for progress, worshipped in the laboratory by a white-coated priesthood. Wells later gave different names to his technocratic caste (the Samurai, the Open Conspiracy, the World Brain), and he eventually opened it up to "any intelligent adult in a reasonably healthy and efficient state." But it always took the form of a brain-worker elite, dedicated to eliminating "friction, conflict and waste" in the name of a religion that was obviously a substitute for Christianity.

(The Samurai even have their own "Bible"—in two testaments.)[167] That religion would have no ends, only means; its followers would abandon "the search for ultimates" and devote themselves solely to fulfilling "a desire, a passion almost, to create and organise, to put in order, to get the maximum result from certain possibilities."[168] No final resting place, no Kingdom of Heaven, would ever be reached. Once the scientists had made the entire earth flawlessly efficient, they would construct spaceships, fly to other planets, and put them in order, world without end. There is the same brushing aside of final objectives in Granville Barker's *Waste*, which simply exhorts us to "use all the energy you find . . . turning it into the nearest channel that points forward." Barker never properly answers the question "Forward to what?"[169] That was the great blind spot of the national efficiency movement. It was the quickest route to nowhere—"politics for politics' sake," as G. K. Chesterton quipped.[170]

The decline of traditional religion, however, left many Edwardians uncertain about the ends of existence, and some of them responded by putting teleology aside and concentrating on their everyday work. Joseph Conrad was happy to embrace the sailor's ethic of doing one's job well and not asking too many questions about the cargo. He "rejoiced in the great security of the sea as compared with the unrest of the land, in my choice of that untempted life presenting no disquieting problems, invested with an elementary moral beauty by the absolute straightforwardness of its appeal and by the singleness of its purpose."[171] Conrad entertained a wry admiration for the dull skipper who somehow manages to bring his ship into port on schedule, like Captain MacWhirr in "Typhoon" (1902). The police in *The Secret Agent* are a plodding crew who never think to question whether the society they protect is worth protecting, but they are at least an "efficient" force for order. The anarchists in that novel question everything, and they succeed only in destroying one another.[172]

Conrad once described his story "Heart of Darkness" (1899) as a fable exposing "the criminality of inefficiency . . . when tackling the civilizing work in Africa."[173] It is specifically an attack on incompetent Belgian colonialism, and an endorsement of British imperial efficiency. Marlow is pleased to see the map painted red "because one knows that some real work is done in there." He admits that imperialism is a dirty business, but "what saves us is efficiency—the devotion to efficiency."[174] The horror of the Congo enterprise is its fantastic

"muddle"—dilapidated machinery, slovenly native troops, "inefficient" native laborers, a railway going nowhere, punctured water pails,
brickmakers who make no bricks, rivets rusting hundreds of miles from
where they are needed. This entropic swamp is relieved only by an
occasional island of good management, like the immaculate company
accountant who keeps his books "in apple-pie order" ("Heart" 63-68).
An obsolete seaman's manual, which Marlow finds in the depths of the
jungle, steadies him like a Bible: "an honest concern for the right way of
going to work . . . made these humble pages . . . luminous with
another than a professional light." Efficiency is an antidote to solipcism:
when we are "cut off from the comprehension of our surroundings,"
then simple "talk of chains and purchases" can convey "a delicious sensation of having come upon something unmistakably real." In the wilderness, where there are no policemen or priests, the thinking man can
preserve his sanity by getting on with the job. Marlow does not find
ultimate truth in repairing a company steamboat, but there is "surface-
truth enough in these things to save a wiser man." He needs rivets to
patch up his metaphysics as well as his boat. Good work creates a sense
of philosophic welds and connections, without which we slip into sav-
agery: "Rivets were what really Mr. Kurtz wanted, if he had only
known it" ("Heart" 84, 96-99).

Some Edwardians treated religion itself as a means of improving efficiency, as a useful myth to promote hard work and cooperation among
believers. That was the central argument of Benjamin Kidd's *Social Evolution*—Christianity had enhanced the "social efficiency" of the human race by teaching individuals to sacrifice themselves for God, for
their fellow man, and for generations yet unborn.[175] This point was explicitly endorsed by the Christian socialist Scott Holland and by Charles
Booth, who would devote seven volumes of his *Life and Labour* to the
sociological influence of religious belief. Kidd was also widely admired
among eugenicists and social imperialists, including Sir Francis Galton,
J. L. Garvin, Joseph Chamberlain, and Lord Milner.[176]

One imperialist who did not necessarily consider Christianity an efficient means of social control was Rudyard Kipling. The district officer
in "The Judgment of Dungara" (1888) is happy to support an indigenous
pagan cult, which keeps his natives contented and obedient, but he recognizes that Christian missionaries are bringing a new, disturbing, and
potentially revolutionary faith to the region. In India, with its volatile
mix of rival creeds, efficiency dictated tolerance and understanding of

all native religions. What could not be tolerated was the introduction of alien ideas that might disrupt the social fabric. That was the principle behind the latitudinarianism of *Kim*: not so much that all religions are equally true but that "each has merit in its own country."[177]

In the absence of religion, some other rule of conduct—Mowgli's Jungle Jaw or the schoolboy code of *Stalky and Co.* (1899)—must be substituted to ensure the efficient functioning of the social machine. It is important to emphasize that the Law of *The Jungle Book* does not mandate a predatory free-for-all. Animal warfare is strictly regulated to guarantee the survival of the pack, the species, and the jungle community as a whole. No wolf cub may be killed until he is old enough to hunt: any adult wolf who breaks that law is punished by death. This is not the social Darwinism of Herbert Spencer; it is more like the social imperialism of Karl Pearson, who wanted to restrain "the internal struggle" for existence to enhance "the efficiency of the herd at large."[178]

Bernard Shaw believed that brain workers needed the stimulation of churchgoing to work at peak "efficiency." He often attended services himself,[179] and he observed that religious people generally "have dignity, conviction, sobriety and force. However impossibly narrow and stupid the mere articles of their creed may be, it is obvious that they are respectable, efficient, and able to do without happiness."[180] For that reason, Shaw and the Webbs were supporters of parochial education. Sidney Webb particularly admired the Catholic church for its emphasis on good works; the Protestant preoccupation with personal salvation struck him as a self-indulgence.[181]

Shaw knew better than the Webbs "that efficiency is obviously not a final term & cannot be held up as an end"—so he warned them in their first flush of enthusiasm over the idea.[182] Most of the Fabians realized that efficiency might only produce a better-run system of economic exploitation: they were very wary of American schemes for scientific management.[183] When the engineers of *John Bull's Other Island* plan to build a resort in a sleepy Irish village, assuring the population that "the world belongs to the efficient," Father Keegan damns the enterprise.

> I do every justice to the efficiency of you and your syndicate. You are both, I am told, thoroughly efficient civil engineers; and I have no doubt that the golf links will be a triumph of your art. . . . You may even build the hotel efficiently if you can find enough efficient masons, carpenters, and plumbers, which I rather doubt. (*Dropping his irony, and beginning to fall into the*

attitude of a priest rebuking sin) When the hotel becomes insolvent . . . your English business habits will secure the thorough efficiency of the liquidation. You will reorganize the scheme efficiently; you will liquidate its second bankruptcy efficiently. . . ; you will get rid of its original stockholders efficiently after efficiently ruining them; and you will finally profit very efficiently by getting that hotel for a few shillings in the pound. (*More and more sternly*) Besides these efficient operations, you will foreclose your mortgages most efficiently. . . ; you will . . . slave-drive your laborers very efficiently; and (*low and bitter*) when at last this poor desolate countryside becomes a busy mint in which we shall all slave to make money for you, with our Polytechnic to teach us how to do it efficiently, . . . then no doubt your English and American shareholders will spend all the money we make for them very efficiently in shooting and hunting, in operations for cancer and appendicitis, in gluttony and gambling; and you will devote what they save to fresh land development schemes. For four wicked centuries the world has dreamed this foolish dream of efficiency; and the end is not yet. But the end will come.

Shaw did not mean to repudiate efficiency; rather, he tried to link it to the spirituality of Father Keegan. Means without ends and ends without means are both futile, and if anything the latter is worse: even Keegan prefers "an efficient devil that knows his own mind and his own business" to a good man "who has no mind and no business."[184] The tragedy of *John Bull's Other Island* is that there is no Forsterian reconciliation of Keegan's vision with the organizing ability of the engineers; however, in Shaw's next play, *Major Barbara*, Barbara and Undershaft arrive at just such an understanding. The weapons manufacturer deliberately undermines his daughter's faith to teach her that even religion must pass the test of practical results.

What do we do here when we spend years of work and thought and thousands of pounds of solid cash on a new gun or an aerial battleship that turns out just a hairsbreadth wrong after all? Scrap it. Scrap it without wasting another hour or another pound on it. Well, you have made for yourself something that you call a morality or a religion or what not. It doesnt fit the facts. Well, scrap it. Scrap it and get one that does fit.[185]

Barbara, on her part, recognizes that it is not enough to provide Undershaft's workers with modern housing and employee benefits, and she resolves to carry her crusade for salvation into her father's factories. That, for Shaw, is true efficiency: power joined with vision. It is the same reconciliation that Rudyard Kipling effected in *Kim*: the lama is free to search for enlightenment because his *chela* is policing the Empire, making it safe "for weaponless dreamers."[186]

Wastage

Although the efficiency men had been accumulating power and influence throughout the Edwardian period, their moment really arrived in August 1914. In order to fight a prolonged global war, the British government was forced to take unprecedented measures to increase productivity, conserve resources, reduce wasteful consumption, and eliminate bottlenecks in every area of industry. The state assumed the right to control the railways, shipping, coal, and any factory engaged in war production. The Asquith government was reluctant to regulate food supplies, but subsidies, price controls, rationing, and fines on waste and profiteering were imposed after the resumption of German submarine warfare in October 1916. The Board of Agriculture and local authorities brought much new acreage under cultivation, and, armed with the threat of dispossession, they ordered farmers to adopt more efficient methods of tillage. Under the pressure of demands for greater production, the science of industrial psychology developed rapidly, and in 1916 the Federation of British Industries was formed by factory owners to standardize and coordinate output. Daylight Savings Time had been proposed in Parliament in 1908, but the wartime necessity of conserving energy made it a reality in 1916. The government was slow to mobilize scientists for the war effort, but appalling shortages of war materiel, together with the prodding of R. B. Haldane and the Royal Society, led to the creation of a well-funded Department of Scientific and Industrial Research in 1916. British scientists (chemists especially) were at last being supported on a really generous scale.[187]

In the war emergency, efficiency was an issue important enough to break one prime minister and make another. Asquith's prosecution of the war was widely perceived as indecisive and lazy, and in December 1916 mounting political pressure and press criticism forced him to resign. He was replaced by Lloyd George, whose handling of a series of crises had won him a reputation for getting things done. Concerned that alcohol impaired the "strength and efficiency" of armament workers, he had induced a reluctant King George to set an example by abstaining for the duration and went on to secure strict government controls over the liquor trade. As early as September 1914 Lloyd George foresaw a frightening shortage of rifles, shells, and artillery, and after several military disasters he persuaded Asquith to set up a special committee to secure "the promptest and most efficient application of all the available resources of the country to the manufacture and supply of munitions of war." (The British public knew nothing of the shell shortage until 14 May 1915, when Colonel Repington of the old Coefficients reported it in the *Times*.) As minister of munitions, Lloyd George built state-owned factories, commandeered private factories, and enforced compulsory arbitration. He swept aside union work rules, employers' prerogatives, bureaucratic red tape, and Lord Kitchener's opposition with an even-handed ruthlessness. He compelled capital and labor to take orders from his staff of brain workers, among them Herbert Llewellyn Smith, W. H. Beveridge, and Seebohm Rowntree. As prime minister, Lloyd George would streamline administration by creating a compact war cabinet. To bypass the cumbersome civil service, the premier and the war cabinet set up their own respective secretariats, which included three young men of the Round Table: Philip Kerr, Leopold Amery, and Waldorf Astor.

From the outset of the war, Lloyd George worked closely with the Conservatives to expedite policymaking. He still cherished the idea of a grand peacetime coalition that would rise above partisan politics and enact a sweeping program of social reform. Immediately after the armistice, he arranged to continue his wartime alliance with the Unionists, and the coalition won an overwhelming victory at the polls. The Party of National Efficiency was at last a reality, though its achievements in the area of welfare legislation would be limited, and it would break up in 1922.[188]

The war gave added force to the old argument that a welfare state produced more efficient fighters and workers, and the Webbs now drove this lesson home relentlessly.[189] In November 1916 Winston Churchill demanded strict food rationing and price controls "to secure to the poorest people in this country who are engaged in fighting this War as comrades with us, a certain modicum of food sufficient to keep up physical war-making efficiency." Noting that a third of all recruits were physically unfit for military service (not a vast improvement over the Boer War), Lord Rhondda and Christopher Addison protested the "in-

efficiency of our public medical services" and secured some limited reforms.[190] In Oliver St. John Gogarty's play *Blight* (1917), an Irish soldier
returns home safe from the front to find that two of his children have
died in slum epidemics. "The strong races that look after their own and
that have homes to fight for will overwhelm ye," he warns the audience.
"How can you win when you're killing your own?"[191]

The War Office was overwhelmed with unsolicited suggestions for
fighting the war more effectively, some of them less hare-brained than
others. H. G. Wells designed a portable conveyor to move supplies up to
the trenches, and he persuaded the government to undertake its development, though it was not perfected soon enough to be used in the fighting.[192] Bernard Shaw unsuccessfully promoted an automated system for
loading and unloading railway freight, later making the grandiose claim
that it would have effected "an enormous saving of labor and smash"
and released "from industry enough men to utterly overwhelm the Central Empires." Shaw did not, as his enemies charged, oppose British
participation in the First World War. He criticized the "muddle" of Sir
Edward Grey's prewar diplomacy, but once the war was on, Shaw resolved to fight it as efficiently as possible. In his skit *Augustus Does His Bit*
(1917), he lampooned jingoes for interfering in other people's work and
bungling their own.[193] "If you have anything to do go and do it," was
Shaw's war slogan; "if not, for heaven's sake get out of the way."[194]

The Fabians responded ambivalently to the war: it was a horrifying
waste of men and wealth, but it also did much to rationalize the British
economy. Beatrice Webb was more depressed than encouraged by current events although (she recorded in August 1917) "to Sidney they are
exhilarating—they stimulate him—he is perpetually thinking of how to
mould them in his own dear disinterested way. He refuses to dwell on
the horrors of the war and he believes that through the war will come
the changes he believes in."[195] H. G. Wells had seen the war coming for
some time, but he had never been able to decide whether it would lead to
a utopia of social efficiency (as predicted in *The World Set Free*, 1913) or
the end of civilization (as predicted in *The War in the Air*, 1907). He
greeted the actual conflict with the same contrary feelings—sometimes
it was "The War That Will End War," sometimes it was the "final and
absolute smash."[196] Although Shaw appreciated "the hideous cost of
Neuve Chapelle, Ypres, and the Gallipoli landing," he saw no alternative.

Our most efficient soldiers . . . left their creative work to drudge at destruction, exactly as they would have left it to take their turn at the pumps in a sinking ship. They did not, like some of the conscientious objectors, hold back because the ship had been neglected by its officers and scuttled by its wreckers. The ship had to be saved, even if Newton had to leave his fluxions and Michael Angelo his marbles to save it; so they threw away the tools of their beneficent and ennobling trades, . . . forcing themselves to pervert . . . their economic faculty for organization to the contriving of ruin and slaughter.

Britain's deadliest enemies, however, were not Germans, but incompetents at home: "Whilst all the efficiency of England was silent and invisible, all its imbecility was deafening the heavens with its clamor and blotting out the sun with its dust." Real power was in the hands of "Noisy Incapables," like Boss Mangan of *Heartbreak House. Major Barbara* made a hero of the practical businessman, but that is precisely how Mangan describes himself, and as a member of the war government he protects his job by sabotaging the work of his colleagues. "I may not know anything about my own machinery," he admits, "but I know how to stick a ramrod into the other fellow's. . . . If that isnt a triumph of practical business, what is?" Shaw's faith in efficiency had always rested on the happy assumption that power could be harnessed to vision, but in *Heartbreak House* Mangan has all the power, Captain Shotover has all the vision, and the two are never reconciled.[197]

A war in which there had been so much talk of practical business and so much actual waste and bungling, a war in which *wastage* was the official euphemism for casualties, was bound to produce a revulsion against the idea of efficiency.[198] It was frequently assailed as a Prussian ideal: in his last book, Benjamin Kidd condemned eugenics as a policy that could "only be applied to the world by the methods of the German General Staff!"[199] The notorious canard that the Germans were rendering human cadavers into oil and pig fodder was publicized as "an illustration of their much-vaunted efficiency! . . . Proof of the zeal to waste nothing!"[200] The *New Statesman*, in which Clifford Sharp and the Webbs editorialized for a level-headed war, only disgusted E. M. Forster: "efficiency as absurd as incompetence."[201] D. H. Lawrence, whose prewar writings were not hostile to "machinery," turned violently against all forms of scientific organization in *Women in Love*, vilifying the cost-effective management that Gerald Crich introduces into his mining operations.

The miners were reduced to mere mechanical instruments. . . . The joy went out of their lives, the hope seemed to perish as they became more and more mechanised. . . . A great and perfect system . . . subjected life to pure mathematical principles. . . . It was the first great step in undoing, the first great phase of chaos, the substitution of the mechanical principle for the organic.[202]

The temporary removal of Germany as a military and economic threat after 1918 eliminated the most compelling argument for national efficiency. In *The Economic Consequences of the Peace* John Maynard Keynes actually stood the old logic of imperial efficiency on its head. Keynes insisted that excessive reparations would so impoverish German workers that they would lack the physical "efficiency" to manufacture enough goods to pay those reparations.[203] The postwar revival of aestheticism and dandyism among Martin Green's "Children of the Sun" produced cultural manifestoes denouncing "the modern tendency of hysterical revolution—speed and efficiency, in modern Art and Life."[204] H. G. Wells continued to rehash his old technocratic sermons, but his most ambitious effort in this direction, *The World of William Clissold* (1926), was reviled by the critics, and *Clissoldism* became a derisory term for Wells's finicky social tinkering.[205] Diatribes against efficiency—like Aldous Huxley's *Brave New World*, George Orwell's *Coming up for Air* (1939), and the literary criticism produced by the Leavis school—have since become almost a tradition in modern English letters.

Of course, *efficiency* did not disappear from the British vocabulary after 1919. It continued to be a preoccupation with the Fabians, with the left-wing intellectuals who extolled Stalin's Five-Year Plans in the 1930s, with the "boffins" who organized weapons manufacture during the Second World War, with C. P. Snow in his lectures "The Two Cultures" (1959, 1963). In recent years, the sluggishness of the British economy has made efficiency a national fixation. In 1964 the Labour Party came to power promising to vaporize social ills in the "white heat of a technological revolution"—words that would have warmed the heart of H. G. Wells. Films like *The Man in the White Suit* (1951) and *I'm All Right, Jack* (1959) have blamed low productivity on both capital and labor. The hero of the former, by the way, is a brain worker, a chemical engineer who invents an indestructible synthetic textile.

Compared with their counterparts in the United States, Soviet Russia, France, Germany, and Japan, British social planners and technocrats have always enjoyed less in the way of status, salary, political power, and state support. They continue to produce blueprints for national efficiency, but they have been frustrated in their work by a conservative aristocracy, unadventurous capitalists, and a powerful labor movement. They have had to fight that anti-industrial strain in English culture recently described by Martin Wiener.[206] With the steady decline of British power—a decline that began in the Edwardian period—the brain worker has often become an embittered Cassandra. "God damn you all: I told you so" was the epitaph H. G. Wells wrote for himself.[207] "I can't help thinking of the Venetian Republic in their last half-century," said C. P. Snow in 1959.

> Like us, they had once been fabulously lucky. They had become rich, as we did, by accident. They had acquired immense political skill, just as we have. A good many of them were tough-minded, realistic, patriotic men. They knew, just as clearly as we know, that the current of history had begun to flow against them. Many of them gave their minds to working out ways to keep going. It would have meant breaking the pattern into which they had crystallised. They were fond of the pattern, just as we are fond of ours. They never found the will to break it.[208]

5. The Gospel of Fun

"Except for 'God,' " wrote Walter Houghton, "the most popular word in the Victorian vocabulary must have been 'work.' "[1] As for recreation, that, according to J. L. and Barbara Hammond, was considered immoral, or at least a "waste: the man who was kicking a football or playing a fiddle might be wielding a hammer at a forge or superintending a spinning machine."[2] The new industrial economy demanded a sober and disciplined labor force, and the Evangelical revival had produced a public reaction against all forms of frivolity and dissipation. In addition, many Victorian reformers were sincerely appalled by the violence, drunkenness, and blood sports that inevitably accompanied workingmen's holidays, particularly the "wakes"—rowdy local festivals popular in the industrial North. Between (roughly) 1800 and 1870, employers, religious bodies, and government officials collaborated to suppress working-class amusements. Traditional holidays were abolished, work routines were enforced, factory hours were long, and Sunday recreations (except for pubs) were restricted.[3]

This puritanism also dampened British literary and cultural life. Jonathan Swift, Laurence Sterne, Dr. Johnson, the wits of the Restoration, the Georgian coffee houses, and the Regency—none of them regarded fun and intellect as mutually exclusive. But the dominant mood of Victorian thought was set by Thomas Carlyle and his "gospel of work." "Life was never a May-game for men," he thundered in *Past and Present* (1843), "in all times the lot of the dumb millions born to toil was defaced with manifold sufferings, injustices, heavy burdens, avoidable and unavoidable; not play at all, but hard work."[4] Thereafter, the intellectual dandyism that Carlyle attacked went out of fashion, and most of its practitioners, like Benjamin Disraeli, were compelled to assume black coats and an air of sobriety.[5]

It would be wrong to imply that the Victorians had no sense of fun. The virtues of play were vigorously defended by Charles Dickens, Lewis Carroll, and Robert Louis Stevenson, and high comedy was produced by George Meredith and Gilbert and Sullivan. For the most part, however, the Victorians kept fun and intellect in separate compartments. When Matthew Arnold injected humor into his cultural criticism, reviewers roundly condemned his flippancy.[6] Even in Arnold, as Max Beerbohm observed in 1901, "there is perfect secretion" between the jokes and the substance: "The humorous passages are always distinct interludes or 'asides' consciously made, and distinct from the scheme of the essay."

In the case of Beerbohm's good friend Bernard Shaw, however,

> the contrast is still sharper and more striking. For there the two moods are, as it were, arm in arm—inseparable comrades. Mr. Shaw cannot realise his own pertness, nor can he preserve his own gravity, for more than a few moments at a time. Even when he sets out to be funny for fun's sake, he must needs always pretend that there is a serious reason for the emprise; and he pretends so strenuously that he ends by convincing us almost as fully as he convinces himself. . . . Conversely, even when he is really engrossed in some process of serious argument, or moved to real eloquence by one of his social ideals, he emits involuntarily some wild jape which makes the whole thing ridiculous—as ridiculous to himself as to us; and straightway he proceeds to caricature his own thesis till everything is topsy-turvy; and we, rolling with laughter, look up and find him no longer on his head, but on his heels, talking away quite gravely; and this sets us off again. . . . Seriousness and frivolity thus co-exist inseparably.[7]

The same could have been said of a host of other Edwardian authors, including Beerbohm himself. This period produced a menagerie of philosopher-comedians who treated the most serious issues with mischievous humor. Oscar Wilde, who flourished from 1881 to 1895, set the fashion: he was followed by Shaw, Beerbohm, H. G. Wells, G. K. Chesterton, Hilaire Belloc, Maurice Baring, Saki, Sir Walter Raleigh, Lytton Strachey, and James Joyce, among others. They all shared the conviction that play—doing something for the intrinsic enjoyment of the thing—is one of the ultimate ends of art and perhaps of human existence. "It all comes back to that," wrote Henry James in *The Golden Bowl* (1904), "to my and your 'fun'—if we but allow the term its full extension."[8] In a 1939 lecture on the Edwardians, E. M. Forster recalled

> the enormous importance which we then attributed to the sense of humour. People who accept the "comic muse" . . . are all right and will help to get the world right. People who deny the comic muse are all wrong. . . . We

weren't content to find fun funny, we required it to be cleansing and helpful, and the expression "clean fun" is the unfortunate legacy of our hopes.[9]

The Recreational Revolution

The Edwardian gospel of fun was part of a broad social revolution that reversed the early Victorian attack on amusement and made recreation a major mass industry in England. A century of industrial development, particularly the long mid-Victorian boom of 1851–1879, had raised living standards in every segment of British society, and more disposable income was available to spend on entertainment. Trade union agitation and parliamentary legislation had created more leisure time for all working people. The royal example of Edward VII (contrasting with that set by his mother) probably contributed to this change in attitudes: his fondness for hunting, continental resorts, horses, and women only seems to have endeared him to his subjects.

Between 1850 and 1900 the number of legitimate theaters tripled in London and quadrupled in the provinces. The comic operas of Gilbert and Sullivan were succeeded in the Edwardian years by dozens of wildly popular and breathtakingly vacuous musical comedies. Music halls existed in the mid-Victorian period, but they were fairly disreputable and appealed mainly to adult men. In the Edwardian era the music halls were at the height of their popularity, providing clean family entertainment for all classes, every age group, and both sexes. The first British screening of a motion picture took place in 1896; by 1914 there were three thousand cinemas in the United Kingdom. After 1880 resorts like Blackpool, Brighton, Bournemouth, and Southend mushroomed as the vacationing habit spread to the working class. A cycling craze struck in 1895, followed by similar manias for lawn tennis and bridge. The Victorians had certainly made a cult of amateur sports, but the growth of spectator sports as a major leisure industry only took off after the professionalization of association football in 1885.[10]

"By the turn of the century," writes James Walvin, "partly as a result of the proliferation of facilities, it had become generally accepted that everyone had a right to the enjoyment of leisure . . . and considerable efforts went into providing it for those in harsh circumstances." Far from discouraging amusement, municipalities were now delivering free or cheap recreational services to the masses: parks, baths, swimming pools, gymnasiums, athletic stadiums, golf courses, libraries, museums, bandstands, and theaters. Private employers were coming to realize that excessive work hours could be cut back without significantly reducing productivity, and many firms now sponsored employee outings to build morale and company loyalty. Victorian trade unionists rarely demanded holidays with pay for fear that wages would be reduced; but Edwardian workers frequently asked for (and sometimes won) paid vacations, which became an official demand of the Trades Union Congress in 1911.[11] In 1903 Charles Booth noted with approval the growing popular "demand for amusement." "Holiday making is spoken of as 'one of the most remarkable changes in habits in the last ten years,' and the statement is applicable to all classes," he wrote. "To 'What shall we eat, what drink, and wherewithal shall we be clothed?' must now be added the question, 'How shall we be amused?' "[12]

The flowering of literary humor in Edwardian Britain was directly connected with the rapid expansion of one leisure industry in particular—journalism. Between 1881 and 1911 the newspaper-reading public increased fourfold; so did the number of journalists, authors, and editors, a faster rate of growth than any other major professional category. Most of these new career opportunities for writers were created by the rise of what was called the New Journalism, newspapers and magazines that placed a novel emphasis on lightness and entertainment. George Newnes is credited with beginning the trend when he founded the weekly *Tit-Bits* in 1880. He went on to launch colorful middlebrow periodicals like the *Review of Reviews* (1890) and the *Strand Magazine* (1891), as well as the *Westminster Gazette* (1893), a sophisticated evening paper. Each appealed to a different audience, but all were brightly written and laid out. Alfred Harmsworth followed with *Answers* (1888), the *Evening News* (acquired in 1894), and the *Daily Mail* (founded in 1896). Several Radical dailies also followed this trend, notably the *Star* under T. P. O'Connor (from 1888), the *Daily Chronicle* under H. W. Massingham (1891), and the *Daily News* under A. G. Gardiner.[13]

The New Journalism created a demand for feuilletonists—writers who could produce, against a deadline, clever squibs on literature or politics. The demand called into existence a flock of Edwardian wits, who would have been far more solemn or far less successful if the New Journalism had not providentially materialized at the beginning of their literary careers. The *Strand Magazine* appeared just in time to print the first caricatures of Max Beerbohm; he found his first steady literary employment in 1897, writing a weekly essay for the *Daily Mail*, one year after it was founded.[14] A. G. Gardiner took over the *Daily News* in 1901 and gave G. K. Chesterton his first opportunity to write for a mass audience. Also in 1901 Saki, after a false start as a serious historian, found his metier writing satires for the *Westminster Gazette*, then only eight years old.

The first prominent author to follow this path to literary success was the Scottish critic Andrew Lang. As early as 1875 London editors had to satisfy a growing reader interest in sports. Lang knew how to turn out literate, informed articles on cricket, golf, and angling, and this talent gave him an immediate entrée into journalism. He went on to write a column for *Longman's* (a popular literary monthly founded in 1882), spinning out bright little paragraphs of literary gossip, puffery, satire, cultural commentary, and interesting facts about psychology and anthropology—very much the intellectual equivalent of *Tit-Bits*. He also wrote serious anthropology and literary criticism, but in the same jocular, chatty style. He was never afraid to insert a joke into a scholarly discussion, even if that meant sacrificing the respect of straight-faced critics. Some accused him of playing with literature, but Lang insisted that belles lettres ought to be a lark. He was particularly fond of literary games, like writing letters to dead authors or imagining encounters between characters from radically different novels.[15]

The New Journalism launched the career of another ambitious young Scotsman, J. M. Barrie. In 1884 Frederick Greenwood of the *St. James's Gazette* was on the lookout for lively copy. When Barrie sent him a humorous, sentimental piece on Scottish rural life, Greenwood printed it and asked for more, and stories of this type soon became Barrie's stock in trade. Beginning in 1887, the newly founded *British Weekly*, a journal that managed to combine Nonconformist religion with modest humor, serialized Barrie's novel *When a Man's Single*. In 1902 Barrie brought his wit to bear on a serious social issue—the class system—and produced *The Admirable Crichton*, which had an impressive ten-month run.[16] This was an important breakthrough: Bernard Shaw had been trying for years to get his own funny-serious plays produced, with very mixed success, but now he found "the managers hankering after intellectual superiority and even Stage-Societyness, if only it [could] be combined with popularity."[17] Shaw went as far as to admit that he had been outdazzled at his own game of intelligent humor. Barrie's *Little Mary* (1903), he wrote, was "a didactic lark compared to which my most wayward exploits are conventional, stagey, & old fashioned."[18]

Shaw also had worked as a journeyman in the New Journalism. He had arrived in London in 1876 and wasted the next several years producing unpublishable novels. Eventually he managed to earn an irregular income writing light articles for the *Hornet*, the *Pall Mall Gazette*, and Edmund Yates's *World*. In 1888 the *Star* hired Shaw to write leaders, but the incorrigible socialist could not conform to the paper's Radical politics. He was soon shifted to music reviews: writing as "Corno di Bassetto," he was now able to perfect that characteristically Shavian "mixture of tomfoolery with genuine criticism." As a feuilletonist, Shaw learned how to alloy seriousness with "an indescribable levity—not triviality, mind, but levity—something spritelike."[19] He now realized that socialist propaganda had to be sugared with good humor before editors or readers would swallow it, and he never tired of teaching that lesson to his political friends. In 1893 he boasted to a trade union official:

> Have you noticed that one result of the Fabians constantly telling the world how clever they are is that the world is beginning to believe them, and, of course, to pretend that it found out the cleverness for itself. Study us, my boy, and learn how to bounce; for it is only by bouncing that our little stage army can conquer the country.[20]

Robert Blatchford, a provincial Fabian, was meanwhile using the New Journalism to promote socialism among a wider audience. In the 1880s Blatchford had made his reputation writing humorous prolabor articles for a popular sheet, the Manchester *Sunday Chronicle*. In 1891 he founded his own weekly paper, the *Clarion*, which served up an editorial mix of light-hearted socialism, adventure tales, children's stories, comic prose and verse, and literary articles. Two years later the *Clarion* serialized Blatchford's socialist tract *Merrie England*, which in book form sold two million copies. Blatchford contributed as much as any individual to building British socialism into a mass movement, and he did it by organizing a range of socialist-oriented leisure activities: the Clarion Fellowship (a fraternal organization), the Clarion Scouts, Clarion Cycling Clubs, Clarion Choirs and Glee Clubs, Clarion Camera Clubs, Clarion Field Clubs, Clarion Handicraft Guilds, and Clarion Holiday Camps. Blatchford brought to the masses the same message that Bernard Shaw was conveying to a more select audience—that socialism could be fun.[21]

One other important Fabian owed his literary career to the fortunate birth of the New Journalism. In 1893 H. G. Wells was an overworked science teacher struggling to break into literature. He had been contributing items to *Tit-Bits* and *Answers* for two shillings apiece, but he was having difficulty getting his serious work published. His style was stilted and Victorian: "Babu English," he later called it. That summer he happened to read the novel *When a Man's Single*, in which J. M. Barrie revealed that a ready market existed for clever, fluffy articles on everyday topics. Wells immediately dashed off something in the Barrie style entitled "On the Art of Staying at the Seaside," which was instantly snapped up by Henry Cust of the *Pall Mall Gazette*. Cust had just taken over as editor, and he wanted to put some bounce into his paper: before the year was out he had published at least thirty pieces by Wells. He even tried to make a drama critic out of his new discovery, who had hardly seen a play in his life—the idea was to give the readers something amusing and out of the ordinary. Cust introduced Wells to Lewis Hind of the *Pall Mall Budget*, who commissioned a string of science fiction stories and in turn introduced him to W. E. Henley of the *National Observer*, who encouraged him to write *The Time Machine*. Practically overnight, Wells had found his style and his market, and by 1895 he was an established and well-paid author.[22] (In 1901, P. G. Wodehouse would likewise find his formula as a humorist in *When a Man's Single*.)

Editors can play a pivotal (and often neglected) role in the history of ideas, and it should be stressed here that it was a group of innovative editors—men like Cust and Blatchford—who assisted at the birth of the New Journalism and the Edwardian style of literary humor. With his influential *National Observer* and *New Review*, Henley infected many of his contributors (Rudyard Kipling, George Wyndham, Charles Whibley, G. S. Street) with his boyish sense of fun and his cutting epigrammatic wit—a wit much like Wilde's, only more vivid and energetic, and frequently directed against decadent aesthetes like Wilde. In 1894 Frank Harris bought the moribund *Saturday Review*, fired the entire staff, and put together a sparkling circle of contributors from scratch, with H. G. Wells reviewing novels and Bernard Shaw (followed by Max Beerbohm) criticizing the stage. In 1896 a similar operation was performed on the *Academy* by Pearl Craigie, who as "John Oliver Hobbes" wrote dry and witty novels of high society and modern marriage. Her editor was Lewis Hind, formerly of the *Pall Mall Budget*. He took a stuffy weekly review and introduced some highly entertaining material into it, including *The Truth about an Author*, which Arnold Bennett wrote for him in 1898.[23]

Can't Think of a Title

Cleverness was a commodity very much in demand among Edwardian readers. There was an excellent market for fiction about impossibly "smart" aristocrats, such as Anthony Hope's *Dolly Dialogues* (first published in the *Westminster Gazette* in 1893), E. F. Benson's best-selling *Dodo* (1893) and *Dodo the Second* (1913), the novels of Pearl Craigie, and the stories of Saki. There was also a larger readership for a lower class of humor, as produced by Pett Ridge, Barry Pain, W. W. Jacobs, F. Anstey, Jerome K. Jerome, and Neil Lyons.[24]

But Edwardian wit was more than a simple response to changing demands in the literary marketplace. Very often it reflected a disinterested taste for intellectual fun among authors who were not New Journalists and did not write for the masses. The Cambridge Apostles, for instance, began to drift away from high-minded Victorian gravity after the election of Walter Raleigh in 1882 and Henry Cust in 1883. One of Raleigh's first addresses to the group, entitled "Laughter from a Cloud," exalted the value of a "sense of humour" above that of "personal integrity" and a social conscience. Corrupted by Raleigh and Cust, the Apostles began to take a jollier approach to great ideas.[25] In the 1890s they spoofed German philosophy by calling themselves "The World of Reality"; everything else in the universe was mere "Appearance," and persons who were not Apostles were dismissed as "phenomena." Bertrand Russell remembered himself as a "shy prig" when he entered Cambridge, but he was elected to the Apostles in 1892, and within two years he had acquired the sardonic wit that later spiced his philosophical criticism: "I had become gay and flippant. Having been reading pantheism, I announced to my friends that I was God. They placed candles on each side of me and proceeded to acts of mock worship. Philosophy altogether seemed to me great fun."[26]

Henry Cust, as noted, served the muse of literary humor as the editor of the *Pall Mall Gazette*. The general tone of the paper is indicated by the heading he gave one leading article: "Can't Think of a Title." Besides H. G. Wells, his contributors included Robert Louis Stevenson, W. E. Henley, and Rudyard Kipling.[27] Walter Raleigh became a professor of literature at the University of Liverpool, and in an 1895 lecture on Stevenson he noted that "some of his best works," like *The Wrong Box*, are "best described as paper-games." Raleigh contended that "all art . . . is play of a sort; the 'sport' impulse (to translate a German phrase) is deep at the root of the artist's power; Sophocles, Shakespeare, Molière, and Goethe, in a very profound sense, make game of life.'"[28] As an academic Raleigh had to maintain a dignified exterior, but in private he enjoyed concocting word games, parodies, nonsense literature, and comic poems, one of which has passed into immortality.

> I wish I loved the Human Race;
> I wish I loved its silly face;
> I wish I liked the way it walks;
> I wish I liked the way it talks;
> And when I'm introduced to one
> I wish I thought *What Jolly Fun!*

Goldsworthy Lowes Dickinson taught the Edwardian Apostles to make scholarship a recreation;[29] Raleigh taught them the virtue of cleverness. Lytton Strachey particularly admired Raleigh's essay on Stevenson and cultivated an intellectual wit modeled on Voltaire's. In 1918 Strachey brought that wit to bear against his "Eminent Victorians," twitting them for sacrificing their sense of humor to moral rigidity.[30] G. E. Moore, after hearing Raleigh defend indecent humor before the Apostles in 1895, was driven to deliver a response in which he asked whether humor is an absolute good—whether, as he put it, "God could laugh." He concluded, with the thoroughgoing agnosticism of a logical positivist, that "since God . . . is absolutely indeterminate, I cannot say if he has a sense of humour."[31]

That "sport impulse" eventually infected the rest of the Bloomsbury Group. In the celebrated "Dreadnought Hoax" of 1910, Adrian Stephen, his sister Virginia, Duncan Grant, and several friends disguised themselves as the emperor of Abyssinia and suite, and were received in state on the flagship of the Home Fleet.[32] The excessive and ill-humoured official reaction to this prank left its mark on the novels of Virginia Woolf, who would satirize "the great make-believe game of English social life," and who generally depicted public affairs as a solemn charade.[33]

The work of James Joyce, particularly *Ulysses* and *Finnegans Wake*, owed much to the Edwardian climate of philosophic levity. Joyce scoffed at critics who discussed *Finnegan* in terms of "levels of meaning": "No, no," he insisted, "it's meant to make you laugh." He candidly described the book as "a great joke," inspired by Laurence Sterne.[34] As a literary gamesman, Joyce had something in common with G. K. Chesterton, who defended the pun as an aesthetically legitimate pairing of sound and content, like a rhyme.[35]

Joyce was clearly indebted to Oliver St. John Gogarty, the Dublin wit and limerickmonger who composed "The Ballad of Joking Jesus," chanted in *Ulysses* by Buck Mulligan.[36] The *Saturday Review* critic George Saintsbury, whose long literary career extended from the 1870s to his death in 1933, may have also contributed to the flowering of Joycean humor. Saintsbury's articles were rambling causeries, each a stream of free literary association, whimsically tripping from book to book— "interior monologues, almost," John Gross calls them.[37] An editor of Sterne (1894), Saintsbury loved the game of tossing out and identifying literary references. He filled his criticism with jokes, puns, slang, neologisms, facetious parentheses, and madcap digressions. "For those who hate jokes and literary allusions one can only pray, 'God help them!' " he declared in his definitive *History of Criticism* (1900–1904).[38] He especially liked to mimic other literary styles, sometimes changing his technique several times in the course of one essay, in the manner of the "Oxen of the Sun" episode in *Ulysses*.[39] In fact, when Joyce wrote that section, he made use of Saintsbury's *History of English Prose Rhythm* (1912); he also had in his library another useful book by Saintsbury, *A Short History of English Literature* (1898).[40] When *Ulysses* was published, Joyce asked Harriet Shaw Weaver to send Saintsbury a press copy. "I am oldfashioned enough to admire him," Joyce wrote. "He is however quite capable of flinging the tome back through your window."[41]

H. G. Wells recognized in Joyce a kindred spirit: both men were attempting to restore the coarse zaniness of Swift and Sterne to English fiction. Wells referred a literary agent to Joyce, wrote a laudatory review of *A Portrait of the Artist*, signed a petition protesting the suppression of *Ulysses*, and even gave Joyce a walk-on role in his novel *Boon*.[42]

Playing games was a passion with Wells, a passion he shared with his literary friends. With G. K. and Cecil Chesterton, he constructed toy theaters, in which they staged a dramatization of Beatrice Webb's *Minority Report of the Poor Law Commission*. The same trio attempted to fool the national press into reporting a craze for Gype, a game that existed only in their own imaginations.[43] The jolly journalists of the Chesterton-Belloc circle entertained themselves in similar fashion—staging elaborate practical jokes, casting everyday correspondence into verse, and putting out a private newspaper written entirely in clichés.[44]

With their clever banter and in jokes, the Fabian socialists diligently cultivated what Wells and Sydney Olivier called "the playful scientific temper."[45] The Fabian Summer Schools, begun in 1907, devoted only three to four hours a day to classes; the better part of the program was given over to sports, games, dancing, music, revues, fancy-dress balls, and amateur theatricals.[46] Edith Nesbit was attracted to the Fabians by their "very jolly" discussions, and she liked to engage her houseguests in games that involved arranging random words into verse, or writing literary parodies.[47] Many Fabians participated in the mock parliaments that sprang up all over London in the late nineteenth century—the Moderns in Hampstead, the Pharos, the IDK ("I Don't Know") of Bedford Park (led by the Chesterton brothers and E. C. Bentley), and a YMCA group in which H. G. Wells took part. These societies were popular among the impoverished intelligentsia of London, for whom they provided a diversion, a social outlet, a platform, and a training course in the art of government. The Fabians managed to take over the Charing Cross Parliament in 1887 and later organized a model legislature for their own members.[48]

Another mental recreation that enjoyed a notable Edwardian vogue was the detective story.[49] Although a few mid-Victorian writers (like Wilkie Collins) had worked in this genre, it was Conan Doyle, writing in the newly founded *Strand Magazine*, who made it fashionable after 1891. Sherlock Holmes was followed by a horde of imitations, among them G. K. Chesterton's Father Brown and R. Austin Freeman's Dr. Thorndyke. In 1914 Cecil Chesterton brought together a group of eminent wits to conduct a mock Edwin Drood trial and find a solution to Dickens's unfinished mystery. He himself served as counsel for the defense, his brother Gilbert presided as judge, and George Bernard Shaw was foreman of a jury that included William Archer, W. W. Jacobs, and Pett Ridge. Shaw could not resist disrupting the proceedings with wisecracks, and the trial ended with the judge committing everyone for contempt of court.[50] The year before, E. C. Bentley, a friend of the Chestertons' and the inventor of a form of comic biographical verse known as the clerihew, had brought out *Trent's Last Case*, the first detective novel that made some attempt at literary artistry.

Ultimately, Fabian socialism, guild socialism, and the smallholders' populism of Chesterton and Belloc aimed to transform labor into recreation. According to C. R. Ashbee, industrial civilization had divorced work from play, offering the worker only the passive diversion of the music hall, "recreation that is apart from life." To promote "recreation that is a part of life," Ashbee revived traditional country sports at his Arts and Crafts commune at Campden.[51] Oliver Lodge, speaking before the Liverpool Fabians in 1894, defined the "working class" as all those "engaged in dull occupations in which they take no interest." Lodge urged the necessity of making work challenging and enjoyable: "Put a man on a bicycle and he will go blithely for hours, or even days; put him on a treadmill and he is dead beat in twenty minutes."[52] "Look," says an artist in one of Granville Barker's plays, "Men are taught to work. I would have them taught to play and only let work bubble from them. Then we should have in the world only geniuses and children."[53] J. L. Hammond cited anthropological evidence to show that in prehistoric times "play formed as large a part in man's life as work, and that many of his activities"—such as hunting and dancing—"were both work and play."[54] The Edwardian philosophers of fun did not reject the work ethic; as Bernard Shaw explained it, they were attempting to create a world in which "work is play and play is life."[55]

The Universe as a Lark

The gospel of fun, then, was part of that broader Edwardian effort to reconcile opposites. It erased the distinction between work and play and, as well, the boundary separating humor and seriousness. This last point deserves emphasis: Edwardian humorists could be funny and perfectly earnest at the same time. They cracked jokes to illuminate eternal truths: "In risu veritas" was James Joyce's motto.[56] The Cambridge Apostles, Leonard Woolf recalled, "were always ready to laugh at themselves and at the universe, even the serious things in the universe that they took very seriously."[57] Bernard Shaw did not care for purely frivolous humor, and he criticized *The Importance of Being Earnest* (unfairly) for having no message: "Unless comedy touches me as well as amuses me, it leaves me with a sense of having wasted my evening."[58]

The Edwardian impulse to unify the sacred and the profane could lead directly to the conclusion that jokes are deeply serious things—perhaps even expressions of religion, as G. K. Chesterton argued. Like so many of his contemporaries, Chesterton passed through a painful crisis of belief, emerging to proclaim in 1899 that "all good things are one thing." The context of that remark is important: Chesterton was trying to comfort his fiancee on the death of her sister by baldly affirming the "duty" of being funny in the face of death: "All good things are one thing. There is no conflict between the gravestone . . . and a comic-opera tune. . . . But there is everlasting conflict between the gravestone . . . and the obscene pomposity of the hired mute: and there is everlasting conflict between the comic-opera tune and any mean or vulgar words to which it may be set."[59]

If humor was as much a part of God's creation as any other thing, then there had to be a place for it in any sound religion. On that ground, in 1908, Chesterton defended his whimsical discussions of serious theology.

> There seems to be some sort of idea that you are not treating a subject properly if you eulogise it with fantastic terms or defend it by grotesque examples. Yet a truth is equally solemn whatever figure or example its exponent adopts. It is an equally awful truth that four and four make eight, whether you reckon the thing out in eight onions or eight angels, or eight bricks or eight bishops, or eight minor poets or eight pigs. Similarly, if it be true that God made all things, that grave fact can be asserted by pointing at a star or by waving an umbrella. . . . So far from being irreverent to use silly metaphors on serious questions, it is one's duty to use silly metaphors on serious questions. It is the test of one's seriousness. It is the test of a responsible religion or theory whether it can take examples from pots and pans and boots and butter-tubs. It is the test of a good philosophy whether you can defend it grotesquely. It is the test of a good religion whether you can joke about it.[60]

Chesterton cited recent anthropological studies to show that religious ceremonies among primitive peoples took the form of joyful celebrations,[61] and he noted that the gargoyles decorating medieval cathedrals embodied the same type of vulgar comedy as music hall songs.[62] He believed that humor could be a form of worship,[63] and he was not in the least distressed by the idea that God might have created the universe as a joke. On the contrary, he wrote,

> it might reasonably be maintained that the true object of all human life is play. Earth is a task garden; heaven is a playground. To be at last in such secure innocence that one can juggle with the universe and the stars, to be so good that one can treat everything as a joke—that may be, perhaps, the real end and final holiday of human souls. When we are really holy we may regard the Universe as a lark.[64]

Bernard Shaw often attended church for the sake of "*recreation*, in the literal sense of that profoundly significant word."[65] He described the medieval mystery play of Cain and Abel as "outrageously comic" and even "Rabelaisian," and he denounced those "whose idea of being religious is to sit in their best clothes in a condition of solemn paralysis, holding all their affection and sympathy and fun in strained and miserable abeyance." Like Chesterton and James Joyce, Shaw noted that Jesus had used a pun ("super hanc petram") when he commanded Peter to found his church: "Bad taste, on so solemn an occasion, was it not?"[66]

Like other Edwardian movements in secular theology, the gospel of fun was a response to the decline of religion. The growth of popular recreations had depressed church attendance as the English people increasingly devoted their Sundays to worldly diversions, and the churches attempted to lure their parishioners back by sponsoring recreational activities and more lively services. This broadening of religion was advocated most forcefully by such Christian socialists as H. C. Shuttleworth, Percy Alden, and Stewart Headlam. In his sermons, Headlam defended music halls as a healthy and necessary diversion for the working classes. In 1879 he founded the Church and Stage Guild to bring religion to the entertainment industry, and in 1895, with Hubert Bland and the Chesterton brothers, he organized the Anti-Puritan League to defend music halls against attacks by other clergymen.[67] As rector of St. Nicholas Cole Abbey in the City of London, Canon Shuttleworth boosted church attendance by sponsoring glee clubs, bands, coffee rooms, games rooms, children's clubs, monthly dances at the Cannon Street Hotel, and a club of six hundred members (a third of them women) in which alcohol was served and smoking permitted. Charles Booth declared that Shuttleworth's "social methods . . . were . . . highly stamped with originality and success," though he noted that, at St. Nicholas Cole's clubs, "religion was hardly ever mentioned; practically it was excluded."[68]

In 1902 Booth reported that only through social and recreational activities were churches able to attract large numbers of working-class parishioners. In particular, the Nonconformist "Pleasant Sunday Afternoons," inaugurated in 1875, had by this time become quite popular in the London slums. These were short services, generally lasting not much over an hour, and often held outdoors, featuring some rousing songs, an entertaining talk (not a sermon), and an absolute minimum of prayer. They were an attempt by the Dissenting churches to counteract their dour public image (the services were advertised as "Brief, Bright, and Brotherly") and to reach working people who would not attend a conventional church service.[69] Charles Booth suggested that deserted chapels should attract new congregations by sponsoring concerts (not of liturgical music), lectures, conferences, choral groups, and literary societies. Booth attacked the puritan tradition as "a pinched and narrow view of the scope of religion," allowing no room for amusement. He believed firmly in the virtue of leading a "jolly life" and endorsed the work of the High Church "in the organization of the leisure of its people for the service of the Church and for their mutual benefit. Thus does our religion, if successful, put on its week-day clothes." "Religious feeling can never die," Booth asserted, "but it changes expression."[70]

By 1902 religious organizations were already deeply involved in leisure activities. The YMCA and YWCA date from the midnineteenth century, but only around 1880 did they begin to build gymnasiums, an investment that quickly multiplied their membership.[71] The predominantly Nonconformist Boys' Brigade was founded in 1883, followed by the Anglican Church Lads' Brigade (1891), the Catholic Lads' Brigade (1896), the Boys' and Girls' Life Brigades (organized by the Sunday School movement in 1899), and the Jewish Brigade. By 1912 these cadet corps had a combined membership of about 140,000, roughly equal to that of the Boy Scouts.[72] After 1880 a large fraction of the amateur football clubs in the kingdom were organized by churches and clergymen of all denominations.[73] The Labour Churches made a point of encouraging laughter in their services, and the Salvation Army reached out to the slums with brass bands and joyful songs. That is what Bernard Shaw admired in the Salvationists: their "laughing, joking, singing, rejoicing, drumming, and tambourining."[74] Many Anglican churches in the affluent suburbs now offered clever sermons and a range of social activities. This last development moved C. F. G. Masterman to complain that the middle classes "play with [religion] as they play with life," but he himself argued that the working masses would only be brought back to the churches by more colorful services.[75] A. C. Benson warned that no modern religion could flourish unless it recognized "a sense of humour in the Creative Spirit,"[76] and C. R. Ashbee contended that churches "must be planned again to prove that humour, which the puritans cast out of religion, is a need of life, and if we cannot revive the grotesque of the 13th century we must be able to prove to men once again the words of the last of the great mediaeval thinkers, 'A man may be merry and yet go to Heaven.' "[77]

Peter Pan and His Times

Around the turn of the century, Sigmund Freud, Henri Bergson, and (in Britain) James Sully explored the psychology of humor. Each of them concluded that jokes reflect, in part, an impulse to return to childhood, to put aside adult responsibilities and indulge in the pointless messing about of infancy.[78] The Edwardian spirit of play was bound up with just such a reversion to a childlike turn of mind, often an outright refusal to grow up—the theme of one of the most popular plays of the period, *Peter Pan* (1904). One can draw up a long list of eminent Edwardians who seem to have been stuck in childhood—Barrie is the obvious example, but contemporaries observed the same trait in H. G. Wells, G. K. Chesterton, Max Beerbohm, Rudyard Kipling, W. E. Henley, Edith Nesbit, Sir Oliver Lodge, Edward Thomas, G. E. Moore, and T. E. Hulme.[79] Even at age fifty-one Bernard Shaw confessed, "I have never yet been able to feel grown up; and now I never shall. . . . The child remains."[80]

On a more constructive level, this fascination with childhood was manifested in a new concern for child welfare. Ivy Pinchbeck and Margaret Hewitt have shown that the Edwardian period was a turning point in the history of English childhood. For the first time it was widely recognized that children are different from adults; that they have different needs, sensibilities, and habits of thinking; that they cannot be educated, worked, or punished like adults; that they have rights of their own independent of their parents. Five separate investigations conducted from 1889 to 1906 revealed widespread disease and malnutrition among London schoolchildren, leading to the institution of free school meals in 1906, school medical inspections in 1907, Britain's first infant welfare center (in St. Pancras, 1907), and subsidized municipal milk dispensaries (the first set up in 1899). Fabian Tracts presented *The Case for School Nurseries* (1909) and *The Case for School Clinics* (1911), though they met with little response from the government. A series of reforms between 1902 and 1907 doubled the proportion of children attending secondary school—which by 1911–1912 was still only nineteen percent of the population aged fourteen to eighteen.

Such measures were motivated in part by growing anxiety over national efficiency and the falling birth rate, but there were many other reforms that could have only reflected a disinterested concern for the well-being of children. These included a 1903 act restricting child labor and the "Children's Charter" of 1908, a comprehensive child-welfare bill directed against parental abuse and mistreatment of juvenile offenders. Societies for the prevention of cruelty to children began to organize in 1883; the first parliamentary legislation against child abuse was not enacted until 1889, and then in the face of much public criticism. But attitudes toward children's rights soon changed, and when that law was stiffened in 1894 and again in 1904, there was far less opposition. The 1896 Mundella Committee Report on Poor Law Schools and the subsequent efforts of the Local Government Board greatly improved education for pauper children. Thereafter orphans were gradually transferred from workhouses to foster homes, cottage homes, and residential schools. The British Child-Study Association was founded in 1894, inspired by American work in child psychology. Following the advice of William McDougall's *Introduction to Social Psychology* (1908), elementary schools began to allow students more freedom to study at their own pace, choose their own reading, learn by discovery, and indulge in creative art work. The child's right to play was also being recognized, and municipal playgrounds and school athletic programs multiplied after 1880. A number of charitable groups were organized to provide day trips in the country for slum children. The largest of these was C. Arthur Pearson's Fresh Air Fund, founded in 1892, which by 1909 had reached two million children.[81]

The New Liberals took a special interest in the welfare of poor children. C. P. Trevelyan championed their cause in Parliament[82] while J. H. Hammond wrote extensively on the need for improving state schools and providing playgrounds in the cities.[83] A group of Cambridge settlement workers in Camberwell, including C. F. G. Masterman and Reginald Bray, organized "guilds of play" and country vacations for local children. Much of Masterman's *Heart of the Empire* was devoted to the plight of slum children, a subject discussed in greater depth in Bray's volume *The Town Child* (1907).[84]

As a junior minister in Asquith's cabinet, Masterman worked with Winston Churchill to improve treatment of juvenile offenders. In spite of that effort, Masterman was accused by many of his Liberal friends at the *Nation* and by the sensational journalist Horatio Bottomley (himself a reformatory alumnus) of "whitewashing" a government investigation of brutality among reform school guards. The fact that Masterman's career was seriously damaged by allegations of insensitivity to juvenile delinquents[85] shows how radically public attitudes had changed since the early nineteenth century, when children were commonly hanged for minor thefts, or even since 1884, when a royal commission condoned the imprisonment of minors. This last practice was denounced in 1896 by a departmental committee, and after a storm of protest (including a letter by Oscar Wilde in the *Daily Chronicle*) it was ended in 1899. Probation was made an alternative to child imprisonment by acts of Parliament in 1887, 1901, 1907, and the Children's Charter established the first juvenile courts in 1908.[86]

The child welfare movement directly facilitated the arrival of psychoanalysis in Britain. England's first school clinic, at Bow, was organized by Dr. David Eder in 1907. Two years later Eder began reading Freudian psychology, and his work with slum children convinced him that Freud's theory of childhood sexuality was correct. In 1911 Eder began presenting papers on psychoanalysis: medical doctors gave him a frigid reception, but school medical officers and educationists were far more enthusiastic. From 1910 to 1915 Eder was an editor of *School Hygiene*, a journal for school medical officers, and he used that platform to publicize the work of Freud. By 1912 Eder had established the first regular psychoanalytic practice in Britain, and in 1913 he joined with Ernest Jones to found the London Psycho-Analytical Society. During the First World War, Eder was one of several doctors who used psychoanalytic methods to treat battle trauma, and their successes hastened the acceptance of Freudianism in postwar Britain.

Eder had, according to one colleague, "an essentially boyish nature. . . . He was in some of the best senses of the term 'childlike,' " and the analysis of children afforded him "the vicarious enjoyment . . . of a second childhood."[87] That nostalgia for youth was one of the motivating passions behind the Edwardian movement for child welfare. C. F. G. Masterman and his friends threw themselves into organizing games and outings for slum children with an enthusiasm that reveals their own fondness for games. Masterman was almost jealous of the freedom that poor parents allowed their sons and daughters: "The strongest final impression is that of the children, playing quaint games, distorted survivals of the old life of 'Merrie England.' "[88] "Games have a special power and charm," wrote J. H. Hammond in a plea for municipal playgrounds, "and . . . mankind returns to them at all ages as to a lost paradise."[89]

Masterman and Charles Booth admiringly described the closeness and affection of working-class families. Slum children, Masterman observed, were "dirty" and "unhealthy" but generally "happy." Although they had to endure poverty and neglect, they were rarely subjected to parental abuse.[90] "They are more likely to suffer from spoiling than from harshness," Booth concluded. "There are no doubt terrible cases of neglect and cruelty, but on the whole kindness and affection reign, though it may be careless kindness and ill-regulated affection."[91] Historian Paul Thompson paints a less rosy picture of Edwardian child-parent relations, but he confirms that closeness was much more common than abuse in working-class families.[92]

Meanwhile, among the affluent classes, progressive education was gaining a small foothold. The pioneering progressive school was Abbotsholme, founded in 1889 with the aid of Edward Carpenter and the Fellowship of the New Life. In 1893 J. H. Badley, an Abbotsholme master, launched Bedales, where the children of Sir Oliver Lodge and Edward Thomas studied. By 1914 there were fifteen such schools in the kingdom. The progressive movement had no effect on the old public schools, with a few remarkable exceptions: Oundle, headed by F. W. Sanderson from 1892, was an experiment in self-directed education attended by the sons of H. G. Wells.[93]

The Edwardian fascination with games and childhood affected the public school establishment in other ways. Generally speaking, athletics became popular at public schools only after 1860 and were not compulsory until after 1880. By the Edwardian period, games had become a mania, even at girls' schools, and the British upper and middle classes were thoroughly steeped in the cult of sportsmanship. School nostalgia found expression in the old boys' associations, most of them founded between 1885 and 1902. Through these alumni groups graduates supported their old teams, celebrated their old victories, and continued to play cricket and football with their old school rivals.[94]

One extraordinary product of this childhood nostalgia was an unprecedented flowering of children's literature. The Victorians published at least as many children's books as the Edwardians (see appendix), and these included the enduring works of Lewis Carroll and Edward Lear. But no other generation in English history produced so many children's classics as the Edwardians. This was the heyday of J. M. Barrie (*Peter Pan*, 1904), Kenneth Grahame (*The Golden Age*, 1895; *Dream Days*, 1899; *The Wind in the Willows*, 1907), Rudyard Kipling (*The Jungle Book*, 1894; *The Second Jungle Book*, 1895; *Stalky and Co.*, 1899; *Kim*, 1901; *Just So Stories*, 1902; *Puck of Pook's Hill*, 1906), and Edith Nesbit (who published all but one of her children's novels between 1899 and 1913).

Most of the works of Beatrix Potter appeared between 1895 and 1919, as did the majority of H. Rider Haggard's adventure stories. Hilaire Belloc made his reputation with *The Bad Child's Book of Beasts* (1896), and P. G. Wodehouse spent his first years as an author (1900–1910) producing stories for boys. Poetry for children was anthologized by E. V. Lucas and written by Laurence Housman, Walter de la Mare, and Eleanor Farjeon. Bernard Shaw wrote *Androcles and the Lion* (1912) as a Christmas pantomine, and he insisted that his 1904 comedy *The Admirable Bashville*— a wild burlesque of prize fighting in Elizabethan iambic pentameter— could only be appreciated by a young audience.

> The Elizabethan style has many charms for imaginative children. It is bloody, bombastic, violent, senselessly pretentious, barbarous and childish in its humor, and full of music. In short, the taste for it, as anyone can observe at the Old Vic or the Stratford Festival, is essentially half childish, half musical. . . . If our children, when they have been simply taught to read, have plenty of dramatically illustrated Bibles and Shakespears left in their way, with the illustrated passages printed under the pictures, it will soon be possible to find a general audience which can laugh at The Admirable Bashville.[95]

As an anthropologist, Andrew Lang was fascinated by literature that appealed to the primal, childlike nature of the reader. He lavished critical praise on blood-and-thunder penny dreadfuls—the sort devoured by late Victorian children of all classes—and he encouraged the work of Robert Louis Stevenson and H. Rider Haggard. Lang recognized that myths, which speak to the primitive side of the human mind, might be an ideal source for children's stories, and he drew on mythology to compile his twelve colored *Fairy Books*, published between 1889 and 1910. These were immensely popular, and they inspired a whole subgenre of Edwardian children's literature based on folklore—English, Scottish, Welsh, Irish, Arabian, Persian, Indian, American Indian, Nordic, medieval, and classical Greek—written by authors like F. J. Darnton and Ernest Rhys.[96]

This was a period of great prosperity for the children's book industry. For the first time, there were large numbers of publishing houses, imprints, editorial departments, and editors exclusively devoted to the juvenile market.[97] Remarkably, the most avid readers of books like *The Wind in the Willows* and *Stalky and Co.* were adults. Bernard Shaw recognized that *Peter Pan* was really "a play for grown-up people; for, as you know, when we buy toys for children, we take care to select the ones which amuse ourselves." Four days before the premiere of Barrie's confection, Harley Granville Barker and Laurence Housman had opened *Prunella*, billed as a Pierrot play "for Grown-up Children."[98] With so many adult readers attempting to recapture their childhoods, the distinction between adult and juvenile fiction gradually dissolved. How, after all, is one to classify the works of Stevenson, Rider Haggard, and Kipling? Public school stories were staple reading for Victorian children, but *Stalky* was the first such story to appeal successfully to all age groups, and it was followed by many others— *The Hill* by H. A. Vachell (1905), *The Harrovians* by Arnold Lunn (1913), and *The Loom of Youth* by Alec Waugh (1917). In the early 1890s the *Publishers' Circular* found it increasingly difficult to distinguish "adult" and "juvenile" literature in its annual book census. By 1895 the editors declared that "so-called juvenile works are nowadays so well written, that often they suit older readers quite as well as those for whom they are primarily intended."[99] That year they entirely gave up trying to classify literature by age group.

This return to childhood also produced the first attempts in English literature to write from the point of view of a child. The Victorians published some brilliantly perceptive portraits of children, such as *Jane Eyre* (1847) and *David Copperfield* (1849), but they are always narrated by an adult who is remembering what it was like to be a child. Even Lewis Carroll's Alice possesses an adult's sense of logic, reality, causation, and conduct, which she vainly tries to impose on the very childish population of Wonderland. Beginning around 1895, however, more than one author succeeded in casting off adult intelligence and writing with the mind of a child. Kipling did it in his two *Jungle Books* of 1894 and 1895 and *Stalky and Co.* in 1899, and Kenneth Grahame caused a sensation when he effected the same trick in *The Golden Age* in 1895. In 1896 Edith Nesbit commenced a series of childhood reminiscences for the *Girl's Own Paper*, and the following year she began writing the first of her child-oriented novels, *The Story of the Treasure Seekers*.[100] In 1897 Henry James published *What Maisie Knew*, a novel in which the adult world is described with the limited knowledge and understanding of a child. Later on, there was *Peter Pan*: Barrie specified that "All the characters, whether grown-ups or babes, must wear a child's outlook as their only important adornment."[101] The same outlook was incorporated into much of the poetry of Edward Thomas, as well as the opening sections of *A Portrait of the Artist as a Young Man.* A remarkable literary event of 1919 was the publication of *The Young Visiters*, a novel written by nine-year-old Daisy Ashford. J. M. Barrie wrote a preface for it but left the manuscript virtually unedited in order to convey a child's sense of reality, logic, and (as one might gather from the the the title) spelling.

Several Edwardian authors retained an extraordinary, childlike ability to shift effortlessly between reality and fantasy. The striking thing about the fictions of Saki, Edith Nesbit, and Arthur Rackham, about *Peter Pan, The Wind in the Willows, The Jungle Books*, or any science fiction by H. G. Wells, is that they are all so *convincing*. There is a seamless transition from the actual to the make-believe and back again that never jars the reader. Saki preserved this credibility by describing his talking cats and home county fauns with the perfect deadpan of a West End clubman. Edith Nesbit achieved the same effect by superimposing mundane reality on her fantasies—enchanted castles coexist with railway stations, and the Psammead's magic in *Five Children and It* (1905) operates according to internally consistent, logical, almost scientific laws. Wells, whom Joseph Conrad hailed as a "Realist of the Fantastic," confirmed that the secret of his science fiction was to take an incredible premise and then "in every possible unobtrusive way to *domesticate* the impossible hypothesis" by keeping "everything else human and real."[102] Kenneth Grahame held that dreams were as much a part of life as anything else: they might be a vacation or "re-action" from reality, but they were in no way unreal.[103] When Arthur Rackham once referred to the fairies and goblins in his illustrations as "superstitions," he immediately corrected himself—"I should rather have said *beliefs.*"[104] And J. M. Barrie never liked to hear *Peter Pan* described as a fantasy: he thought it was "rather realistic."[105] The first-night audience apparently agreed: when asked to affirm their belief in fairies, they responded with an unprompted and thunderous *credo.*[106]

The Never Never Land

Peter Pan was able to inspire such faith because he afforded theatergoers relief from all those social and spiritual problems that they lumped under the label "decadence." The Edwardian withdrawal into childhood was, in part, a reaction against the Decadent movement in literature. More generally, it was an attempt to rejuvenate—or escape from—a civilization that seemed old, dissolute, and sterile. Lord Baden-

Powell feared that the British Empire was going the way of the Roman Empire, and he organized the Boy Scouts to rebuild the moral and physical fiber of the nation's youth. Baden-Powell was backed by Rudyard Kipling, who had already created literary models for the scouting movement—Mowgli, Stalky, and Kim, who play "the Great Game" by serving the Empire.[107]

Edith Nesbit, Edward Thomas, and Kenneth Grahame all flirted briefly with the Decadent movement, but after the trials of Oscar Wilde they turned their attention to the innocent world of childhood.[108] Grahame's first book was *Pagan Papers* (1893), which included a chapter on the pleasures of narcotics. In *The Wind in the Willows*, however, he would emphasize the dangers of flouting convention. (Peter Green suggests that Toad's disgrace may be an allegory of Wilde's downfall.) Clearly Grahame was mourning the decay of the old social order of rural England, threatened by proletarian ruffians (the weasels who commandeer Toad Hall) and the nuisances of technology (Toad's automobiles). Grahame admitted that he wrote *The Wind in the Willows* to escape the anxieties of the twentieth century, casting the characters as animals in order "to get away . . . from weary sex-problems."[109]

In *The Condition of England* (1909) C. F. G. Masterman painted a depressing portrait of a troubled society. He saw only one cause for hope—the boyish, playful spirit of Kipling, W. E. Henley, and Robert Louis Stevenson.[110] Barrie, Kipling, G. K. Chesterton, and Henry James were among the many Edwardian authors who admired Stevenson as a children's writer, an enemy of decadence, and a refugee from a tired civilization.[111] Rupert Brooke went out to Samoa to see Stevenson's idyll for himself: "It's getting back to one's childhood, somehow," he wrote back breathlessly.[112] Henley, the nemesis of the Decadents, was associated with Stevenson and several other chroniclers of childhood. He was a close friend of Edith Nesbit's and an inspiration for Kipling and Barrie. He prodded Grahame into writing *The Golden Age* (and published excerpts in his *National Observer*), and he serialized *What Maisie Knew* in the *New Review*.[113]

The *Guy Domville* disaster had convinced Henry James that European civilization was "*en décadence*," and he proceeded to write a series of works about children threatened by evil, including *The Other House* (1896) and "The Turn of the Screw" (1898). In *What Maisie Knew* the child becomes the fixed point of observation—"the ironic centre"— from which adults are described and judged.[114] The reader is put into the mind of a young girl who looks on half-comprehendingly as her comfortable world disintegrates. The process of dissolution is as stately and symmetrical as a minuet: her parents divorce, remarry, commit low adulteries, and divorce again, leaving Maisie with her two stepparents, who pair off with each other. The girl faces one of the primal terrors of childhood, the fear of being abandoned by one's parents. That horror was a metaphor for the cultural despair that oppressed James in the nineties, the sense that civilization was giving way beneath his feet. But when Maisie confronts this loss, "as if she were sinking with a slip from a foothold, her arms made a short jerk. What this jerk represented," writes James, "was the spasm within her of something still deeper than a moral sense."[115] It represented what Kenneth Grahame called "the innate conservatism of youth."[116] An instinctive need for security impels Maisie to reject her fashionably dissolute stepparents and live instead with her stuffy, Victorian, but reliable nurse.

In several works of Edwardian fiction, children entirely escape a decadent civilization and lose themselves in a fantasy world of timeless fun and youth. H. G. Wells's short story "The Door in the Wall" was as cloying as anything Barrie wrote, as was W. H. Hudson's *A Little Boy Lost* (1905) and E. F. Benson's *David Blaize and the Blue Door* (1918). Two works on this theme achieved such phenomenal popularity that they may be taken as indicators of popular attitudes. One was *Peter Pan*, which was revived every year after it opened in 1904. The other was *The Blue Lagoon*, a best-selling novel of 1908, in which two children are marooned on an island "Wonderland" of "eternal morning . . . , eternal happiness, eternal youth."[117] All of these owe an obvious debt to Lewis Carroll, but they paint a much starker contrast between the gloriousness of children's fantasies and the misery of adulthood. Alice eventually returns to reality and grows up without much fuss, but Peter Pan clings to endless childhood, and the sad grownup of "The Door in the Wall" kills himself in a desperate attempt to find his way back to infancy. The tragedy of *The Blue Lagoon* is that the children are ultimately rescued; after they have lived in a blissful state of nature, it is "cruelty to bring them back to what we call civilization."[118]

Edwardian artists also found an escape from decadence in childhood. Those who felt that art had become too refined and ornamented saw one way out of this cul-de-sac—to start again at the beginning, to return to a primitive art based on the untrained vision of the child. A generation before, William Morris had blamed capitalism for leading art into decadence, and his response was the storybook medievalism of *News from Nowhere* (1890). "It is the child-like part of us that produces works of imagination," Morris declared. The utopia of *News from Nowhere* is a "second childhood" for mankind: there is no longer any distinction between work and play, and manufactured articles are called "toys."[119]

The Arts and Crafts movement carried Morris's childlike primitivism into the Edwardian era. In a lecture at the 1896 Arts and Crafts Exhibition, W. R. Lethaby argued that

> art is not the pride of the eye and the purse, it is a link with the child-spirit and the child-ages of the world. The Greek drama grew up out of the village dance; the Greek theatre was developed from the stone-paved circles where the dance took place. If we gather the children who now dance at the street corners into some better dancing-ground, might we not hope for a new music, a new drama, and a new architecture?[120]

Walter Crane worked with the Board of Education to introduce more creative art work (as opposed to simple copying) into school art classes. A friend of Morris's and a leading children's book illustrator, Crane modeled his work on primitive Japanese and Egyptian art. "Children," he wrote in 1913,

> like the ancient Egyptians, appear to see most things in profile, and like definite statement in design. They prefer well defined forms and bright frank colour. They don't want to bother about three dimensions. They can accept symbolic representations. They themselves employ drawing . . . as a kind of picture-writing, and eagerly follow a pictured story. . . . The best of designing for children is that the imagination and fancy may be let loose and roam freely, and there is always room for humour and even pathos, sure of being followed by that ever-living sense of wonder and romance in the child heart—a heart which in some cases, happily, never grows up or grows old.[121]

Postimpressionism, as championed by Roger Fry, also reacted against artistic decadence by recapturing the "perfect sincerity" of children. By 1902 Fry concluded that English art had arrived "at a dead point in the revolutions of our culture" and could only move forward "by going back to an earlier tradition." He therefore plunged into the study of Italian primitives and African art, and he urged artists to unlearn their conventions and view the world with the virgin eye of an infant. "The untaught child," Fry proclaimed, "is artistically in a state of grace," a "genuine primitive artist," and art education should preserve "the ebullient fancy and vitality of youth." This is the idea embodied in Fry's oft-quoted rationale for postimpressionism—that "a good rocking-horse has often more of the true horse about it than an instantaneous photograph of a Derby winner."[122]

As an artist, G. K. Chesterton had distinctly childish tastes—a fondness for vivid images, slashes of color, grotesque caricatures, and primitive innocence.[123] He hated Decadent art because it would not accept limits, and all art, he protested, depends on limits—we must simplify art until it is literally child's play.[124] Chesterton frequently wrote on the artistry of fairy tales and nonsense literature, which he described as allegories of Christianity: like religion, they demand faith, they arouse a childlike sense of wonder, and they bestow magnificent gifts on those who obey seemingly arbitrary laws.[125] The *"carpe diem* religion" of Wilde and Pater leads inevitably to satiation and boredom, Chesterton warned. Only the wonderful fun of *Tristram Shandy* and *The Pickwick Papers* can make us feel happy and immortal.[126]

Edwardian jolliness, then, was in part an attempt to dispel the gloom of decadence. It overlay a profound pessimism, and sometimes the smile cracked. In *Tono-Bungay* there is an almost manic-depressive vacillation between bouncy Wellsian fun and total despair, as aristocratic England gives way to a commercial civilization of patent-medicine tycoons and mass-market advertising. G. K. Chesterton observed the same "jovial pessimism" in C. F. G. Masterman, who, in his frustrating career as a political reformer, alternated between cheery humor and the black gloom of *The Condition of England.*[127] In such cases laughter served the function that the psychologist William McDougall ascribed to it in 1903: it was a natural anaesthetic to relieve the misery of living, actuated not by joy, but by pain.[128]

Of course, the decay of English civilization did not depress everyone: Saki was one Edwardian who found it all rather amusing. His childhood nostalgia was far from a rejection of decadence. On the contrary, Saki romanticized children as "naturally depraved"—not "Nature's raw material" but "Nature's highly finished product."[129] "People talk vaguely about the innocence of a little child," he wrote, "but they take mighty good care not to let it out of their sight for twenty minutes."[130] Fun, as pursued by the gilded youth of his short stories and *The Unbearable Bassington* (1913), consists of refined dissolution, cruel practical jokes, and public-school sadism. Saki's boys, like Barrie's, "never do grow up," but it is the amorality of youth, not its innocence, that they refuse to leave behind. For the good little children of *Peter Pan*, Saki had only polite sarcasm.

> With all reverence for the author of that masterpiece I should say that he had a wonderful and tender insight into the child mind and knew nothing whatever about boys. To make only one criticism on that particular work, can you imagine a lot of British boys, or boys of any country that one knows of, who would stay contentedly playing children's games in an underground cave when there were wolves and pirates and Red Indians to be had for the asking on the other side of the trap door? . . . The "Boy who would not grow up" must have been written by a "grownup who could never have been a boy." Perhaps that is the meaning of the "Never-never Land."[131]

Jokes and Rebellion

Comedians, psychologists, historians, novelists, political revolutionaries, and government censors alike have long appreciated the subversive potential of games and humor. In 1905 Sigmund Freud suggested that jokes could be a socially acceptable means of venting repressed desires and assaulting the existing order of things. "The object of the joke's attack," Freud wrote, "may . . . be institutions, people in their capacity as vehicles of institutions, dogmas of morality or religion, views of life which enjoy so much respect that objections to them can only be made under the mask of a joke."[132] Historians like Emmanuel Le Roy Ladurie have chronicled popular revolts that began as carnivals and turned violent: the French revolution of 1848 has been explained in those terms.[133] Some French radicals of the 1960s frankly described their own revolt as "*une fête*": "Play is the ultimate rationale of this *fête*, to live outside of dead time and to act without inhibitions."[134]

In Edwardian literature, rebellion could often take the form of jokes or games. James Joyce had heard of Freud's theory of humor, and Stephen Dedalus uses laughter "to free his mind from his mind's bondage."[135] The joke was Bernard Shaw's prime weapon for socialism, as deployed in *Pygmalion* (1914). When Alfred Doolittle demands five pounds from Prof. Higgins, with the solemn assurance that the money will be squandered on high living, he exposes the arrogance behind the phrase "the deserving poor," so often invoked by Victorian charity officials. That joke is an explicit attack on the hypocrisy of "middle class morality"—which, as Doolittle says, is "just an excuse for never giving me anything."[136] Shaw was a comedian, but he fairly warned his audience that "every jest is an earnest in the womb of Time."[137]

In G. K. Chesterton's first novel, *The Napoleon of Notting Hill* (1904), a game precipitates a revolt against a bureaucratic despotism. The story begins sometime in the future, when the king of England whimsically orders all the London boroughs to incorporate as free medieval cities, each with fake heraldry, costumes, and local customs. It is all a stupendous practical joke, but two Londoners take it quite seriously. One of them is a psychological Peter Pan: he has never outgrown playing soldiers, and he solemnly vows to defend Notting Hill against a plan to run a highway through the district. The other is a toyshop owner who has already fought the battle of Notting Hill several times—with lead soldiers on a scale model of the area. The two of them rouse the men of the neighborhood, who, armed with halberds and poleaxes, successfully engage the king's forces. The king joins in the fun himself, writing sensational dispatches from the front and anonymous leading articles denouncing his own misrule. Notting Hill triumphs, but not before it infects its enemies with the spirit of parish patriotism, dissolving London into a Chestertonian utopia of autonomous medieval burghs.

In *The Napoleon of Notting Hill*, fun and revolution are two sides of the same coin. Much like Freud, Chesterton argues that humor expresses frustrated human desires; once some "madman" treats a joke seriously, he is capable of transforming society.[138] That, wrote Bernard Shaw, is the history of every revolutionary idea: "First it is generally a joke. Next it is a blasphemy. The third time it is a troublesome call to work. It is never solemn until its time is past."[139] *The Napoleon of Notting Hill* became something of a cult book among the guild socialists, who understood the revolutionary power of fun. They concluded their meetings by singing Chesterton's jolly ballads; they wrote the satiric socialist ditties of *The Bolo Book*; they even composed agitprop comic operas parodying Gilbert and Sullivan.[140]

Following George Meredith, E. M. Forster used humor to disrupt the social order. In *A Room with a View* Cecil Vyse mischievously refers the Emersons, who are hopelessly bohemian, to a stuffy landlord who yearns for "respectable" tenants. That prank, as Cecil half-seriously proclaims, is a blow for equality and fellowship: "I, even I, have won a great victory for the Comic Muse. George Meredith's right—the cause of Comedy and the cause of Truth are really the same. . . . The classes ought to mix. . . . There ought to be intermarriage—all sorts of things. I believe in democracy."[141] Sure enough, the joke throws the socialists and philistines of the novel together and leads to the reconciliation of George Emerson and Lucy Honeychurch. That, for Forster, was the great virtue of humor: it was a catalyst that made people connect.

When H. G. Wells tried to remake the world according to his own personal blueprint, he was partly acting out the games of his boyhood, when he would imagine himself a Cromwell or a Napoleon fighting brilliant campaigns. The Martian attack on London in *The War of the Worlds* was very much a projection of these fantasies,[142] just as *The Napoleon of Notting Hill* originated in the imaginary street battles Chesterton fought as a boy.[143] At age seventy Wells recalled that he had always approached the task of social reform like "a little boy at a lovely party, who has been given quite a lot of jolly toys and who has spread his play about the floor." Wells was spoiled as a child—"Woe betide if toys his highness wanted were denied him," his brother Frank remembered—and in that respect he never really grew up. With a boyish enthusiasm, he concocted fantastic schemes for remodeling society, but when others would not play the game entirely according to his rules, he was likely to throw a tantrum and walk off in high dudgeon. In 1906 he dazzled the Fabian Society with a grandiose plan to build a mass socialist political party, with an imposing block of offices, a profitable publishing subsidiary, and a national weekly magazine. The rank and file was eager to follow him, but Wells sabotaged his own revolution by indulging in personal attacks, petty and obvious lies, and (in the words of Bernard Shaw) "every other petulance of which a spoiled child" is capable.[144]

Even as an adult, Wells was addicted to playing with toy soldiers. He wrote two books on the subject, and he admitted that in constructing his socialist utopias, he had always pushed around individuals, classes, and societies like so many lead pieces. The same, he added, was true of Winston Churchill, Leopold Amery, George Trevelyan, and C. F. G. Masterman (he might have also mentioned G. K. Chesterton): they all shared his passion for tabletop wars and carried that passion over to their politics.[145]

Winston Churchill turned this toy-soldier mania to counterrevolutionary ends—as in his notorious 1911 assault on Sidney Street. As home secretary, he mobilized a platoon of Scots Guards to assist 750 policemen and the Horse Artillery in assaulting an anarchist hideout in the East End, which, it was later discovered, was garrisoned by exactly two men. Churchill personally oversaw the siege in a conspicuous silk hat that made him a perfect target for anarchist fire. Afterward he soothed a frantic Charles Masterman: "*Now* Charlie. Don't be croth. It was such fun."[146] George Dangerfield notes that Churchill brought the same *Boy's Own Paper* mentality to the post of first lord of the Admiralty: "Fleet, and squadron, and flotilla, the guns, the tubes, the 'murderous queens' of steel, all these were his to play with . . . ; the administration of these precise and sanguinary toys touched some rich, secret place in his imagination. [He was] lost in a drama as solitary as that of a child which plays by itself."[147]

The prewar social unrest described in *The Strange Death of Liberal England* was aroused by deadly serious issues, but it was often treated by contemporary onlookers as an amusing lark. By 1914, writes Dangerfield,

> the public was . . . so accustomed to thrills—from motors cars and aeroplanes to the cinematograph, ragtime, and the menace of Germany— that . . . it declined to take even the palpable prospects of an Irish Civil War with any sort of seriousness. Civil War was a game, it was a dangerous and exciting game. . . .
>
> Indeed the confusions of 1914 are hardly more curious than the detachment of the public. The loudest cries, the most lamentable predictions, failed to arouse in its bosom any stronger emotion than one of pleasant excitement.[148]

For Saki the riotous events of the day were only inspiration for his farcical short stories: the suffragettes provided especially good material.[149] H. W. Nevinson, a supporter of the WSPU, was disgusted to find that their Albert Hall rallies were filled with West End sympathizers who cheered the suffrage battle as a sort of "bull-fight." They enjoyed the delicious "thrill of vicarious danger, implying no risk whatever to themselves. . . . If the Liberal Government had burnt one of the leaders alive on the stage, they would have shrieked with indignant delight, and gone home to tea."[150]

The Wicket We Must Defend

The public schools had promoted the cult of gamesmanship for the explicit purpose of preparing their boys for war. Sports were supposed to teach the military virtues of self-sacrifice, teamwork, and esprit de corps. The myth that "the battle of Waterloo was won on the playing fields of Eton" was invented in 1889, and the same moral was taught in "Vitaï Lampada," Henry Newbolt's popular poem of 1898.

> The sand of the desert is sodden red—
>   Red with the wreck of a square that broke;
> The Gatling's jammed and the Colonel dead,
>   And the regiment blind with dust and smoke;
> The river of death has brimmed his banks,
>   And England's far, and Honor a name;
> But the voice of a schoolboy rallies the ranks:
>   "Play up! play up! and play the game!"

With that sort of indoctrination, the British plunged into the First World War as a magnificent sport, something "not too far distant from playing games, running races, and competing in a thoroughly decent way," as Paul Fussell has written. One music-hall actor performed a patriotic turn wearing a naval uniform and carrying a cricket bat. "Cricket for the time must end," he sang; "This is the wicket we must defend." "It's all great fun," Rupert Brooke wrote home, and he was not an exceptional case: regimental histories record any number of heroic moments when British infantrymen dribbled footballs as they charged enemy trenches.[151] This sort of behavior becomes more comprehensible when one discovers that a large portion of the British army was recruited at football matches. Before it shut down for the duration in April 1915, professional football aided the war effort by staging enlistment rallies at matches where speakers would exhort the crowd to join in the greatest game of all. The results were spectacular: of the nearly 1.2 million volunteers who had signed up by the end of 1914, football accounted for half a million. Bear in mind also that many war recruits were graduates of the scouting movement—four hundred thousand from the Boys' Brigade alone.[152]

Saki enlisted in August 1914 at the age of forty-three, and he fought as a foot soldier with tremendous enthusiasm. The war brought him back to his boyhood: the battles he had once fought with lead soldiers were now gloriously real. "No one could really forget those wonderful leaden cavalry soldiers; the horses were as sleek and prancing as though they had never left the parade-ground, and the uniforms were correspondingly spick and span," he recalled, not long before he was killed in

France. "Nearly every red-blooded human boy has had war, in some shape or form, for his first love; if his blood has remained red and he has kept some of his boyishness in after life, that first love will never have been forgotten."[153]

War correspondents liked to report the mordant trench humor cultivated by British soldiers. E. T. Cook suggested that the nicknames they gave to various weapons—*plum puddings* for bombs and *grandmother* for a 15-inch gun—reflected a habit of "wrapping up a death-dealing contrivance in a cover of domestic humour. In their choice of words, as in their songs and in their everyday philosophy, the British soldiers are of one mind with the sergeant who, sitting in a trench knee-deep in water, explained to one of the press correspondents, 'You know, sir, it doesn't do to take this war seriously.' "[154]

Quotations of this sort should be read skeptically. Paul Fussell has warned us that Allied journalists continued to write about jolly Tommies treating the war as a great lark long after the picture had ceased to conform to reality. There was still humor in the trenches; but as the conflict dragged on, it became increasingly cynical, pessimistic, and rebellious in tone.[155]

In fact, the effect of the war was to chill the Edwardian spirit of play. The government and the press relentlessly drove home the message that fun and extravagance were not to be thought of while men were fighting and dying in France. Nearly all professional sports suspended operations, and most other leisure activities were drastically curtailed.[156] Of all categories of book publishing, "Games and Sports" suffered the greatest proportional decline during the war years.

Heartbreak House was the only full-length play Bernard Shaw wrote during the war, and it is also his saddest story, modeled closely on *King Lear*. It begins deceptively as a typical Shavian farce, but the mood darkens as the drama proceeds, and by the final act the cast has descended into total despair. Not growing up, that Edwardian obsession, here means the horrors of senility, as Captain Shotover slips into his "second childhood": "In old age [your] vessel dries up: . . . you are a child again."[157] As Shaw explained in his preface, the dark comedy of *Heartbreak House* made it unsuitable for production until after the armistice.

War cannot bear the terrible castigation of comedy, the ruthless light of laughter that glares on the stage. When men are heroically dying for their country, it is not the time to shew their lovers and wives and fathers and mothers how they are being sacrificed to the blunders of boobies, the cupidity of capitalists, the ambition of conquerors, the electioneering of demagogues, the Pharisaism of patriots, the lusts and lies and rancors and bloodthirsts that love war because it opens their prison doors, and sets them in the thrones of power and popularity. . . . That is why comedy, though sorely tempted, had to be loyally silent. . . . That is why I had to withhold Heartbreak House from the footlights during the war; for the Germans might on any night have turned the last act from play to earnest, and even then might not have waited for their cues.[158]

For the same reason, Max Beerbohm cancelled an exhibition of his cartoons scheduled for April 1915.

My caricatures, exhibited while England is in the throes of a life-and-death struggle, would not merely fall flat: they would be an offence against decency. In time of peace, they are delightful, no doubt; but imagine a nation being called on, in the midst of a whole world's tragedy of suffering and horror, to enjoy my little jokes about Mr Hall Caine and Sir Gilbert Parker and Mr Bonar Law and Mr Sydney [sic] Webb. . . . The idea is inconceivable. So long as the war lasts (and, indeed, I think, for some months after peace has been declared) my caricatures must be kept locked up in a drawer.[159]

In fact, Beerbohm all but ceased drawing for the rest of his life. Somehow the postwar world did not lend itself to light humor: after 1918 the satire of Shaw, Wells, and Belloc would grow scolding and pessimistic. Among the younger generation of writers, new styles of comedy were emerging: the decadent dandyism of Ronald Firbank and the Children of the Sun, and the black irony of Aldous Huxley, Evelyn Waugh, and Robert Graves's best-selling *Good-bye to All That* (1929). In 1939 E. M. Forster mourned the passing of the Edwardian "fetich of humour—D. H. Lawrence killed it though you can still find its corpse weekly in *Punch.*" Nowadays, Forster declared, "the Comic Muse looks too like a governess, . . . and the expression 'clean fun' . . . has naturally evolved the dirty joke as its corrective."[160] Actually, Edwardian whimsy left a permanent mark on Britain, where it is still important to be clever as well as competent, and there is an appreciative audience for the educated comedy of Tom Stoppard and Woody Allen. But the war did sour the tone of British humor, at least for a time, and it introduced into English literature the ghastly, sardonic, unclean fun of the trenches.

As for children's literature, historians of that genre generally agree that the brilliance of the Edwardian age was followed by a remarkably dull period, producing nothing above the level of Winnie the Pooh and Hugh Lofting's Doctor Doolittle.[161] Barrie, Grahame, and Edith Nesbit were no longer productive, and no postwar author of comparable talent bothered to write for children. Refusing to grow up continued to be a common theme in the literature of the 1920s, especially among the Children of the Sun, but it was a puerilism very different from the Edwardian variety. It was more a perpetual adolescence than a perpetual childhood, more an Oedipal revolt than a quest for lost innocence, a glorification of decadence rather than an escape from it. It was, in other words, a cult of *jeunesse dorée* that, among the Edwardians, had been anticipated only by Saki.[162]

"Oh, for an hour of Herod," sighed Anthony Hope after the premiere of *Peter Pan*,[163] and it is impossible not to sympathize with him. Granted, the Edwardian cult of childhood brought forth some delightful books and a more humane approach to childrearing. But it also had a precious side, as reflected in the upper-class fad for having tea with the children in the playroom. Max Beerbohm warned that this sort of slumming in the nursery would only make children neurotic,[164] and in fact it could be very damaging, as we are now beginning to discover. J. M. Barrie took the Llewellyn Davies orphans under his wing and worked them into several of his books, but his possessiveness and suppressed pedophilia eventually drove one of the boys—the model for Peter Pan—to kill himself.[165] Kenneth Grahame and his wife put terrific academic pressure on their only son, though he was sickly and half blind, and he too found an escape in suicide.[166]

The psychologist T. W. Mitchell noted that reversion to immature behavior was a common affliction among his Edwardian patients: "Weaker spirits, when they find life hard, know well the craving for the dependence and irresponsibility of childhood."[167] Wishful thinking was one of the infirmities of the Edwardian intellect, and the gospel of fun reflected that unhealthy softness. Confronted by difficult issues, some Edwardians insisted on reconciling everything; others, like Dickens's Mr. Skimpole, evaded those problems by not growing up. G. K. Chesterton tried to conjure away hard questions with clever paradoxes, while Kenneth Grahame simply shut out reality and withdrew into a fantasy world. Certainly there was a touch of easy self-delusion in the

Fabian notion that Britain could be tickled into socialism—that, as Rupert Brooke exclaimed, "acting on one's conscience is always rather fun."[168] H. G. Wells, for one, despised the Fabians for treating "this grave high business of Socialism [as] an idiotic middle-class joke."

> Perhaps our worst pettiness, and the one most offensive and deterrent to the serious newcomer, is our little stock-in-trade of jokes, our little special style of joking. It is quite after the manner of the jokes one finds in a large, lax family. . . . I can assure you that constant flow of rather foolish laughter, of rather forced jesting, is no small defect in our work. It flows over and obscures all sorts of grave issues, it chills and kills enthusiasm. Its particular victim in this society is Mr. Bernard Shaw.[169]

But Shaw himself occasionally grew tired of playing the "poor silly-clever Irishman." He blamed his Irish upbringing for instilling the habit of answering serious questions with

> a horrible, senseless, mischievous laughter. When youre young, you exchange drinks with other young men; and you exchange vile stories with them; and as youre too futile to be able to help or cheer them, you chaff and sneer and taunt them for not doing the things you darent do yourself. And all the time you laugh! laugh! laugh! eternal derision, eternal envy, eternal folly, eternal fouling and staining and degrading, until, when you come at last to a country where men take a question seriously and give a serious answer to it, you deride them for having no sense of humor, and plume yourself on your own worthlessness as if it made you better than them.[170]

Chesterton, in his autobiography, recalled an incident that exposes the rank silliness of the age. It involved an inane mock-western film produced by J. M. Barrie and directed by Harley Granville Barker, in which Barrie, Shaw, Chesterton, and William Archer appeared as cowboys. The film was shown at a gala supper at the Savoy Theatre, attended by political and cultural celebrities (including the prime minister), who pelted each other with bits of bread. Speaking from the stage, Shaw vilified his collaborators and then brandished a huge sword, whereupon they also produced swords and chased Shaw behind the scenery. For those who like dramatic irony in their history, this farce was perfectly timed: it was staged five days after the assassination of Franz Ferdinand of Austria. It may be trite to say that the Edwardians were dancing atop a volcano, but they did have an inordinate weakness for playing with ideas, with religion, with social reform, and, finally, with war. "There really had been a sort of unearthly unreality in all the levity of those last hours," wrote Chesterton, "like something high and shrill that might crack; and it did crack."[171]

6. The Undivided Self

In 1925 Alfred North Whitehead described the nineteenth century as "a perplexed century," a peculiar era in which

> each individual was divided against himself. In the earlier times there were opposing camps, bitterly at variance on questions which they deemed fundamental. But, except for a few stragglers, either camp was whole-hearted. . . . The deep thinkers were the clear thinkers,—Descartes, Spinoza, Locke, Leibniz. They knew exactly what they meant and said it. In the nineteenth century, some of the deeper thinkers among theologians and philosophers were muddled thinkers. Their assent was claimed by incompatible doctrines; and their efforts at reconciliation produced inevitable confusion.[1]

The "Divided Self" has since become a favorite concept among critics of Victorian literature. Masao Miyoshi has traced the theme from the Gothic novelists to the Decadents, climaxing with *The Strange Case of Dr. Jekyll and Mr. Hyde* (1886) and *The Picture of Dorian Gray* (1891).[2] Self-division was the psychological product of the great intellectual conflicts of the Victorian age: the clash of science and religion, reason and emotion, morality and desire, society and individuality. "Can I ever again compact my shattered self into a definite ego whose mind shall reflect the mind of Christ?" wailed the young James Ward in 1870, as he grappled with terrifying religious doubts. Ward longed "to be taken up into a higher life and delivered from the teacherous self. . . . I have no dread of God, no fear of the Devil, no fear of man," he wrote in 1872, "but my head swims as I write it—*I fear myself.*"[3]

Milder forms of the same disease were not unknown among the Edwardians. Kenneth Grahame was never quite able to reconcile the two sides of his personality: the respectable officer of the Bank of England and the bohemian who wrote for the *Yellow Book*. As "an introspective intellectual," forever watching himself with a cold objectivity, Leonard Woolf could not help but see himself "as 'I' and yet at the same time . . . as a 'not I', a stranger acting a part upon a stage."[4] Beatrice Webb also felt painfully divided over questions of religion, free will, mortality, sexuality, and civic responsibility. "Beneath the surface of our daily life, in the personal history of many of us," she wrote, "there runs a continuous controversy between an Ego that affirms and an Ego that denies."[5]

Centaurs

For all that, the Divided Self was only a minor theme in Edwardian literature. It was eclipsed by a stronger emphasis on inner unity and the balanced development of the whole personality. Dr. Jekyll gave way to Kim, who struggles with his identity ("Who is Kim?") but finally reconciles his European and Asian selves. "With an almost audible click" his mind reintegrates, and "the wheels of his being lock up anew on the world without."[6] *Many-sidedness* became a popular catchword among educated people, as E. M. Forster noted. (He derived the idea from Goldsworthy Lowes Dickinson, who in turn absorbed it from Goethe.)[7] That was the context in which Forster proclaimed his gospel: "Only connect! . . . Only connect the prose and the passion, and both will be exalted, and human love will be seen at its height. Live in fragments no longer. Only connect, and the beast and the monk, robbed of the isolation that is life to either, will die."[8]

Connecting ideas, connecting people, connecting opposing sides of the personality—all were parts of the same Edwardian current. The reconciliation of the sacred and the secular, the rich and the poor, sexuality and spirituality, the child and the adult brought with it an inner reconciliation of the self. Young Havelock Ellis was torn between the conflicting claims of science and the spirit, but his conversion to a religion of "life" at once ended that "painful sense of strain and division": "The dull aching tension was removed; the two opposing psychic tendencies were fused in delicious harmony. . . . My self was one with the Not-self, my will one with the universal will."[9]

The ideal, as Kenneth Grahame saw it, was to live as a centaur, allowing expression to both the animal and the social halves of the human personality. Grahame could not assert that freedom in his own life, but he attained it vicariously in *The Wind in the Willows*. As he explained it, he deliberately populated that book with animals—very human animals, like centaurs—because "every animal, by nature, lives according to his nature," undivided.[10]

That was the aim of the Edwardian movement to restore craftsman-

ship in industry. By introducing an element of play into our work, wrote
J. L. Hammond, we make labor "an equable balancing effort of the body
and muscles," and we create "that harmony of the whole being which
constitutes happiness."[11] According to A. J. Penty, capitalism forced the
laborer to "live a conscious double life," split between the drudgery of
his job and the empty commercialized recreation of his leisure time.
Guild socialism, by reviving traditional crafts, would "unite these warring forces in man and . . . make him once more simple, harmonious,
and whole."[12]

Many Edwardian authors and psychologists recognized the existence of a subconscious mind, but not the subconscious of Sigmund
Freud. They regarded the second self as a good self, a creative self, not so
much a hiding place for perverse impulses. Whether or not they read
Freud, they rejected the inevitability of repression and psychic conflict:
they preferred, once again, to believe in the reconciliation of opposites.
Their solution to self-division was perfectly simple: the subconscious
should be liberated and united with the conscious mind. The way to
psychic health, as W. H. Hudson wrote in 1903, was through the "revelation of an unfamiliar and unsuspected nature hidden under the nature
we are conscious of."[13]

Even Henry James succeeded in liberating that hidden self. From the
very beginning of *The Ambassadors*, Strether feels the ambivalent pull of
"a double consciousness." Already something tells him that Chad should
not be brought home to Massachusetts and a career in advertising.[14]
Years before, Strether had toured Paris and brought back twelve yellow
volumes, a precious sampling of European belles lettres. Those books,
forgotten over the decades, have stuck in Strether's "subconsciousness"
ever since. Now the sight of lemon covers on a bookshelf reawakens his
hunger for European culture, "the general stirred life of connexions
long since individually dropped" (*Ambass.* 21:85–88). Strether is relieved
to discover that "he didn't want . . . to prevent Chad from living;
 . . . if he had he would himself have thoroughly gone to pieces," but by
following his own "wild native impulses," Strether "held together"
(*Ambass.* 22:212). He urges Waymarsh not to deny a part of himself: "*Let
yourself, on the contrary, go*—in all agreeable directions" (*Ambass.*
22:194). Ultimately, Strether has to rein himself in and return to America, but he cannot completely undo his own transformation: he will be
going home "to a great difference" (*Ambass.* 22:325).

Joseph Conrad was more adventurous in "The Secret Sharer" (1909), a story told by a curiously dissociated sea captain. He is "a stranger" to his ship: it is a new command, and he does not yet have the feel of it. He is also "somewhat of a stranger to myself," at least until he rescues a fellow seaman, named Leggatt, from the ocean. The captain is astonished to find that he has pulled on deck "my other self." The two men have an immediate rapport, "a mysterious communication," though Leggatt is much more aggressive and impulsive. He has, in fact, murdered a sailor who was threatening the safety of his ship. Leggatt is an incarnation of the vital subconscious, and by aiding his escape, the captain achieves a healthy integration of his own personality. He is at last one with himself and with his ship, "the perfect communion of a seaman with his first command."[15]

Edwardian explorers of the subconscious generally owed more to Samuel Butler than to Sigmund Freud. In *The Way of All Flesh*, Ernest Pontifex tries to follow his "reasoning and reflecting self," the priggish superego that his father beat into him. But there is also an "other Ernest that dwelt within him, and was so much stronger and more real than the Ernest of which he was conscious." "Obey *me*, your true self, and things will go tolerably well with you," whispers the subconscious, "but only listen to that outward and visible old husk of yours which is called your father, and I will rend you in pieces even unto the third and fourth generation as one who has hated God; for I, Ernest, am the God who made you."[16] Fortunately, Ernest loses his inheritance, accosts a respectable girl he mistakes for a prostitute, and is sent to prison, which experience shocks his unconscious into consciousness and fuses his two selves. The result is not an Oedipal patricide, but a very Edwardian synthesis. The undivided Ernest asserts his independence from his father but is reconciled with him; he thinks Radical but votes Conservative; he is no longer a clergyman, but he writes essays defending the Established Church as a fair approximation of the true faith, at least as long as it remains a "lukewarm" Broad Church open to different viewpoints.[17]

Bernard Shaw inherited Butler's faith in the second self. Sergius Saranoff and Raina Petkoff (*Arms and the Man*), Dick Dudgeon and the Reverend Anderson (*The Devil's Disciple*), and Adolphus Cusins (*Major Barbara*) are each momentarily upset when his or her subconscious clashes with the social roles he or she plays, but they all make peace with themselves by sloughing off their old personalities and assuming new vocations more suited to their true temperaments. E. M. Forster, another admirer of Butler, made the same point in *A Room with a View*.

Charlotte Bartlett, Lucy Honeychurch's spinster chaperone, consciously tries to keep her away from George Emerson, but everything she does has the practical result of bringing them together, and that, Forster implies, is the surreptitious work of the subconscious Charlotte.[18]

In 1909 James Joyce began buying pamphlets on psychoanalysis, including Freud's *Childhood Memory of Leonardo da Vinci*. Joyce, however, was always dismissive of Freud and denied his influence. Although Freudianism may have had some impact on his later work, the fact is that Joyce had been exploring the subconscious well before he encountered the psychoanalysts.[19] Back in 1906 he had resolved to "put down a bucket into my own soul's well, sexual department,"[20] and he had been interpreting dreams even earlier than that. It is true that Joyce later acquired a copy of *The Problem of Hamlet and the Oedipus Conflict* by Ernest Jones. But there is no Oedipal conflict in *Ulysses*; on the contrary, there is a reunion of Odysseus and Telemachus. That final rapprochement between father and son, as well as the universal synthesizing of *Ulysses*, is more reminiscent of another book in Joyce's library, *The Way of All Flesh*.[21]

Many early admirers of *Sons and Lovers*, including David Eder, read it as a psychoanalytic novel about the Oedipus complex, but the book owes little if anything to Freud. Lawrence did not care much for Freudianism, which he found too clinical; he had been far more enthusiastic about *Erewhon*.[22] The conflicts in *Sons and Lovers* are not so much Oedipal as spiritual. In Lawrence's own outline of the story, the Morel brothers are split between their religious and their sexual selves. "William gives his sex to a fribble, and his mother holds his soul," a division of loyalties that literally kills him. Paul begins to fracture along the same lines when he becomes involved with Clara Dawes.[23] In *Women in Love* Gerald Crich tries to evade that conflict by indulging his passional self in meaningless sex and "scorning his other self." But the religious side of his personality cannot be cast aside: "Somewhere far off and small, the other hovered."[24] Rupert Birkin is caught in that same ambivalence, an "oscillation" that will "at length be too violent for his coherency, and he would smash and be dead. . . . This violent and directionless reaction between animalism and spiritual truth would go on in him till he tore himself in two between opposite directions, and disappeared meaninglessly out of life" (*Women* 289). (Lawrence in fact defined death as the coming apart of the self, the undoing of "the last knot which held the human being in its unity" [*Women* 275].)

Lawrence was able to reconcile religion and sexuality in the balance of "star-equilibrium," which made the spiritual and passional selves "whole again" (*Women* 337). By releasing the "dark, powerful under-life" of the subconscious, men and women can purge all the hermaphroditic elements in their personalities—another kind of self-division that Lawrence dreaded. Then we are no longer

> broken fragments of one whole. Rather we are the singling away into purity and clear being, of things that were mixed. . . . And passion is the further separating of this mixture, that which is manly being taken into the being of the man, that which is womanly passing to the woman, till the two are clear and whole as angels, the admixture of sex in the highest sense surpassed, leaving the two single beings constellated together like two stars. (*Women* 192–93)

When Birkin and Ursula achieve this balance, he feels "the tension of his consciousness broken," and she at last finds "her complete self." Birkin is now "awake and potent in that other basic mind, the deepest physical mind." While his conscious self thinks of other things, his "second consciousness" is even capable of steering his car to the perfect spot in Sherwood Forest where he and Ursula can spend the night together (*Women* chap. 23).

Earlier, at the turn of the century, F. W. H. Myers had built an entire theory of psychology on the concept of a benign and almost magical subconscious. Myers and his colleagues in the Society for Psychical Research were quite familiar with the Divided Self: in seances and hypnotism sessions they frequently observed subjects assuming other personalities and speaking with other voices. From 1885 until his death in 1901 Myers worked out his "theory of the subliminal self," which postulated that every individual has several different selves, each a separate stream of consciousness. Usually, only one of these selves is conscious; the rest remain subliminal. But shock, hypnosis, psychopathology, or some special psychic gift can bring the subliminal to consciousness, where it manifests itself as mesmeric trances, dreams, somnambulism, automatic writing, visions, apparitions, mediumism, or schizophrenia. Very often, the subliminal can be a pool of artistic, philosophical, or religious inspiration. Andrew Lang, an SPR member who read Myers's work, used it to explain the visions and military genius of Joan of Arc, and Bernard Shaw in turn borrowed from Lang when he wrote *Saint Joan* (1923).[25] The finished version of Myers's theory was published posthumously in

1902 under the title *Human Personality and Its Survival of Bodily Death*. William McDougall and G. F. Stout reviewed the book skeptically, but Oliver Lodge and F. C. S. Schiller were more approving, and thereafter much of the SPR *Proceedings* was given over to discussions of the subliminal self.[26]

The emerging science of psychology was closely bound up with psychical research inasmuch as both disciplines were investigating the subconscious. The SPR was heavily represented at the International Congress of Experimental Psychology, first convened in Paris in 1889. Among pioneer psychologists, William James, G. Stanley Hall, Henri Bergson, Jean Charcot, Pierre Janet, Alfred Binet, Charles Richet, Théodore Ribot, Cesare Lombroso, Sándor Ferenczi, Théodore Flournoy, and Carl Jung were all affiliated with the SPR. James Strachey discovered psychoanalysis when he heard a paper by Freud read at an SPR meeting; Strachey later became a psychoanalyst and translated the collected works of Freud.[27] Freud himself was a corresponding member of the SPR, and the first British account of his research was published by F. W. H. Myers, in the SPR *Proceedings* for June 1893.

Myers also knew the work of another explorer of the subconscious: Robert Louis Stevenson, who joined the SPR in 1893.[28] But Myers disagreed with Stevenson and Freud on one crucial point—he did not regard the subconscious primarily as a mental cesspool. Myers's subliminal was sometimes pathological, but more often it was a mine of psychic riches. One subliminal self might be a poet, another a saint, yet another an artist or a philosopher. Myers, in fact, explained human genius as the ability to tap into the subliminal. If all these streams of subconsciousness could somehow be made conscious (and the SPR appeared to be doing promising work in this area), the powers of the human personality could be multiplied many times over.

Other SPR psychologists took the same approach to Freud: they admired and publicized his work, but they frequently dissented from his dark view of the subconscious. T. W. Mitchell pointed out that schizophrenics often manifested extraordinary psychic or mathematical talents. "If there is any transcendental world," Mitchell speculated, "and if it is possible for us to get into relation with it, it may well be that such intercommunication is possible only during states of mental dissociation." Some dissociations are "helpful," producing "enhancements of the natural powers," and schizophrenics may be, in that respect, "more fully adjusted to their environment than ordinary men and women are."[29] Mitchell, May Sinclair, and several other SPR members took an interest in Carl Jung, who saw a treasure trove of archetypes and collective memories in the subconscious.[30] Jung presented a paper to the SPR in 1919; two years earlier Constance Long had praised his work in the SPR *Proceedings*. Dr. Long disliked Freud's emphasis on the censor, and she found his "interpretation of symbols . . . monotonous and stultifying." She favorably cited both Jung and Samuel Butler on the subject of collective memory. Jungian analysis, she wrote, "reveals a richness in the content of dreams which is fully in accordance with the creative and evolutional character of the human mind." Long wanted to deemphasize psychic conflict, to stress "the synthetic or reconstructive side of analysis," to "bring about that co-operation between good and evil, spiritual and animal, white and black, without which no life can be lived satisfactorily."[31] (Long had been brought into the London Psycho-Analytical Society by David Eder, who had reservations concerning the Oedipus conflict and passed through a Jungian phase of his own.)

In traditional Christianity, as in Freudian psychology, there is inevitable tension between the impulses of the body and the ideals of the soul: the self is always somewhat divided. But there was no necessary conflict between the body and these various Edwardian models of the secular soul. George Moore's Father Gogarty learns that "body and mind are not two things, but one thing, . . . that the best thinking is done when the whole man thinks, the flesh and the brain together."[32] The great fault of Western civilization, according to Edward Carpenter, was that it overemphasized the soul at the expense of the body whereas happiness "consists in combining and harmonizing *both* body and soul, the outer and inner."[33]

Happy Hypocrites

Carpenter chose to live undivided in one other important respect. He refused to conceal his homosexuality, and he published some groundbreaking tracts advocating tolerance of homosexuals, including *Homogenic Love* (1895) and *The Intermediate Sex* (1908). He declined to lead the double life of an Oscar Wilde, concealing his real self behind a flamboyant public persona.

Wilde's second self, however, was more than just a camouflage for his homosexuality: it was the artistic product of what the Decadents called "the Doctrine of the Mask." According to this theory, "being oneself" is either an impossibility or a bore. The human personality cannot freely blossom and develop of its own accord, Wilde argued; it has to be constructed deliberately, like a work of art. The so-called real self, unformed and uninteresting, needs a beautiful false front. One must therefore create a second self, a mask for presentation to the outside world, as Wilde did when he invented his outlandish aesthetical "pose."[34]

After Wilde's downfall Max Beerbohm took the Doctrine of the Mask and inverted it, using it not to divide the personality but to make it whole again. "The Happy Hypocrite" (1897) is Beerbohm's fable of the evil Lord George Hell, who has an angelic mask fashioned to hide his diabolical features in order that he may woo an innocent young actress. He wins her hand and, after several months of pure and blissful Arcadian marriage, the face of Lord George softens until it becomes indistinguishable from the mask. "The Happy Hypocrite" is a spoof of *The Picture of Dorian Gray*, a retelling of that story in reverse. It also conveys the opposite message—that if we maintain a facade long enough, we become the part we are playing, and the division between our pose and our "natural" self disappears.

William Butler Yeats made use of the Doctrine of the Mask in grappling with a more difficult problem of self-division. It was a split rooted in many personal and philosophical dilemmas, among them his revolt against his father's agnosticism, his sexual anxieties, and his frustrating pursuit of the charismatic Fenian heroine Maud Gonne. Yeats's loyalties were divided between the dreamy languor of Ireland and the stimulating literary life of London. In his 1888 story *John Sherman*, he assigned his Hibernian and metropolitan selves to the characters of Sherman and the Reverend William Howard. After 1895 he wrote a series of stories and poems around the antipodal figures of Michael Robartes and Owen Aherne. Each embodied an opposing side of himself, the first mystical, bohemian, and adventurous, the other Catholic, thoughtful, conventional, and retiring. To conceal this inner ambivalence, Yeats, much like Wilde, adopted a public mask, creating the character of a mystic Celtic poet and playing that role to the hilt. As an answer to his religious dilemmas, he invented an Irish mystical order in which novitiates would be enjoined to unite the opposing spirits of Aengus and Edain, representing the spiritual and the aesthetic. "The Candidate's Mind," he wrote, "must become able to blend the two forces together, so as to create completeness" and to enter "the country where the contraries are equally true." Around 1914 Yeats's psychical experiments led him to suspect that he was accompanied through life by an "anti-self," a spirit who might reveal to him the unity he had been seeking.[35]

> I call to the mysterious one who yet
> Shall walk the wet sands by the edge of the stream
> And look most like me, being indeed my double,
> And prove of all imaginable things
> The most unlike, being my anti-self,
> And, standing by these characters, disclose
> All that I seek. . . .[36]

In 1917 Yeats discovered the perfect symbol of the metaphysical synthesis for which he was searching—a pair of opposing and interpenetrating cones or "gyres," each tapering as the other broadened. In *A Vision*, begun that same year, Yeats used his gyres, together with a fantastic menagerie of spirits and antispirits and recurring cycles, to sort the entire universe into ordered pairs of opposites. This impossibly abstruse synthesizing cosmology apparently resolved Yeats's self-division. The individual could attain wholeness by coming to rest at the point where the two gyres intersected, where all opposing tendencies were perfectly balanced. Yeats had at last achieved "Unity of Being." For years he had worn the mask of a moody poet, but now, like the Happy Hypocrite, he had grown into his mask and become one with his antiself. The world around him was coming apart, Irishmen and Europeans were killing one another on a monstrous scale; but Yeats was sure that the artist could find psychic harmony simply by retiring behind his mask, "to hide from itself and others this separation and disorder."[37]

In the early 1890s G. K. Chesterton had been locked in his own struggle with his second self. He was profoundly troubled by the Decadent philosophy fashionable among his fellow students at the Slade, and he came close to insanity when he began to perceive a depraved side emerging in his own personality. "I have never indeed felt the faintest temptation to the peculiar madness of Wilde," he later recalled, "but I could at this time imagine the worst and wildest disproportions and distortions of more normal passion." To be explicit, Chesterton's Mr. Hyde was a sadist: his notebooks of those years are filled with sketches of horrifying violence and torture. The example of Robert Louis Stevenson, who as a student in Paris had also grappled with decadence, aided Chesterton in exorcising his other self and regaining his psychic balance.[38] He later paid homage to Stevenson in his dedication to *The Man Who Was Thursday* (1908), which can be read as an inversion of *Dr. Jekyll and Mr. Hyde.* Chesterton's tale is a fable of masks—not angelic masks that hide an evil self, but evil masks that hide the radical goodness of the "ordinary healthy person." It is the story of an undercover agent for Scotland Yard's "philosophical police" who infiltrates a demonic anarchist conspiracy only to discover that all but one of the conspirators are fellow infiltrators. (The exception conceals himself behind the cleverest mask of all: he poses as a parlor anarchist, spouting "the old cant of the lawlessness of art and the art of lawlessness" at suburban teas, and no one suspects him of being a real anarchist.)[39]

Beerbohm, Yeats, Chesterton, Bernard Shaw, James Joyce, Augustus John—each of them assumed a colorful mask for presentation to the general public. At the same time they were all able to avoid or overcome the personality split that afflicted so many Victorian writers. The new century, as Masao Miyoshi notes, took a "more relaxed attitude towards the art of the lie."[40] Bernard Shaw fully recognized that Bernard Shaw was "one of the most successful of my fictions,"[41] but this was a matter for easy joking, not something over which to agonize. His mask was a perfect, seamless, thoroughly comfortable fit.

Who Is the Third Who Walks Always beside You?

After 1918 the Doctrine of the Mask would be revived, in all its Decadent glory, by the Children of the Sun, who reveled in gorgeous costumes and flamboyant role playing. The war, which had wreaked havoc with all the other reconciling movements in Edwardian thought, had had the same effect on the quest for psychological unity. Paul Fussell describes the resurgence of the schizoid theme in English literature after 1914. In order to live with the indescribable horrors of the war, soldiers often had to insulate themselves psychologically from their surroundings. They were, so to speak, "beside themselves," split into two personalities, one looking on dispassionately while the other fought the Germans. The regimental rituals, patriotic niceties, and class roles that the troops acted out only reinforced the sense that they were players on a stage watching themselves perform in a "Theatre of War."[42]

Civilians also took refuge from the war and the postwar world in the "dissociation of sensibility." T. S. Eliot coined the term in 1921, and it quickly became a catchphrase among critics. Eliot, Huxley, Waugh,

Virginia Woolf, and war veterans like Robert Graves wrote as strangely distant observers, as if they could only bear to watch modern life by treating it as a play in which they were at once actors and audience. "Who is the third who walks always beside you?" Eliot asked in *The Waste Land* (lines 360–66):

> When I count, there are only you and I together
> But when I look up ahead up the white road
> There is always another one walking beside you
> Gliding wrapt in a brown mantle, hooded
> I do not know whether a man or a woman
> —But who is that on the other side of you?

And Aldous Huxley would open *Point Counter Point* with a quotation from Fulke Greville.

> Oh, wearisome, condition of humanity,
> Born under one law, to another bound,
> Vainly begot and yet forbidden vanity,
> Created sick, commanded to be sound.
> What meaneth nature by these diverse laws,
> Passion and reason, self-division's cause?

Before we lament self-division in the modern consciousness, we should remember the faults of the well-integrated personality. The undivided Edwardians achieved inner wholeness by affirming unity everywhere; but in so doing, they sacrificed philosophical integrity. They resolved psychic conflict by believing in everything, however slack that sort of thinking might be. Samuel Butler, who taught the Edwardians so much about the subconscious, assured his readers that they should never feel divided between rival convictions because all ideas are one. "Life is like a fugue," a continual reworking of the same theme. It is impossible "to say where one idea ends and another begins, . . . there being an unity in spite of infinite multitude, and an infinite multitude in spite of unity." Life is an ongoing "process of fusion and accommodation," constantly adjusting the individual to his environment. That rule also applies to intellectual life: adjust, absorb, compromise, never be dogmatic or inflexible. Butler realized that this synthesizing impulse, carried to its final conclusion, would dissolve all intellectual distinctions whatsoever into metaphysical slush. But he was not single-minded about anything, not even reconciliation, and he avoided this difficulty by reconciling unity and diversity, nonchalantly suggesting that we believe in one when it suits us and the other when it doesn't. "This is illogical," he admitted, "but extremes alone are logical, and they are always absurd, the mean alone is practicable and it is always illogical."[43]

Winston Churchill was just as eager to cast aside logic and believe in opposites. He had followed a typically Edwardian path of spiritual development. Until 1896 he regularly attended church and "dutifully accepted everything I had been told" about religion; then he began reading Darwin, Schopenhauer, Gibbon, and Lecky. At this time he was a cavalry officer stationed in India, where "the deities of a hundred creeds were placed by respectful routine in the Imperial Pantheon." His fellow officers believed in a Kiplingesque ecumenicism: they approved of any Eastern or Western faith that had "a disciplinary value, . . . made people want to be respectable, to keep up appearances, and so saved lots of scandals. From this standpoint ceremonies and rituals ceased to be of importance. They were merely the same idea translated into different languages to suit different races and temperaments." Churchill himself briefly "passed through a violent and aggressive anti-religious phase," but he soon realized that,

> whatever I might think and argue, I did not hesitate to ask for special protection when about to come under the fire of the enemy: nor to feel sincerely grateful when I got safely home to tea. . . . This practice seemed perfectly natural, and just as strong and real as the reasoning process which contradicted it so sharply. Moreover the practice was comforting and the reasoning led nowhere. I therefore acted in accordance with my feelings without troubling to square such conduct with the conclusions of thought.
>   . . . It seemed to me that it would be very foolish to discard the reasons of the heart for those of the head. Indeed I could not see why I should not enjoy them both. I did not worry about the inconsistency of thinking one way and believing the other. . . . I could not feel that the Supreme Creator who gave us our minds as well as our souls would be offended if they did not always run smoothly together in double harness.
>   . . . The idea that nothing is true except what we comprehend is silly, and that ideas which our minds cannot reconcile are mutually destructive, sillier still. . . . I therefore adopted quite early in life a system of believing whatever I wanted to believe.[44]

That was the soft center of the undivided Edwardians. They were like Lambert Strether, who, liberated from Massachusetts puritanism, suddenly felt "free to believe in anything that from hour to hour kept him going" (*Ambass.* 22:173). Some Edwardians were even willing to believe in contradictions in order to fit together a comfortable secular faith. Like John Galsworthy, they tried "to worship Mystery with one lobe of the brain, and with the other to explain it."[45]

In that light, the postwar return of the Divided Self looks like a healthy development. It was a sign of intellectual honesty, the inevitable result of facing up to hard philosophical choices. The Victorians are often called complacent, but many of them squarely confronted the conflict between science and religion. Some of them ultimately wrenched away from their sustaining beliefs, though they tore themselves apart in the process. They had more courage than those Edwardians who purchased inner peace by glossing over difficult questions and only connecting everywhere. In that respect, Carlyle, Mill, Sidgwick, and Tennyson were made of sterner stuff than Bernard Shaw, who once bragged that he "never gave up an old belief without feeling inclined to give three cheers and jump into the air."[46] The Undivided Self was the product of what Arthur Lovejoy called "*esprits simplistes*—minds which habitually tend to assume that simple solutions can be found for the problems they deal with."[47] That mentality was all too common in Edwardian Britain, and it never recovered from the shock of the Great War. Since then, like E. M. Forster's George Emerson, we have had to live with the uncomfortable fact that "things won't fit."

Appendix

Census of Books Published in Britain 1870–1924

The *Publishers' Circular*, a trade journal, compiled an annual census of book titles published in Britain, breaking down the returns by subject matter. This table lists the results in terms of both absolute numbers and, immediately below that, in italics, a percentage of the total for each category. Some subject areas have been omitted, so the categories reported here add up to less than 100 percent. The totals at the bottom of the table represent all titles published in a given year. These figures do not include ephemera, leaflets, local government publications, musical scores or texts, or books imported from America; they do include pamphlets, books about music, and important government publications of some interest to the general public. The compilers may have missed a few books published privately or by very obscure presses, but otherwise the returns appear to be reasonably complete.

The following notes apply throughout the run of tables.

a The majority were reprints rather than new books.

b In these years the *Publishers' Circular* had difficulty distinguishing between juvenile and adult books, so these figures may not be reliable.

c Increase here was mainly among art books.

d This decline was due entirely to a reduction of reprints; the number of new novels and children's books remained constant.

e Includes many books on or relevant to the Boer War.

f Includes many books and pamphlets on Joseph Chamberlain's tariff proposals.

	1870	1871	1872	1873	1874	1875	1876
Theology	754	726	752	756	649	757	693
	16.2	*15.0*	*16.6*	*15.9*	*15.1*	*15.4*	*14.2*
Philological,	548	645	429	407	359	335	470
Educational,	*11.8*	*13.3*	*9.5*	*8.6*	*8.3*	*6.8*	*9.6*
& Classical							
Juvenile	657	694	229	255	229	217	419
	14.1	*14.4*	*5.1*	*5.4*	*5.3*	*4.4*	*8.6*
Fiction	362	315	708	803	798	974	857
	7.8	*6.5*	*15.7*	*16.9*	*18.5*	*19.9*	*17.6*
Law	103	119	101	119	94	114	164
	2.2	*2.5*	*2.2*	*2.5*	*2.2*	*2.3*	*3.4*
Political &	103	146	172	142	120	101	337
Social Economy,	*2.2*	*3.0*	*3.8*	*3.0*	*2.8*	*2.1*	*6.9*
Trade, Commerce							
Arts, Science,	288	283	487	559	546	622	252
Illustrated	*6.2*	*5.9*	*10.8*	*11.8*	*12.7*	*12.7*	*5.2*
Works							
History &	341	286	318	407	247	391	347
Biography	*7.3*	*5.9*	*7.0*	*8.6*	*5.7*	*8.0*	*7.1*
Poetry &	346	309	371	313	275	348	323
Drama	*7.4*	*6.4*	*8.2*	*6.6*	*6.4*	*7.1*	*6.6*
Belles Lettres,	226	264	185	183	198	177	176
Essays, &	*4.9*	*5.5*	*4.1*	*3.9*	*4.6*	*3.6*	*3.6*
Monographs							
Medicine	155	165	137	155	119	115	181
	3.3	*3.4*	*3.0*	*3.3*	*2.8*	*2.3*	*3.7*
Total	4,656	4,835	4,519	4,749	4,312	4,904	4,888

	1877	*1878*	*1879*	*1880*	*1881*	*1882*	*1883*
Theology	737	739	1086	975	945	789	912
	14.5	*13.9*	*18.6*	*17.1*	*17.5*	*15.4*	*14.8*
Philological, Educational, & Classical	529	586	828	675	682	525	691
	10.4	*11.0*	*14.2*	*11.8*	*12.6*	*10.2*	*11.2*
Juvenile	522	448	214	719	500	987	939
	10.2	*8.4*	*3.7*	*12.6*	*9.2*	*19.3*	*15.3*
Fiction	854	879	1013	580	674	420	578
	16.8	*16.5*	*17.4*	*10.2*	*12.5*	*8.2*	*9.4*
Law	118	129	157	145	133	75	223
	2.3	*2.4*	*2.7*	*2.5*	*2.5*	*1.5*	*3.6*
Political & Social Economy, Trade, Commerce	189	181	121	226	162	189	225
	3.7	*3.4*	*2.1*	*4.0*	*3.0*	*3.7*	*3.7*
Arts, Science, Illustrated Works	189	147	353	479	452	344	491
	3.7	*2.8*	*6.1*	*8.4*	*8.4*	*6.7*	*8.0*
History & Biography	373	430	403	363	437	452	536
	7.3	*8.1*	*6.9*	*6.4*	*8.1*	*8.8*	*8.7*
Poetry & Drama	358	356	191	187	148	181	159
	7.0	*6.7*	*3.3*	*3.3*	*2.7*	*3.5*	*2.6*
Belles Lettres, Essays, & Monographs	364	531	179	166[a]	247	106	304
	7.1	*10.0*	*3.1*	*2.9*	*4.6*	*2.1*	*4.9*
Medicine	215	233	189	202	164	177	253
	4.2	*4.4*	*3.2*	*3.5*	*3.0*	*3.5*	*4.1*
Total	5,095	5,314	5,834	5,708	5,406	5,124	6,145

	1884	*1885*	*1886*	*1887*	*1888*	*1889*	*1890*
Theology	929	847	752	815	912	764	708
	14.6	*15.0*	*14.4*	*14.3*	*13.8*	*12.6*	*12.3*
Philological,	683	652	572	684	779	681	703
Educational,	*10.7*	*11.6*	*11.0*	*12.0*	*11.8*	*11.2*	*12.3*
& Classical							
Juvenile	757	813	445	539	460[b]	511	538
	11.9	*14.4*	*8.5*	*9.5*	*7.0*	*8.4*	*9.4*
Fiction	697	695	969	1050	1314[b]	1404	1204
	10.9	*12.3*	*18.6*	*18.5*	*19.9*	*23.1*	*21.0*
Law	279	129	33	122	172	106	79
	4.4	*2.3*	*0.6*	*2.1*	*2.6*	*1.7*	*1.4*
Political &	239	253	246	138	135	126	109
Social Economy,	*3.8*	*4.5*	*4.7*	*2.4*	*2.0*	*2.1*	*1.9*
Trade, Commerce							
Arts, Science,	591	373	178	178	253	146	73
Illustrated	*9.3*	*6.6*	*3.4*	*3.1*	*3.8*	*2.4*	*1.3*
Works							
History &	623	481	350	465	486	424	391
Biography	*9.8*	*8.5*	*6.7*	*8.2*	*7.4*	*7.0*	*6.8*
Poetry &	228	164	93	126	231	187	188
Drama	*3.6*	*2.9*	*1.8*	*2.2*	*3.5*	*3.1*	*3.3*
Belles Lettres,	239	220	479[a]	375[a]	389[a]	340[a]	362[a]
Essays, &	*3.8*	*3.9*	*9.2*	*6.6*	*5.9*	*5.6*	*6.3*
Monographs							
Medicine	215	187	171	210	199	182	193
	3.4	*3.3*	*3.3*	*3.7*	*3.0*	*3.0*	*3.4*
Total	6,373	5,640	5,210	5,686	6,591	6,067	5,735

	1891	*1892*	*1893*	*1894*		*1895*	*1896*
Theology	627	673	533	556		570	603
	11.0	10.8	8.4	8.6		8.7	9.2
Philological, Educational, & Classical	694	694	622	742		771	643
	12.2	11.1	9.7	11.4		11.8	9.8
Juvenile	447[b]	345[b]	695[b]	298[b]			
	7.8	5.5	9.7	4.6			
						1891	2179
						29.0	33.2
Fiction	1216[b]	1537[b]	1328[b]	1652[b]			
	21.3	24.6	20.8	25.5			
Law	109	65	50	149		90	182
	1.9	1.0	0.8	2.3		1.4	2.8
Political & Social Economy, Trade, Commerce	136	175	85	162		186	346
	2.4	2.8	1.3	2.5		2.9	5.3
Arts, Science, Illustrated Works	116	209	123	128		112	380[c]
	2.0	3.3	1.9	2.0		1.9	5.8
History & Biography	413	368	334	314		421	717
	7.2	5.9	5.2	4.8		6.5	10.9
Poetry & Drama	201	227	234	181		247	407
	3.5	3.6	3.7	2.8		3.8	6.2
Belles Lettres, Essays, & Monographs	254	139	107	485		442	153
	4.5	2.2	1.7	7.5		6.8	2.3
Medicine	175	177	151	156		206	162
	3.1	2.8	2.4	2.4		3.2	2.5
Total	5,706	6,254	6,382	6,485		6,516	6,573

	1897	1898	1899	1900	1901	1902	1903
Theology	703	688	693	708	519	648	702
	8.9	*9.2*	*9.2*	*9.9*	*8.6*	*8.8*	*8.4*
Philological,	928	921	990	732	618	572	748
Educational,	*11.7*	*12.3*	*13.1*	*10.2*	*10.2*	*7.7*	*8.9*
& Classical							
Fiction &	2677	2402	2561	2109	1992[d]	2470	2650
Juvenile	*33.8*	*32.0*	*33.8*	*29.5*	*33.0*	*33.5*	*31.6*
Law	140	163	160	147	146	134	87
	1.8	*2.2*	*2.1*	*2.1*	*2.4*	*1.8*	*1.0*
Political &	641	534	464	487	455	593[e]	609
Social Economy,	*8.1*	*7.1*	*6.1*	*6.8*	*7.5*	*8.0*	*7.3*
Trade, Commerce							
Arts, Science,	318	295	339	448[e]	338	464	445
Illustrated	*4.0*	*3.9*	*4.5*	*6.3*	*5.6*	*6.3*	*5.3*
Works							
History &	745	743	654	716[e]	531[e]	537	573
Biography	*9.4*	*9.9*	*8.6*	*10.0*	*8.8*	*7.3*	*6.8*
Poetry &	427	371	394	370	262	348	391
Drama	*5.4*	*4.9*	*5.2*	*5.2*	*4.3*	*4.7*	*4.7*
Belles Lettres,	275	218	320	330	325	271	315
Essays, &	*3.5*	*2.9*	*4.2*	*4.6*	*5.4*	*3.7*	*3.8*
Monographs							
Medicine	211	196	228	266[e]	237	237	282
	2.7	*2.6*	*3.0*	*3.7*	*3.9*	*3.2*	*3.4*
Total	7,926	7,516	7,567	7,149	6,044	7,381	8,381

	1904	1905	1906	1907	1908	1909	1910
Theology	666	745	737	950	922	1022	1064
	8.0	*9.0*	*8.6*	*9.6*	*9.4*	*9.5*	*9.8*
Philological,	836	734	916	697	637	629	659
Educational,	*10.0*	*8.9*	*10.6*	*7.0*	*6.5*	*5.9*	*6.1*
& Classical							
Fiction &	2548	2360	2883	2782	2787	2881	2833
Juvenile	*30.6*	*28.6*	*33.5*	*28.1*	*28.4*	*26.9*	*26.2*
Law	103	107	98	243	260	243	248
	1.2	*1.3*	*1.1*	*2.5*	*2.6*	*2.3*	*2.3*
Political &	775[f]	637	760	763	671	752	816
Social Economy,	*9.3*	*7.7*	*8.8*	*7.7*	*6.8*	*7.0*	*7.6*
Trade, Commerce							
Arts, Science,	532	581	499	1109	1164	1201	1254
Illustrated	*6.4*	*7.0*	*5.8*	*11.2*	*11.9*	*11.2*	*11.6*
Works							
History &	653	636	641	873	860	913	860
Biography	*7.8*	*7.7*	*7.5*	*8.8*	*8.8*	*8.5*	*8.0*
Poetry &	407	473	458	527	569	475	590
Drama	*4.9*	*5.7*	*5.3*	*5.3*	*5.8*	*4.4*	*5.5*
Belles Lettres,	220	381	307	336	257	304	272
Essays, &	*2.6*	*4.6*	*3.6*	*3.4*	*2.6*	*2.8*	*2.5*
Monographs							
Medicine	219	251	279	342	310	347	398
	2.6	*3.0*	*3.2*	*3.4*	*3.2*	*3.2*	*3.7*
Total	8,334	8,252	8,603	9,914	9,821	10,725	10,804

NOTE: Through 1906 books on philosophy were classified under "Philological, Educational, and Classical"; beginning in 1907 they were included under "Theology."

	1911	*1912*	*1913*	*1914*	*1915*	*1916*	*1917*
Philosophy	273	332	280	179	237	249	201
	2.5	*2.8*	*2.3*	*1.6*	*2.2*	*2.7*	*2.5*
Religion	930	798	889	969	896	785	759
	8.5	*6.6*	*7.2*	*8.4*	*8.4*	*8.6*	*9.3*
Sociology	725	705	921	699	694	575	550
	6.6	*5.8*	*7.4*	*6.1*	*6.5*	*6.3*	*6.8*
Law	303	304	319	279	258	172	146
	2.8	*2.5*	*2.6*	*2.4*	*2.4*	*1.9*	*1.8*
Education	250	311	307	315	293	211	211
	2.3	*2.6*	*2.5*	*2.7*	*2.7*	*2.3*	*2.6*
Philology	187	206	197	185	216	148	151
	1.7	*1.7*	*1.6*	*1.6*	*2.0*	*1.6*	*1.9*
Science	650	827	732	840	698	374	346
	6.0	*6.9*	*5.9*	*7.3*	*6.5*	*4.1*	*4.3*
Technology	525	586	699	687	520	275	268
	4.8	*4.9*	*5.6*	*6.0*	*4.9*	*3.0*	*3.3*
Medicine &	413	440	478	454	356	293	300
Public Health	*3.8*	*3.6*	*3.9*	*3.9*	*3.3*	*3.2*	*3.7*
Business	151	198	230	155	186	199	217
	1.4	*1.6*	*1.9*	*1.3*	*1.7*	*2.2*	*2.7*
Fine Arts	232	261	254	204	225	200	125
	2.1	*2.2*	*2.1*	*1.8*	*2.1*	*2.2*	*1.5*
Music	52	83	73	55	45	54	46
	0.5	*0.7*	*0.6*	*0.5*	*0.4*	*0.6*	*0.6*
Games &	122	152	174	149	75	55	47
Sports	*1.1*	*1.3*	*1.4*	*1.3*	*0.7*	*0.6*	*0.6*
Literature	345	505	448	480	378	319	216
	3.2	*4.2*	*3.6*	*4.2*	*3.5*	*3.5*	*2.7*
Poetry &	668	721	697	642	567	551	544
Drama	*6.1*	*6.0*	*5.6*	*5.6*	*5.3*	*6.0*	*6.7*
Fiction	2215	2464	2504	2112	1693	1830	1537
	20.3	*20.4*	*20.2*	*18.3*	*15.9*	*20.0*	*18.9*
Juvenile	648	805	668	631	582	559	539
	5.9	*6.7*	*5.4*	*5.5*	*5.5*	*6.1*	*6.6*

(*continued*)	1911	1912	1913	1914	1915	1916	1917
Biography	476	554	543	442	394	285	230
	4.4	*4.6*	*4.4*	*3.8*	*3.7*	*3.1*	*2.8*
History	429	491	523	454	763	539	686
	3.9	*4.1*	*4.2*	*3.9*	*7.2*	*5.9*	*8.4*
Military	—	—	—	402	467	495	313
& Naval	—	—	—	*3.5*	*4.4*	*5.4*	*3.8*
Total	10,914	12,067	12,379	11,537	10,665	9,149	8,131

	1918	1919	1920	1921	1922	1923	1924
Philosophy	206	229	279	274	292	319	317
	2.7	*2.7*	*2.5*	*2.5*	*2.7*	*2.6*	*2.5*
Religion	783	766	679	775	743	869	956
	10.1	*8.9*	*6.3*	*7.0*	*6.9*	*7.1*	*7.5*
Sociology	662	824	870	823	836	864	920
	8.6	*9.6*	*7.9*	*7.5*	*7.7*	*7.0*	*7.2*
Law	130	261	363	274	264	231	230
	1.7	*3.0*	*3.3*	*2.5*	*2.4*	*1.9*	*1.8*
Education	187	259	253	261	207	244	223
	2.4	*3.0*	*2.3*	*2.4*	*1.9*	*2.0*	*1.8*
Philology	142	182	205	148	189	223	203
	1.8	*2.1*	*1.9*	*1.3*	*1.7*	*1.8*	*1.6*
Science	329	434	597	600	597	678	585
	4.3	*5.0*	*5.4*	*5.4*	*5.5*	*5.5*	*4.6*
Technology	378	686	720	743	686	689	586
	4.9	*8.0*	*6.5*	*6.7*	*6.3*	*5.6*	*4.6*
Medicine &	380	367	446	436	360	433	388
Public Health	*4.9*	*4.3*	*4.1*	*4.0*	*3.3*	*3.5*	*3.1*
Business	179	139	138	182	157	130	134
	2.3	*1.6*	*1.3*	*1.7*	*1.4*	*1.1*	*1.1*
Fine Arts	138	127	184	267	248	294	325
	1.8	*1.5*	*1.7*	*2.4*	*2.3*	*2.4*	*2.6*

(*continued*)	*1918*	*1919*	*1920*	*1921*	*1922*	*1923*	*1924*
Music	27	29	65	73	95	114	131
	0.3	*0.3*	*0.6*	*0.7*	*0.9*	*0.9*	*1.0*
Games &	41	96	161	148	222	165	220
Sports	*0.5*	*1.1*	*1.5*	*1.3*	*2.0*	*1.3*	*1.7*
Literature	250	281	366	403	411	496	525
	3.2	*3.3*	*3.3*	*3.7*	*3.8*	*4.0*	*4.1*
Poetry &	642	495	563	617	702	746	810
Drama	*8.3*	*5.7*	*5.1*	*5.6*	*6.5*	*6.1*	*6.4*
Fiction	1014	1217	2104	1926	1931	2487	2801
	13.1	*14.1*	*19.1*	*17.5*	*17.8*	*20.3*	*22.0*
Juvenile	384	564	770	757	776	1048	1016
	5.0	*6.5*	*7.0*	*6.9*	*7.2*	*8.5*	*8.0*
Biography	221	295	374	397	398	466	577
	2.9	*3.4*	*3.4*	*3.6*	*3.7*	*3.8*	*4.5*
History	629	422	525	478	372	515	468
	8.2	*4.9*	*4.8*	*4.3*	*3.4*	*4.2*	*3.7*
Military	341	216	269	307	210	206	188
& Naval	*4.4*	*2.5*	*2.4*	*2.8*	*1.9*	*1.7*	*1.5*
Total	7,716	8,622	11,004	11,026	10,842	12,274	12,706

Notes

Introduction

1. Samuel Hynes, *The Edwardian Turn of Mind* (Princeton: Princeton Univ. Press, 1968), chap. 1, pp. vii–viii, 345–59.

2. Walter E. Houghton, *The Victorian Frame of Mind 1830–1870* (New Haven: Yale Univ. Press, 1973), xiii.

3. Arthur O. Lovejoy, *The Great Chain of Being* (New York: Harper and Row, 1960), 7–14.

Chapter 1

1. For a census of British book publishing, see appendix.

2. W. J. Reader, *Professional Men* (New York: Basic, 1966), 208.

3. K. S. Inglis, *Churches and the Working Classes in Victorian England* (London: Routledge and Kegan Paul, 1963), 37. Melvin Richter, *The Politics of Conscience: T. H. Green and His Age* (Cambridge: Harvard Univ. Press, 1964), 69.

4. Samuel Hynes, *The Edwardian Turn of Mind* (Princeton: Princeton Univ. Press, 1968), chap. 2.

5. "The Function of Criticism at the Present Time," in *The Complete Prose Works of Matthew Arnold*, ed. R. H. Super (Ann Arbor: Univ. of Michigan Press, 1960–1974), 3:260–70.

6. E. M. Forster, *Howards End* (New York: Vintage, 1954), 195.

7. John Galsworthy, *The Inn of Tranquillity* (New York: Scribner's, 1913), 260–62.

8. See, for example, Hynes, *Edwardian Turn of Mind*, chap. 5, and Alan Gauld, *The Founders of Psychical Research* (London: Routledge and Kegan Paul, 1968).

9. Leon Edel, *Henry James* (New York: Avon, 1978), 4:89. Joseph Conrad, "The Life Beyond," in *Notes on Life and Letters* (Garden City: Doubleday, 1924).

10. Membership lists were published regularly in the *Proceedings* and *Journal* of the SPR. Gauld, *Psychical Research*, 316.

11. Bernard Shaw diary, 29 Oct. 1885, 6–7 Mar. 1886, 3 May 1886, British Library of Political and Economic Science. *The Diary of Beatrice Webb*, 16 Sept. to 15 Nov. 1877 (Teaneck, N.J.: Somerset House, 1978, microfiche). Doris Langley Moore, *E. Nesbit*, rev. ed. (Philadelphia: Chilton, 1966), 160–61.

12. "Sonnet," in *The Poetical Works of Rupert Brooke*, ed. Geoffrey Keynes, 2d ed. (London: Faber and Faber, 1970), 40.

13. A. J. Balfour, *A Defence of Philosophic Doubt* (London: Macmillan, 1879), v, and *The Foundations of Belief* (New York: Longmans, Green, 1895), pt. 4.

14. Kenneth Young, *Arthur James Balfour* (London: G. Bell, 1963), 160–62.

15. *Proceedings of the Society for Psychical Research* 2 (1884): 191; 10 (1894): 2–8; 14 (1898): 3.

16. W. P. Jolly, *Sir Oliver Lodge* (London: Constable, 1974), 39, 59–60, 87–88, 97, 110–11.

17. Heaviside to Lodge, 1 Jan. 1895, 28 July, 26 Aug. 1896, Oliver Lodge Papers, University College London Library, MS. Add. 89/50.

18. Oliver Lodge, "Professor Heinrich Hertz," *Journal of the Society for Psychical Research* 6 (Feb. 1894): 198. A. J. Balfour, "Address by the President," *Proceedings of the Society for Psychical Research* 10 (1894): 2–3.

19. A. J. Penty, *The Restoration of the Gild System* (London: Swan Sonnenschein, 1906), 84–86.

20. Edward Carpenter, *The Drama of Love and Death* (New York: Mitchell Kennerley, 1912), 113.

21. Sir Edmund Whittaker, *A History of the Theories of Aether and Electricity* (London: Thomas Nelson, 1951–1953), vol. 1.

22. Sir Oliver Lodge, *Continuity* (London: J. M. Dent, 1913), 22–42, 92–93, 102–6, 116.

23. Thomas S. Kuhn, *The Structure of Scientific Revolutions*, 2d ed. (Chicago: Univ. of Chicago Press, 1970), 155–56.

24. Lodge to "Theodora," 2 Dec. 1916, Oliver Lodge Papers, Society for Psychical Research, London, 1105.

25. L. P. Jacks and G. Dawes Hicks, editorial, *Hibbert Journal* 1 (Oct. 1902): 1–4.

26. Jacks to Lodge, 7 July 1904, Lodge Papers, Society for Psychical Research, 795.

27. Jacks to Lodge, 13 Sept. 1901, 12 June 1904, 2 Dec. 1908, ibid., 786, 794, 840.

28. E. M. Forster, *Goldsworthy Lowes Dickinson* (London: Edward Arnold, 1962), 74, 111, 119–20.

29. Sir Arthur Conan Doyle, *The Complete Sherlock Holmes* (Garden City: Doubleday, 1930), 23, 109, 317. Ronald Pearsall, *Conan Doyle: A Biographical Solution* (New York: St. Martin's, 1977), 34, 58.

30. Doyle, *Holmes*, 681, 684, 713–14, 958–60, 1034.

31. Ibid., 455, 901.

32. Doyle to Lodge, 12 Sept. 1913, Lodge Papers, Society for Psychical Research, 402.

33. G. K. Chesterton, "The Honour of Israel Gow" and "The Insoluble Problem," in *Father Brown: Selected Stories* (London: Oxford Univ. Press, 1971).

34. G. K. Nelson, *Spiritualism and Society* (London: Routledge and Kegan Paul, 1969), chaps. 6–7.

35. Richard Ellmann, *Yeats: The Man and the Masks* (New York: W. W. Norton, 1978), pp. 25–26, 42–44, 196–205, chaps. 5, 7.

36. Quoted in ibid., 241.

37. Ibid., 19–20, 42–44, 119–26.

38. Richard Ellmann, "Two Faces of Edward," in *Edwardians and Late Victorians* (New York: Columbia Univ. Press, 1960), 191–98.

39. D. H. Lawrence, *Sons and Lovers* (Harmondsworth: Penguin, 1980), 227.

40. James Joyce, *A Portrait of the Artist as a Young Man* (New York: Viking, 1970), 221.

41. Ibid., 189, 240, 244.

42. Joyce to Harriet Shaw Weaver, 27 Jan. 1925, *Letters of James Joyce*, ed. Stuart Gilbert, new ed. (New York: Viking, 1966), 1:226.

43. James Joyce, *Ulysses* (New York: Modern Library, 1961), 17.

44. Oliver St. John Gogarty, *Many Lines to Thee*, ed. James F. Carens (Dublin: Dolmen, 1971), 94–95.

45. Richard Ellmann, *James Joyce*, rev. ed. (New York: Oxford Univ. Press, 1982), 416–17, 435–36. Joyce to Carlo Linati, 21 Sept. 1920, Joyce to Harriet Shaw Weaver, 24 June 1921, *Letters*, 1:146–47, 167.

46. John Gross, *James Joyce* (New York: Viking, 1970), 66, 69–70.

47. Joyce, *Portrait*, 217–18.

48. James Joyce, *Stephen Hero* (New York: New Directions, 1955), 210–13.

49. G. K. Chesterton, preface, "What I Found in My Pocket," and "The Prehistoric Railway Station," in *Tremendous Trifles* (Philadelphia: Dufour, 1968).

50. Virginia Woolf, "A Sketch of the Past," in *Moments of Being and Other Autobiographical Writings* (New York: Harcourt Brace Jovanovich, 1976), 71–73.

51. Virginia Woolf, *Night and Day* (New York: Harcourt Brace Jovanovich, 1967), 506, and *The Voyage Out* (New York: Harcourt Brace Jovanovich, 1976), 292–93, 314.

52. In Richard Mudie-Smith, ed., *The Religious Life of London* (London: Hodder and Stoughton, 1904), 19–22, 39–42.

53. "The Church and the World," *Hibbert Journal* 5 (Oct. 1906): 2.

54. William Charles Braithwaite, in Mudie-Smith, *Religious Life*, 332–33.

55. T. H. Green, *Prolegomena to Ethics*, 5th ed. (Oxford: Clarendon, 1907), 13–62.

56. Richter, *Politics of Conscience*, chap. 1, pp. 90–91, 118–21, 163–81, 292–98.

57. Green to Sidgwick, 28 Dec. 18??, Henry Sidgwick Papers, Trinity College Library, Cambridge University, box 94, 18.

58. James Ward, *The Realm of Ends* (Cambridge: Cambridge Univ. Press, 1911), 434–35.

59. Bernard Bosanquet, *The Philosophical Theory of the State*, 4th ed. (London: Macmillan, 1965), 167–68.

60. Richter, *Politics of Conscience*, chap. 9.

61. Henry Pelling, *The Origins of the Labour Party*, 2d ed. (Oxford: Clarendon, 1974), 128.

62. Charles Gore, *The Solidarity of the Faith* (London: Longmans, Green, 1914), 8.

63. James Carpenter, *Gore: A Study in Liberal Catholic Thought* (London: Faith, 1960), chap. 6. G. L. Prestige, *The Life of Charles Gore* (London: Heinemann, 1935), 272.

64. Carpenter, *Gore*, 35.

65. Charles Gore, *The Body of Christ*, 4th ed. (London: John Murray, 1920), 7, 47.

66. Penty, *Gild System*, 45–51.

67. C. R. Ashbee, "Memoirs," 1938, Victoria and Albert Museum Library, 1:48–49, 102, and *Craftsmanship in Competitive Industry* (London: Essex House, 1908), 122.

68. Norman MacKenzie and Jeanne MacKenzie, *The Fabians* (New York: Simon and Schuster, 1977), chap. 12. Warren Sylvester Smith, *The London Heretics 1870–1914* (New York: Dodd, Mead, 1968), 176–78, 207–23. Peter d'A. Jones, *The Christian Socialist Revival 1877–1914* (Princeton: Princeton Univ. Press, 1968), 450.

69. Pelling, *Origins of the Labour Party*, 137.

70. MacKenzie and MacKenzie, *Fabians*, 60–62.

71. Smith, *London Heretics*, 118–26.

72. MacKenzie and MacKenzie, *Fabians*, 21–27, 179–83.

73. Sydney Olivier, *Letters and Selected Writings*, ed. Margaret Olivier (London: George Allen and Unwin, 1948), 63.

74. Ibid., 144–45.

75. "On Going to Church," in *Selected Non-Dramatic Writings of Bernard Shaw*, ed. Dan H. Laurence (Boston: Houghton Mifflin, 1965), 389–90.

76. Bernard Shaw, *Man and Superman*, vol. 2 of *Complete Plays with Their Prefaces* (New York, 1975), 658.

77. Bernard Shaw, *John Bull's Other Island*, in ibid., 1021.

78. MacKenzie and MacKenzie, *Fabians*, 122–25.

79. "Church and the World," 3.

80. Beatrice Webb to H. G. Wells, Sept. 1904, and to Bertrand Russell, 16 Oct. 1904, *The Letters of Sidney and Beatrice Webb*, ed. Norman MacKenzie (Cambridge: Cambridge Univ. Press, 1978), 2:208–9.

81. Charles Booth, *Life and Labour of the People in London* (1902–1904; reprint, New York: AMS, 1970), 3d ser., 7:432.

82. T. S. Simey and M. B. Simey, *Charles Booth* (London: Oxford Univ. Press, 1960), 41–42, 45–49, 60.

83. Charles Booth, "Positivism," Jan. 1870, Charles and Mary Booth Papers, University of London Library, MS. 797, II/24, 6.

84. Charles Booth, "Positivism," 5 Aug. 1883, ibid., II/26/15/xi–xiv.

85. Booth, *Life and Labour*, 3d ser., 3:52.

86. Simey and Simey, *Booth*, 64–67, 77–79, 100. Philip Abrams, *The Origins of British Sociology 1834–1914* (Chicago: Univ. of Chicago Press, 1968), chaps. 3, 4, 7.

87. Booth to Beatrice Potter, 31 July 1886, Booth Papers, I, 1308.

88. Booth, *Life and Labour*, 3d ser., 7:38, 422–23, 429–32.

89. Ibid., 5:29, 7:424. Mudie-Smith, *Religious Life*, 28–29.

90. In Mudie-Smith, *Religious Life*, 193–94.

91. Gauld, *Psychical Research*, 74–77. Nelson, *Spiritualism*, pp. 140–42, chap. 15.

92. Booth, *Life and Labour*, 3d ser., 7:37, 424–25.

93. Jones, *Christian Socialist Revival*, 419, 444.

94. Werner Picht, *Toynbee Hall and the English Settlement Movement*, trans. Lilian A. Cowell, rev. ed. (London: G. Bell, 1914), 109–12.

95. Philip Snowden, *The Christ That Is to Be* (London: Independent Labour Party, 1905).

96. Jones, *Christian Socialist Revival*, 396–97, 401. Pelling, *Origins of the Labour Party*, chap. 7.

97. Richard Hoggart, *The Uses of Literacy* (New York: Oxford Univ. Press, 1970), 93–99.

98. *The Autobiography of Bertrand Russell* (London: Unwin, 1978), 129–31. Victor Lowe, *Understanding Whitehead* (Baltimore: Johns Hopkins Press, 1966), 6, 231–32.

99. Alfred North Whitehead, *A Treatise on Universal Algebra* (Cambridge: Cambridge Univ. Press, 1898), viii.

100. Victor Lowe, "The Development of Whitehead's Philosophy," in *The Philosophy of Alfred North Whitehead*, ed. Paul Arthur Schlipp, 2d ed. (New York: Tudor, 1951), 30.

101. Alfred North Whitehead, "On Mathematical Concepts of the Material World," *Philosophical Transactions of the Royal Society of London*, ser. A, 205 (May 1906): 525.

102. Alfred North Whitehead and Bertrand Russell, *Principia Mathematica*, 2d ed. (Cambridge: Cambridge Univ. Press, 1957), 1:v.

103. Alfred North Whitehead, *Process and Reality* (Cambridge: Cambridge Univ. Press, 1929), 461.

104. Alfred North Whitehead, *The Concept of Nature* (Cambridge: Cambridge Univ. Press, 1930), 2.

105. Lowe, *Understanding Whitehead*, 254–56.

106. Robert F. Whitman, *Shaw and the Play of Ideas* (Ithaca: Cornell Univ. Press, 1977), chaps. 5–7.

107. Murray to Lodge, 8 Feb. 1910, in Jolly, *Lodge*, 174.

108. Bernard Shaw, *Major Barbara*, vol. 3 of *Complete Plays*, 183–84.

109. Murray to Bertrand Russell, 20 Dec. 1902, Gilbert Murray Papers, Bodleian Library, Oxford University.

110. H. H. Munro, "The Music on the Hill," in *The Complete Short Stories of Saki* (New York: Modern Library, 1958), 180.

111. Hewlett to Milton Bronner, 5 June 1905, and introduction by Edward Hewlett, in *The Letters of Maurice Hewlett*, ed. Laurence Binyon (London: Methuen, 1926), 5, 17, 84.

112. Jacks to Oliver Lodge, 10 May 1906, Lodge Papers, Society for Psychical Research, 820. Percy Alden, in Mudie-Smith, *Religious Life*, 39–42. Samuel A. Barnett, "The Religion of the People," *Hibbert Journal* 5 (July 1907): 888.

113. Helen Meller, *Leisure and the Changing City 1870–1914* (London: Routledge and Kegan Paul, 1976), 77–79.

114. H. G. Wells, *A Modern Utopia*, vol. 9 of *Works* (New York, 1924–1925), 267.

115. Prestige, *Gore*, 269–71.

116. Charles Gore, *The New Theology and the Old Religion* (London: John Murray, 1907), 43–50. G. K. Chesterton, "The Priest of Spring" and "The Separatist and Sacred Things," in *A Miscellany of Men* (1912; reprint, Freeport, N.Y.: Books for Libraries, 1969).

117. Russell, *Autobiography*, 60, 192–94.

118. Bertrand Russell, *Scientific Method in Philosophy* (Oxford: Clarendon, 1914), 5, 16–19.

119. Russell, *Autobiography*, 162.

120. G. E. Moore, *Principia Ethica* (Cambridge: Cambridge Univ. Press, 1922), 30–31, 183–86, 222–23.

121. T. E. Hulme, *Speculations*, ed. Herbert Read, 2d ed. (London: Routledge and Kegan Paul, 1936), 228–29.

122. Ibid., 219.

123. Ibid., 3–11, 39–45, 62–63. Hulme's emphasis.

124. George Dangerfield, *The Strange Death of Liberal England 1910–1914* (New York: Putnam's, 1961), viii. See also Hynes, *Edwardian Turn of Mind*, chaps. 9–10.

125. Crites [T.S. Eliot], "A Commentary," *Criterion* 2 (Apr. 1924): 231.

126. Russell, *Scientific Method*, 5. The subquotation is from Bernard Bosanquet's *Logic*.

127. Paul Fussell, *The Great War and Modern Memory* (London: Oxford Univ. Press, 1975), chap. 3.

128. Bernard Shaw, *Heartbreak House*, vol. 5 of *Complete Plays*, 29.

129. Richter, *Politics of Conscience*, 375–76.

130. Huxley to Jelly d'Aranyi, late June 1915, *Letters of Aldous Huxley*, ed. Grover Smith (New York: Harper and Row, 1969), 73.

131. Aldous Huxley, *Antic Hay* (New York: Harper and Row, 1964), 230, 267.

132. Ibid., 4.

133. Aldous Huxley, *Point Counter Point* (New York: Modern Library, 1928), 27–28.

134. Ellmann, "Two Faces of Edward," 200–6.

135. Lines 301–2.

136. "The Second Coming," in *The Collected Poems of W. B. Yeats* (New York: Macmillan, 1974), 184.

137. Ellmann, *Yeats*, chap. 15, p. 294. H. G. Wells, *Experiment in Autobiography* (New York: Macmillan, 1934), 612–13, 616. Stanley Weintraub, *Journey to Heartbreak* (New York: Weybright and Talley, 1971), 294–99. Ellmann, *Joyce*, 537, 544.

138. Dorothy Emmet, *Whitehead's Philosophy of Organism*, 2d ed. (London: Macmillan, 1966), chap. 10.

139. Whitehead, *Process and Reality*, 23.

140. Nelson, *Spiritualism*, chap. 9.

141. Jolly, *Lodge*, 205, 210–11.

142. Sir Arthur Conan Doyle, *The New Revelation* (New York: Doran, 1918), 39.

143. Galsworthy, *Tranquillity*, 8–11.

144. Anthony Quinton, "Thought," in Simon Nowell-Smith, ed., *Edwardian England 1901–1914* (London: Oxford Univ. Press, 1965), 259.

145. Jolly, *Lodge*, 205–12.

146. Sir Arthur Conan Doyle, "My Religious Evolution," *Daily Express*, 17 Sept. 1925.

147. Walter E. Houghton, *The Victorian Frame of Mind 1830–1870* (New Haven: Yale Univ. Press, 1957), chap. 7. See also Raymond Williams, *Culture and Society 1780–1950* (New York: Harper and Row, 1966), 71–77, 105–6, 119–20, 138–40, 156–57; John A. Lester, Jr., *Journey through Despair 1880–1914* (Princeton: Princeton Univ. Press, 1968), 25–30; and Frank Miller Turner, *Between Science and Religion* (New Haven: Yale Univ. Press, 1974), 1–3.

148. James Martineau, *Studies of Christianity* (London: Longmans, Green, 1895), 395.

149. Houghton, *Victorian Frame of Mind*, 176–80.

150. Virginia Woolf, *To the Lighthouse* (New York: Harcourt, Brace, 1958), 53–56.

Chapter 2

1. Virginia Woolf, *Night and Day* (New York: Harcourt Brace Jovanovich, 1967), 506.

2. E. M. Forster, "Three Generations," lecture at University College, Nottingham, 28 Jan. 1939, E. M. Forster Papers, King's College Library, Cambridge University, vol. 16, fols. 183–86.

3. G. E. Moore, *Principia Ethica* (Cambridge: Cambridge Univ. Press, 1922), 188–207.

4. Paul Levy, *Moore: G. E. Moore and the Cambridge Apostles* (New York: Holt, Rinehart and Winston, 1979), 1–9, 14–16, 116–18.

5. Ibid., 236–44.

6. P. N. Furbank, *E. M. Forster: A Life* (New York: Harcourt Brace Jovanovich, 1978), 1:49, 76–77.

7. Levy, *Moore*, 222–25.

8. Leonard Woolf, *Sowing* (New York: Harcourt Brace Jovanovich, 1975), 146–48. John Maynard Keynes, *Essays and Sketches in Biography* (New York: Meridian, 1956), 241–52.

9. E. M. Forster, *A Room with a View* (New York: New Directions, n.d.), pp. 29, 47–50, chap. 4. Hereafter cited in text as *Room*.

10. E. M. Forster, *Howards End* (New York: Vintage, 1954), 81, 241.

11. E. M. Forster diary, 8 Apr. 1911, Forster Papers, F1/1.

12. Virginia Woolf to Vanessa Bell, 11 Nov. 1918, *The Letters of Virginia Woolf*, ed. Nigel Nicholson and Joanne Trautmann (New York: Harcourt Brace Jovanovich, 1975–1980), 2:292.

13. Virginia Woolf, *The Voyage Out* (New York: Harcourt Brace Jovanovich, 1976), 74. Hereafter cited in text as *Voyage*.

14. Virginia Woolf to Lady Robert Cecil, 12 Apr. 1909, *Letters*, 1:389–90.

15. *Journal of the Society for Psychical Research* 5 (Oct. 1891): 131–33.

16. Ibid., 6 (Apr. 1894): 229. Synopsis of Myers's remarks at SPR meeting, 9 March 1894.

17. F. W. H. Myers, *Human Personality and Its Survival of Bodily Death* (London: Longmans, Green, 1903), 1:112.

18. Noel Annan, *Leslie Stephen* (London: MacGibbon and Kee, 1951), 75.

19. Virginia Woolf, "Leslie Stephen," in *The Captain's Death Bed and Other Essays* (New York: Harcourt Brace Jovanovich, 1978), 75.

20. "Dover Beach," lines 29–30.

21. Alan Wood, *Bertrand Russell: The Passionate Skeptic* (New York: Simon and Schuster, 1958), chap. 1.

22. *The Autobiography of Bertrand Russell* (London: George Allen and Unwin, 1978), 149. Hereafter cited in text as *Autobio.*

23. Furbank, *Forster*, 1:104–7.

24. John Galsworthy, *The Inn of Tranquillity* (New York: Scribner's 1913), 258.

25. Joseph Conrad, *The Nigger of the "Narcissus"* (Garden City: Doubleday, 1924), preface.

26. Frederick Karl, *Joseph Conrad: The Three Lives* (New York: Farrar, Straus and Giroux, 1979), 308–21, 345, 349–50, 368, 394–96. Joseph Conrad, *Victory* (Garden City: Doubleday, 1924), 91–92, 173–75, 195–96, 218–20.

27. Karl, *Conrad*, 486, 491–93, 502.

28. Joseph Conrad, *Lord Jim* (Garden City: Doubleday, 1924), 157, 180. Hereafter cited in text as *Jim.*

29. Conrad, *Victory*, 198–200.

30. Edward Caird, *The Critical Philosophy of Immanuel Kant* (Glasgow: J. Maclehose, 1889), 2:371. Quoted approvingly in James Ward, *The Realm of Ends* (Cambridge: Cambridge Univ. Press, 1911), 128–29.

31. Leon Edel, *Henry James* (New York: Avon, 1978), 1:109–12, 115–17, 140–42, 156; 2:84; 3:84–85, 104, 149–53, 167–71, 235–36, 258–59, 322–23.

32. Henry James, *The Princess Casamassima*, vol. 6 of *Novels and Tales* (New York, 1936–1937), chap. 30.

33. Edel, *James*, 3:378–80; 4:79, 83–85, 89–95, 139–40, 153–55, 178–79, 231–32, 238–39, 248–60, 274–84, 328; 5:86–90.

34. Ibid., 2:345–49; 3:356–72; 4:108–15, 148–50, 300, 350–55; 5:77–78, 160, 330, 333. Henry James, *The Ambassadors*, vol. 22 of *Novels and Tales*, 201.

35. James to Bernard Shaw, 20 Jan. 1909, *Bernard Shaw: Collected Letters*, ed. Dan H. Laurence (London: Max Reinhardt, 1965–1972), 2:829.

36. James, *Ambassadors*, 21:189, 22:129, 172. Hereafter cited in text as *Ambass.*

37. Bernard Shaw, *Heartbreak House*, vol. 5 of *Complete Plays with Their Prefaces* (New York, 1975), 101. William Morris, *A Dream of John Ball*, vol. 16 of *Collected Works* (London, 1912), 230.

38. Raymond Williams, *Culture and Society 1780–1950* (New York: Harper and Row, 1966), 63–65, 84–85, 98–102, 146. Ben Knights, *The Idea of the Clerisy in the Nineteenth Century* (Cambridge: Cambridge Univ. Press, 1978).

39. Philip Whitwell Wilson, in Richard Mudie-Smith, ed., *The Religious Life of London* (London: Hodder and Stoughton, 1904), 294–96.

40. Werner Picht, *Toynbee Hall and the English Settlement Movement*, trans. Lilian A. Cowell, rev. ed. (London: G. Bell, 1914), appendix. J. A. R. Pimlott, *Toynbee Hall* (London: J. M. Dent, 1935), 269–72.

41. Charles Booth, *Life and Labour of the People in London* (1902–1904; reprint, New York: AMS, 1970), 3d ser., 7:377–79.

42. Pimlott, *Toynbee Hall*, 51–52.

43. Booth, *Life and Labour*, 3d ser., 2:58.

44. Lucy Masterman, *C. F. G. Masterman* (London: Frank Cass, 1968), 19–34. H. G. Abel to C. F. G. Masterman, 8 Dec. 1923, C. F. G. Masterman Papers, in possession of Masterman family.

45. Booth, *Life and Labour*, 3d ser., 4:26–27.

46. Picht, *Toynbee Hall*, 100–1, 127.

47. Booth, *Life and Labour*, 3d ser., 2:57, 4:26–27, 7:381.

48. Pimlott, *Toynbee Hall*, pp. x–xi, 30–31, 36–37, 51–56, chap. 9.

49. Booth, *Life and Labour*, 3d ser., 7:383–93.

50. Helen Meller, *Leisure and the Changing City 1870–1914* (London: Routledge and Kegan Paul, 1976), 6–11.

51. T. H. Green, *Prolegomena to Ethics*, 5th ed. (Oxford: Clarendon, 1907), 237–53.

52. John E. Kendle, *The Round Table Movement and Imperial Union* (Toronto: Univ. of Toronto Press, 1975), 17–18, 171–74. C. R. Ashbee, "Memoirs," 1938, Victoria and Albert Museum Library, 2:188–91.

53. Charles Gore, *St. Paul's Epistle to the Ephesians* (London: John Murray, 1898), 271–74.

54. C. F. G. Masterman, ed., *The Heart of the Empire* (London: T. Fisher Unwin, 1901), 50–51.

55. Ashbee, "Memoirs," 1:5–7.

56. C. R. Ashbee, *Craftsmanship in Competitive Industry* (London: Essex House, 1908), 165. Ashbee's emphasis.

57. D. H. Lawrence, *The Rainbow* (New York: Modern Library, n.d.), 223–24.

58. A. J. Penty, *The Restoration of the Gild System* (London: Swan Sonnenschein, 1906), vii–viii, 45–55.

59. Peter d'A. Jones, *The Christian Socialist Revival 1877–1914* (Princeton: Princeton Univ. Press, 1968), pp. 92–94, 159–63, 277–78, 436–47, chap. 6. Wallace Martin, *The "New Age" under Orage* (Manchester: Manchester Univ. Press, 1967), 190.

60. Robert Speaight, *The Life of Eric Gill* (London: Methuen, 1966), 16–20, 29–35, 42–43, 51–53, 60–67. Ananda K. Coomaraswami, "The Purpose of Art," *The Path* (Mar. 1913): 3.

61. Martin J. Wiener, *Between Two Worlds: The Political Thought of Graham Wallas* (Oxford: Clarendon, 1971), 3–12, 17–18, 26–28, 103, 176, 182–85, 199–201, 210.

62. E. M. Forster, *Goldsworthy Lowes Dickinson* (London: Edward Arnold, 1962), 35–36.

63. Angus Wilson, *The Strange Ride of Rudyard Kipling* (Harmondsworth: Penguin, 1979), 314.

64. Rudyard Kipling, *Kim*, vol. 16 of *The Writings in Prose and Verse* (New York, 1925), chaps. 5–6.

65. Gilbert Murray, "The Stoic Philosophy," in *Essays and Addresses* (London: George Allen and Unwin, 1921), 98.

66. Richard Taylor, ed., *The Personal Notebooks of Thomas Hardy* (New York: Columbia Univ. Press, 1979), 243–44.

67. Stephen Winsten, *Salt and His Circle* (London: Hutchinson, 1951), 86–88, 91–92, 114, 118, 122, 131, 185.

68. Edward Carpenter, *My Days and Dreams* (New York: Scribner's, 1916), 143, 202, 207–9, 264–65.

69. Furbank, *Forster*, 1:256–58. John Batchelor, *The Edwardian Novelists* (New York: St. Martin's, 1982), 209.

70. Ashbee, "Memoirs," 2:123, 127.

71. Timothy d'Arch Smith, *Love in Earnest* (London: Routledge and Kegan Paul, 1970).

72. Levy, *Moore*, 237–39.

73. Paul Fussell, *The Great War and Modern Memory* (London: Oxford Univ. Press, 1979), chap. 8.

74. George Dangerfield, *The Strange Death of Liberal England 1910–1914* (New York: Putnam's, 1961), 387–88, 400–402, 422–25.

75. Carpenter, *Days and Dreams*, 319–20.

76. Gilbert Murray, *Faith, War, and Policy* (Boston: Houghton Mifflin, 1918), 3–6, 175–76.

77. Jason [J. L. Hammond], *Past and Future* (London: Chatto and Windus, 1918), chaps. 8–12. Stephen Koss, *Fleet Street Radical: A. G. Gardiner and the "Daily News"* (Hamden, Conn.: Archon, 1973), 229.

78. L. P. Carpenter, *G. D. H. Cole: An Intellectual Biography* (Cambridge: Cambridge Univ. Press, 1973), 71–73, 77–78.

79. Ashbee, "Memoirs," 4:30, 33.

80. Kendle, *Round Table*, 181–82, 248–60.

81. Henry R. Winkler, *The League of Nations Movement in Great Britain 1914–1919* (New Brunswick: Rutgers Univ. Press, 1952).

82. Kendle, *Round Table*, chaps. 8, 11.

83. Margaret Cole, *The Life of G. D. H. Cole* (London: Macmillan, 1971), 82–84, 102–3, 120–24.

84. Arthur Marwick, *The Deluge: British Society and the First World War* (New York: W. W. Norton, 1970), chap. 6. C. L. Mowat, *Britain between the Wars 1918–1940* (Boston: Beacon, 1971), chaps. 1–2. Fussell, *Great War*, chap. 3. Martin Green, *Children of the Sun* (New York: Basic, 1976), chap. 2.

85. Keynes, "Dr. Melchior," in *Essays and Sketches*.

86. John Maynard Keynes, *The Economic Consequences of the Peace* (London: Macmillan, 1971), 2.

87. Ibid., 5–10, 22–23, 170, 185–87.

88. Forster to Dickinson, 5 Apr. 1916, Forster Papers, A1.

89. E. M. Forster, *Arctic Summer and Other Fiction* (New York: Holmes and Meier, 1981), 162.

90. Furbank, *Forster*, 2:106.

91. D. H. Lawrence, *Aaron's Rod* (New York: Viking, 1970), chap. 20.

92. Virginia Woolf to Gerald Brennan, 25 Dec. 1922, *Letters*, 2:598–600.

93. Huxley to Jelly d'Aranyi, Oct. 1915, *Letters of Aldous Huxley*, ed. Grover Smith (New York: Harper and Row, 1969), 83.

94. Aldous Huxley, *Antic Hay* (New York: Harper and Row, 1964), 88.

95. *The Waste Land*, lines 412–17.

96. Eliot's footnote to line 412 of *The Waste Land*.

97. Stephen Spender, *T. S. Eliot* (Harmondsworth: Penguin, 1976), 24–29.

98. Goronwy Rees, *A Chapter of Accidents* (London: Chatto and Windus, 1972), 95. Fussell, *Great War*, 106.

99. L. T. Hobhouse, *Liberalism* (London: Oxford Univ. Press, 1964), 121.

100. C. F. G. Masterman, *The Condition of England* (London: Methuen, 1909), 303.

Chapter 3

1. Alun R. Jones, *The Life and Opinions of T. E. Hulme* (London: Gollancz, 1960), 199.

2. He invoked it 330 times, to be exact, or 516 if we count cognates like *live, lived, living, alive*, and *liveth*.

3. *A Supplement to the Oxford English Dictionary*, s.v. "life force."

4. Samuel Butler, *Luck or Cunning?* (London: Jonathan Cape, 1924), 111.

5. Samuel Butler, "God the Known and God the Unknown," in *Collected Essays* (London: Jonathan Cape, 1925), 1:30.

6. Samuel Butler, *The Way of All Flesh* (New York: Holt, Rinehart and Winston, 1948), chap. 86.

7. Leonard Woolf, *Sowing* (New York: Harcourt Brace Jovanovich, 1975), 152, 166.

8. Sydney Cockerell to Bernard Shaw, 27 Aug. 1903, British Library, Add. MS. 50531, fols. 63–64.

9. William C. Frierson, *The English Novel in Transition 1885–1940* (Norman: Univ. of Oklahoma Press, 1942), 189.

10. L. E. Holt, "Samuel Butler's Rise to Fame," *PMLA* 57 (1942): 867–78.

11. Olivier to Bernard Shaw, 31 Jan. 1921, BL, Add. MS. 50543, fol. 156.

12. E. M. Forster, "Samuel Butler 1835–1902," E. M. Forster Papers, King's College Library, Cambridge University, E3, vol. 16, fols. 159–60.

13. St. John Ervine, *Bernard Shaw: His Life, Work and Friends* (New York: William Morrow, 1956), 49, 92.

14. Bernard Shaw, *Immaturity*, vol. 1 of *Collected Works* (London, 1930), 438.

15. Bernard Shaw, *Back to Methuselah*, vol. 5 of *Complete Plays with Their Prefaces* (New York, 1975), 294.

16. Shaw to Frederick H. Evans, 27 Aug. 1895, *Collected Letters*, ed. Dan H. Laurence (London: Max Reinhardt, 1965–1972), 1:551.

17. Bernard Shaw, *Man and Superman*, vol. 2 of *Complete Plays*, 661–62.

18. Warren Sylvester Smith, *The London Heretics 1870–1914* (New York: Dodd, Mead, 1968), 187, 210–11.

19. Bernard Shaw, *The Perfect Wagnerite* (1923; reprint, New York: Dover, 1967), 11, 21.

20. Ibid., 11–12, 23.

21. Bernard Shaw, *Androcles and the Lion*, vol. 4 of *Complete Plays*, 530, 563–64.

22. Frierson, *Novel in Transition*, 148.

23. Shaw, *Androcles*, 530, and *Methuselah*, 302–7.

24. Beatrice Bateson, *William Bateson, F.R.S.* (Cambridge: Cambridge Univ. Press, 1928), 232, 422, 454.

25. William Bateson, *The Problems of Genetics* (New Haven: Yale Univ. Press, 1916), 189.

26. Patrick Geddes and J. Arthur Thomson, *Evolution* (New York: Henry Holt, 1911), 188–92, 197–99, 202, 207–11.

27. Shaw, *Man and Superman*, 668, 675, 689.

28. Ibid., 728.

29. Shaw, *Perfect Wagnerite*, 21.

30. George Moore, *The Lake* (New York: Appleton, 1906), 7–8.

31. Ibid., 49–50. (In later editions Rose's name was changed to Nora Glynn.) Hereafter cited in text as *Lake*.

32. James F. Carens, *Surpassing Wit: The Life and Work of Oliver St. John Gogarty* (New York: Columbia Univ. Press, 1979), chap. 1.

33. Richard Ellmann, *James Joyce*, rev. ed. (New York: Oxford Univ. Press, 1982), 234.

34. James Joyce, *A Portrait of the Artist as a Young Man* (New York: Viking, 1970), 169–71. Hereafter cited in text as *Portrait*.

35. Joyce to Lady Gregory, Nov. 1902, *Letters of James Joyce*, ed. Stuart Gilbert, new ed. (New York: Viking, 1966), 1:53.

36. Lawrence to Blanche Jennings, 25 June, 17 July 1908, *The Letters of D. H. Lawrence*, ed. James T. Boulton (Cambridge: Cambridge Univ. Press, 1979), 1:57–58, 62.

37. Lawrence to Reid, 15 Oct., 3 Dec. 1907, ibid., 36–37, 39–41.

38. E. T. [Jessie Chambers], *D. H. Lawrence: A Personal Record* (New York: Barnes and Noble, 1965), 83–85, 112–13.

39. Lawrence to Smith, 5 Dec. 1909, *Letters*, 1:7, 147.

40. Lawrence to Reid, 3 Dec. 1907, ibid., 39.

41. Lawrence to Blanche Jennings, 1 Sept. 1908, and to Louie Burrows, 20 Nov. 1909, ibid., 72, 145.

42. D. H. Lawrence, *The Rainbow* (New York: Modern Library, n.d.), 106, 147–48. Hereafter cited in text as *Rainbow*.

43. D. H. Lawrence to Ada Lawrence, 9 Apr. 1911, *Letters*, 1:255–56.

44. Lawrence to Reid, 27 Mar. 1911, ibid., 244.

45. Lawrence to Blanche Jennings, 17, 30 July 1908, ibid., 62, 66–67.

46. Lawrence to Blanche Jennings, 15 Dec. 1908, ibid., 99.

47. W. H. Hudson, *Idle Days in Patagonia* (London: J. M. Dent, 1923), 48–49. E. M. Forster, *Howards End* (New York: Vintage, 1954), 186.

48. D. H. Lawrence, *Women in Love* (New York: Viking, 1975), 164, 192.

49. John E. Stoll, *The Novels of D. H. Lawrence: A Search for Integration* (Columbia: Univ. of Missouri Press, 1971), chap. 2.

50. Lawrence, *Women in Love*, chap. 13, pp. 191–93, 302–8, 361.

51. Havelock Ellis, *My Life* (Boston: Houghton Mifflin, 1939), 114–15, 131–33.

52. Ibid., 156, 163–68.

53. Phyllis Grosskurth, *Havelock Ellis: A Biography* (New York: Knopf, 1980), 57–58, 64–65, 105.

54. Havelock Ellis, *Studies in the Psychology of Sex* (Philadelphia: F. A. Davis, 1900–1928), 1:310–25, and *Life*, 433.

55. Edward Carpenter, *My Days and Dreams* (New York: Scribner's, 1916), 49–51.

56. Ibid., 86, 264–65.

57. Emile Delavenay, *D. H. Lawrence and Edward Carpenter* (New York: Taplinger, 1971), 21–43.

58. D. H. Lawrence, *The White Peacock* (Cambridge: Cambridge Univ. Press, 1983), 29–30.

59. D. H. Lawrence, "Pan in America," in *Phoenix*, ed. Edward McDonald (New York: Viking, 1968).

60. Ellis, *Life*, 103–4.

61. P. N. Furbank, *E. M. Forster: A Life* (New York: Harcourt Brace Jovanovich, 1978), 1:113–14.

62. Arnold Bennett, *The Old Wives' Tale* (New York: Modern Library, n.d.), 187–89.

63. Norman MacKenzie and Jeanne MacKenzie, *H. G. Wells* (New York: Simon and Schuster, 1973), 258.

64. H. de Vere Stacpoole, *The Blue Lagoon*, 21st ed. (London: Ernest Benn, 1951), 153–55, 227–28, 244–45.

65. Ronald Pearsall, *Edwardian Life and Leisure* (Newton Abbot, Eng.: David

and Charles, 1973), 143–54. Donald Read, ed., *Documents from Edwardian England 1901–1915* (London: Harrap, 1973), 14–19.

66. Forster, *Howards End*, chap. 6.

67. H. G. Wells, *Tono-Bungay*, vol. 13 of *Works* (New York, 1924–1925), 519.

68. Ted Morgan, *Maugham: A Biography* (New York: Simon and Schuster, 1980), 181–99.

69. Shaw, *Man and Superman*, 560–61, 581–84, 672.

70. Havelock Ellis, *The Nineteenth Century* (London: Grant Richards, 1900), 39–53.

71. T. E. Hulme, *Speculations*, ed. Herbert Read, 2d ed. (London: Routledge and Kegan Paul, 1936), 202–13.

72. McDougall to Lodge, 10 Aug. 1912, Oliver Lodge Papers, Society for Psychical Research, London, 1217.

73. Balfour to Lodge, 16 Oct. 1905, BL, Add. MS. 49798, fol. 133.

74. Sir Oliver Lodge, *Continuity* (London: J. M. Dent, 1913), 69–79. J. H. Poynting, "Physical Law and Life," *Hibbert Journal* 1 (July 1903): 728–46.

75. Myers to Lodge, 21 June 1894, Lodge Papers, Society for Psychical Research, 1400.

76. Hulme, *Speculations*, 185–97, 202–13.

77. Shaw, *Perfect Wagernite*, 60.

78. Sydney Olivier, "Moral," in *Fabian Essays in Socialism*, ed. Bernard Shaw (Gloucester, Mass.: Peter Smith, 1967), 134–46.

79. Sydney Olivier, *Letters and Selected Writings*, ed. Margaret Olivier (London: George Allen and Unwin, 1948), 191–95.

80. Ibid., 127–29. Olivier to Shaw, undated (1899), BL, Add. MS. 50543, fols. 122–30.

81. John Cerullo, *The Secularization of the Soul: Psychical Research in Modern Britain* (Philadelphia: Institute for the Study of Human Issues, 1982).

82. Alan Gauld, *The Founders of Psychical Research* (London: Routledge and Kegan Paul, 1968), 58–62. Frank Miller Turner, *Between Science and Religion* (New Haven: Yale Univ. Press, 1974), 212–13.

83. Reba N. Soffer, *Ethics and Society in England: The Revolution in the Social Sciences 1870–1914* (Berkeley: Univ. of California Press, 1978), 142–43, 147–49. Stefan Collini, *Liberalism and Sociology: L. T. Hobhouse and Political Argument in England 1880–1914* (Cambridge: Cambridge Univ. Press, 1979), chap. 5.

84. Turner, *Science and Religion*, 201–6. Olwen Ward Campbell, "Memoir," in James Ward, *Essays in Philosophy*, ed. W. R. Sorley and G. F. Stout (Cambridge: Cambridge Univ. Press, 1927), 32.

85. Turner, *Science and Religion*, 206–8. Campbell, "Memoir," 64.

86. Turner, *Science and Religion*, 209–17.

87. James Ward, *Psychological Principles* (Cambridge: Cambridge Univ. Press, 1919), 17, 28, 35.

88. Ibid., chap. 15.

89. Turner, *Science and Religion*, 225–27.

90. James Ward, *The Realm of Ends* (Cambridge: Cambridge Univ. Press, 1911), 11, 75–76

91. Ibid., 9, 97–112, 203–4, 361.

92. Hulme, *Speculations*, 191–97.

93. Thomas Hardy, *Jude the Obscure* (New York: New American Library, 1961), 331, 398. Frierson, *Novel in Transition*, chaps. 2–4.

94. Oscar Wilde, "The Critic as Artist," in *The Soul of Man under Socialism and Other Essays* (New York: Harper and Row, 1970), 124–25, 155–58.

95. May Sinclair, *Audrey Craven* (New York: Henry Holt, 1907), 11.

96. Lawrence to Blanche Jennings, 28 Jan. 1910, and to Louie Burrows, 1 Apr. 1911, *Letters*, 1:154, 248. H. G. Wells, *A Modern Utopia*, vol. 9 in *Works*, 252.

97. Jerome Buckley, *William Ernest Henley* (Princeton: Princeton Univ. Press, 1958), chap. 10, pp. 196–97.

98. C. F. G. Masterman, *In Peril of Change* (New York: B. W. Huebsch, 1907), 39–40.

99. H. G. Wells, *Complete Short Stories* (London: Ernest Benn, 1974), 91. Lovat Dickson, *H. G. Wells* (Harmondsworth: Penguin, 1972), 82.

100. H. G. Wells, *The History of Mr. Polly*, vol. 17 of *Works*, chap. 9.

101. Henry James, *The Portrait of a Lady*, vol. 3 of *Novels and Tales* (New York, 1936–1937), chap. 54.

102. Ibid., chap. 53.

103. Henry James, *What Maisie Knew*, vol. 11 of *Novels and Tales*, chap. 31.

104. Alan Friedman, *The Turn of the Novel* (New York: Oxford Univ. Press, 1966). Robert M. Adams, *Strains of Discord: Studies in Literary Openness* (Ithaca: Cornell Univ. Press, 1958).

105. Joseph Conrad, "Henry James," in *Notes on Life and Letters* (Garden City: Doubleday, 1924), 18–19.

106. Henry James, *Roderick Hudson*, vol. 1 of *Novels and Tales*, vii.

107. Virginia Woolf to Lytton Strachey, 28 Feb. 1916, *The Letters of Virginia Woolf*, ed. Nigel Nicolson and Joanne Trautmann (New York: Harcourt Brace Jovanovich, 1975–1980), 2:82.

108. Wells, *Tono-Bungay*, bk. 1, chap. 1.

109. Ibid., bk. 4, chap. 3.

110. E. M. Forster, *Aspects of the Novel* (New York: Harcourt, Brace, 1927), 145, 233–34, 241–42.

111. Furbank, *Forster*, 1:132–33, 147–48.

112. Lawrence, *White Peacock*, 120.

113. D. H. Lawrence, *The Trespasser* (Cambridge: Cambridge Univ. Press, 1981), 45.

114. Lawrence to Louie Burrows, 13 Mar. 1911, *Letters*, 1:238.

115. Lawrence to Sallie Hopkin, 2 June 1912, ibid., 414.

116. Lawrence to Arthur McLeod, 15 June 1912, ibid., 418.

117. Lawrence to Edward Garnett, 30 Oct.–2 Nov. 1912, ibid., 465.

118. D. H. Lawrence, introduction to the American edition of *New Poems*, in *Phoenix*.

119. Frierson, *Novel in Transition*, 131–35, 183–210.

120. Arthur Waugh, "The New Realism," *Fortnightly Review*, n.s. 99 (May 1916): 849–58.

121. William James, *The Principles of Psychology* (Cambridge: Harvard Univ. Press, 1981), 233.

122. William James, *Talks to Teachers on Psychology* (Cambridge: Harvard Univ. Press, 1981), chap. 2.

123. Hulme, *Speculations*, 184–213.

124. Edouard Dujardin, *Le Monologue intérieur* (Paris: Albert Messein, 1931), 58.

125. Gloria G. Fromm, *Dorothy Richardson* (Urbana: Univ. of Illinois Press, 1977), 61, 65–67, 76.

126. Dorothy Richardson, *Pilgrimage* (London: J. M. Dent and Cresset, 1938), 1:302.

127. In Stanley J. Kunitz, ed., *Authors Today and Yesterday* (New York: H. W. Wilson, 1933), 562.

128. May Sinclair, "The Novels of Dorothy Richardson," *Egoist* 5 (Apr. 1918): 58.

129. Virginia Woolf, "The Tunnel," in *Contemporary Writers* (New York: Harcourt, Brace and World, 1966), and "Modern Fiction," in *Collected Essays* (London: Hogarth, 1966), vol. 2.

130. Oscar Wilde, "The Decay of Lying," in *Soul of Man*, 46–50, 53, 60, 71.

131. Wilde, "Critic as Artist," 145, 151.

132. Henry James, *The Golden Bowl*, vol. 23 of *Novels and Tales*, xix.

133. Leon Edel and Gordon N. Ray, eds., *Henry James and H. G. Wells* (Urbana: Univ. of Illinois Press, 1958), 182–85. MacKenzie and MacKenzie, *Wells*, 282.

134. Wells, *Tono-Bungay*, 7–8.

135. H. G. Wells, *Boon*, vol. 13 of *Works*, 454.

136. Bernard Shaw, *Candida*, vol. 1 of *Complete Plays*, 593–94.

137. Shaw, *Man and Superman*, 646, 727.

138. Lawrence, *Women in Love*, chaps. 6–7, 28.

139. W. Somerset Maugham, *Of Human Bondage* (Garden City: Doubleday, 1936), chaps. 51, 81, 88.

140. Michael Holroyd, *Augustus John* (New York: Holt, Rinehart and Winston, 1975), 77–80, 112, 122–23, 131, 266–67, 280, 312–13, 360.

141. Holbrook Jackson, *The Eighteen Nineties* (New York: Putnam's, 1966), 196.

142. Richard Aldington, *Life for Life's Sake* (London: Cassell, 1968), 57, 86.

143. Murray to Bertrand Russell, 5 Apr. 1902, Gilbert Murray Papers, Bodleian Library, Oxford University.

144. D. H. Lawrence, *Sons and Lovers* (Harmondsworth: Penguin, 1980), 257.

145. Shaw, *Man and Superman*, 545.

146. Ibid., 650–52.

147. Shaw to Eva Christy, Dec. 1900, *Letters*, 2:203.

148. George Dangerfield, *The Strange Death of Liberal England 1910–1914* (New York: Putnam's, 1961), 144–45, 149. See also John A. Lester, Jr., *Journey through Despair 1880–1914* (Princeton: Princeton Univ. Press, 1968), 10–11.

149. Richardson, *Pilgrimage*, 1:303.

150. Dora Marsden, "Views and Comment: The Chastity of Women," *Egoist* 1 (2 Feb. 1914): 44–46. Elaine Showalter, *A Literature of Their Own* (Princeton: Princeton Univ. Press, 1977), 232–38.

151. Gordon N. Ray, *H. G. Wells and Rebecca West* (New Haven: Yale Univ. Press, 1974), 15–18, 25–27, 30, 32, 41–42.

152. H. G. Wells, *Ann Veronica*, vol. 13 of *Works*, 6–7, 36, 133, 146, 252, 354, 364, 370, 376–77.

153. Ibid., 174, 179–80, 202, 297, 373–74.

154. Carrington to Mark Gertler, May 1915, *Carrington: Letters and Extracts from Her Diaries*, ed. David Garnett (New York: Holt, Rinehart and Winston, 1971), 19.

155. Virginia Woolf, *Night and Day* (New York: Harcourt Brace Jovanovich, 1976), 130. Hereafter cited in text as *Night*.

156. D. H. Lawrence, "Study of Thomas Hardy," in *Phoenix*, 404–6.

157. C. R. Ashbee, "Memoirs," 1938, Victoria and Albert Museum Library, 4:15, 18.

158. Carpenter, *Days and Dreams*, 310–15.

159. Brooke to Dudley Ward, 13 or 14 Jan. 1915, *The Letters of Rupert Brooke*, ed. Geoffrey Keynes (London: Faber and Faber, 1968), 654.

160. Alan Seeger, "The Aisne" and "Rendezvous," in *Up the Line to Death: The War Poets 1914–1918*, ed. Brian Gardner (London: Methuen, 1966), 31–32.

161. Julian Grenfell, "Into Battle," in ibid., 34.

162. Francis Ledwidge, "Soliloquy," in ibid., 28–29.

163. Robert Graves, "Two Fusileers," in ibid., 148.

164. "An Irish Airman Foresees His Death," in *The Collected Poems of W. B. Yeats* (New York: Macmillan, 1974), 133–34.

165. Jones, *Hulme*, 137–38.

166. Bernard Shaw, *Heartbreak House*, vol. 5 of *Complete Plays*, 146–48.

167. Shaw, *Man and Superman*, 674.

168. Stanley Weintraub, *Journey to Heartbreak* (New York: Weybright and Talley, 1971), 179, 251.

169. D. H. Lawrence, *Studies in Classic American Literature* (New York: Viking, 1964), 116.

170. D. H. Lawrence, *Psychoanalysis and the Unconscious* and *Fantasia of the Unconscious* (New York: Viking, 1974), 18–25.

171. Aldous Huxley, *Antic Hay* (New York: Harper and Row, 1964), 133–34.

172. Ibid., 70–73.

173. T. S. Eliot, *The Waste Land*, lines 62–63.

174. Virginia Woolf, "The Art of Fiction," in *Collected Essays*, 2:53.

175. Charles Booth, *Life and Labour of the People in London* (1902–1904; reprint, New York: AMS, 1970), final vol., p. 206.

176. R. C. K. Ensor, *England 1870–1914* (Oxford: Clarendon, 1936), 527.

Chapter 4

1. H. W. Nevinson, *More Changes, More Chances* (London: Nisbet, 1925), 232.

2. Philip Snowden, *The Living Wage* (London: Hodder and Stoughton, 1912), 49.

3. Stanley Wolpert, *A New History of India* (New York: Oxford Univ. Press, 1977), 269–74.

4. Elie Halévy, *The Rule of Democracy 1905–1914*, trans. E. I. Watkin (New York: Barnes and Noble, 1961), 154–232.

5. See G. R. Searle, *The Quest for National Efficiency* (Oxford: Basil Blackwell, 1971), chap. 2; Bernard Semmel, *Imperialism and Social Reform* (Garden City: Doubleday, 1968), chaps. 4–5; Samuel Hynes, *The Edwardian Turn of Mind* (Princeton: Princeton Univ. Press, 1968), chap. 2; and H. C. G. Matthew, *The Liberal Imperialists* (London: Oxford Univ. Press, 1973).

6. Samuel Haber, *Efficiency and Uplift: Scientific Management in the Progressive Era 1890–1920* (Chicago: Univ. of Chicago Press, 1973).

7. W. J. Reader, *Professional Men* (New York: Basic, 1966), chap. 4.

8. Ibid., 140. D. S. L. Cardwell, *The Organisation of Science in England* (London: Heinemann, 1974), 80–82, 111–13, 119. W. H. G. Armytage, *A Social History of Engineering* (Cambridge: MIT Press, 1966), chap. 21, and *The Rise of the Technocrats* (London: Routledge and Kegan Paul, 1969), 108.

9. Between 1860 and 1900, journals of professional scientific societies in Britain increased from (roughly) 12 to 70, and general technical periodicals multiplied from about 40 to over 130. Engineering societies formed between

1880 and 1914 included the Society of Chemical Industry (1881), the National Association of Colliery Managers (1887), the Institute of Marine Engineers (1889), the Cycle Engineers Institute (1898), the Institute of Refrigeration (1900), the Institute of Brewing (1903), the Faraday Society (1903), the Concrete Institute (1908), the Institute of Metals (1908), the Illuminating Engineering Society (1909), the Institution of Automobile Engineers (1910), the Junior Institution of Locomotive Engineers (1911), the British Foundrymen's Association (chartered 1912), the Institution of Railway Signal Engineers (1912), the Institution of Petroleum Technologists (1914), and the Association of Supervising Electrical Engineers (1914). Simultaneously, American engineers were moving toward professionalization and organizing a national efficiency movement of their own. W. H. G. Armytage, *Engineering*, chap. 21, and *Technocrats*, 108. Haber, *Efficiency and Uplift*, 8–12. Edwin T. Layton, Jr., *The Revolt of the Engineers* (Cleveland: Press of Case Western Reserve Univ., 1971), 55–68.

10. Rollo Appleyard, *The History of the Institution of Electrical Engineers* (London: Institution of Electrical Engineers, 1939), chap. 3.

11. Armytage, *Technocrats*, 119, 125–26.

12. Richard Heathcote Heindel, *The American Impact on Great Britain 1898–1914* (1940; reprint, New York: Octagon, 1968), chaps. 6–9.

13. Cardwell, *Science in England*, 162, 177–78, 183–84, 194–95, 204–6, 211.

14. A. J. Balfour, *Decadence* (Cambridge: Cambridge Univ. Press, 1908), 49–57.

15. Halévy, *Rule of Democracy*, 262. Charles Booth, *Life and Labour of the People in London* (1902–1904; reprint, New York: AMS, 1970), 2d ser., 4:16, 179–82.

16. Armytage, *Engineering*, 244–45.

17. L. F. Haber, *The Chemical Industry during the Nineteenth Century* (Oxford: Clarendon, 1958), 206–8.

18. Oliver MacDonagh, "The Nineteenth Century Revolution in Government: A Reappraisal," *Historical Journal* 1 (1958): 52–67.

19. Bernard Shaw, ed., *Fabian Essays in Socialism* (Gloucester, Mass.: Peter Smith, 1967), 230.

20. *Fabian News* 10 (July 1900): 19; 17 (Feb. 1907): 20; 18 (Aug. 1907): 61; 25 (Sept. 1914): 74.

21. Bernard Shaw, *The Fabian Society* (London: Fabian Society, 1892), 26–28.

22. "On Going to Church," in *Selected Non-Dramatic Writings of Bernard Shaw*, ed. Dan H. Laurence (Boston: Houghton Mifflin, 1965), 378.

23. Bernard Shaw, *Sixteen Self-Sketches* (New York: Dodd, Mead, 1949), 97, 132.

24. E. J. Hobsbawm, "The Fabians Reconsidered," in *Labouring Men* (London: Weidenfeld and Nicolson, 1968), 257–59, 264–65.

25. *Fabian News* 2 (Jan. 1893): 1–2; 10 (Feb. 1901): 47–48; 19 (Dec. 1907): 96; 24 (Jan. 1913): 14–15.

26. H. G. Wells, *Anticipations*, vol. 4 of *Works* (New York, 1924–1925), 77–78.

27. Beatrice Webb to Georgina Meinertzhagen, 9 Aug. 1909, *The Letters of Sidney and Beatrice Webb*, ed. Norman MacKenzie (Cambridge: Cambridge Univ. Press, 1978), 2:333.

28. G. D. H. Cole, *Guild Socialism* (London: Fabian Society, 1920), 9–10, 17–18.

29. Bernard Shaw, *The Irrational Knot*, vol. 2 of *Collected Works* (London: 1931), 137–38.

30. R. F. Dietrich, *Portrait of the Artist as a Young Superman* (Gainesville: Univ. of Florida Press, 1969), 93–96.

31. Sidney Webb to Beatrice Potter, 13 Aug. 1890, *Letters*, 1:168.

32. Sydney Olivier, *Letters and Selected Writings*, ed. Margaret Olivier (London: George Allen and Unwin, 1948), 61.

33. H. G. Wells, *Anticipations*, 44–46, 236–38, and *Experiment in Autobiography* (New York: Macmillan, 1934), 203.

34. *Fabian News* 16 (May 1906): 23–24.

35. *Fabian News* 11 (May 1901): 11.

36. Beatrice Webb to Mary Playne, 29 July 1906, *Letters*, 2:234.

37. Sidney Webb to Rev. Archibald Robertson, 3 Jan. 1903, ibid., 176, 350.

38. Sidney Webb to Beatrice Webb, 12 July 1902, ibid., 159.

39. Beatrice Webb to Sidney Webb, 11 July 1902, ibid., 158–59.

40. Wells, *Anticipations*, p. 88, chap. 5.

41. Sidney Webb to Bernard Shaw, 26 Apr. 1898, Beatrice Webb to Catherine Courtney, 29 Apr., 2 July 1898, *Letters*, 2:62, 64, 72–73.

42. Sidney Webb and Beatrice Webb, *English Local Government from the Revolution to the Municipal Corporations Act: The Manor and the Borough* (London: Longmans, Green, 1908), 729–30.

43. Sidney Webb and Beatrice Webb, *English Local Government from the Revolution to the Municipal Corporations Act: The Parish and the County* (London: Longmans, Green, 1906), 360–68.

44. Wells, *Anticipations*, 77–81.

45. H. G. Wells, *The New Machiavelli*, vol. 14 of *Works*, 66–69, 347–48; "The Faults of the Fabian," in Hynes, *Edwardian Turn of Mind*, appendix C; and "Socialism and the Middle Classes," *Fabian News* 16 (Nov. 1906): 45–47.

46. Shaw proposed to organize a middle-class socialist party at a Fabian Society meeting, 1 Feb. 1907. He was supported by Cecil Chesterton and S. G. Hobson and opposed by Edward Pease and R. C. K. Ensor. The proposal was voted down. *Fabian News* 17 (Mar. 1907): 27–28. Shaw to Sidney Webb, 25 Nov. 1906, 21 Oct. 1907, *Collected Letters*, ed. Dan H. Laurence (London: Max Rein-

hardt, 1965–1972), 2:661–62, 717–18. Shaw to Emil Davies, 13 Dec. 1911, British Library, Add. MS. 50557, fols. 190–94.

47. Sidney Webb and Beatrice Webb, *Industrial Democracy* (London: Longmans, Green, 1920), xx. Margaret Cole, *The Life of G. D. H. Cole* (London: Macmillan, 1971), 100–2.

48. J. M. Winter, *Socialism and the Challenge of War: Ideas and Politics in Britain 1912–1918* (London: Routledge and Kegan Paul, 1974), 272.

49. *Fabian Essays*, 267.

50. Hobsbawm, "Fabians Reconsidered," 257.

51. *Fabian Essays*, 79, 136, 138, 168, 175, 178, 195–96, 223, 227, 230.

52. A. M. McBriar, *Fabian Socialism and English Politics 1884–1918* (Cambridge: Cambridge Univ. Press, 1962), 11–12.

53. Bernard Shaw, *Report on Fabian Policy* (London: Fabian Society, 1896), 3.

54. Shaw to Norman, 4 Oct. 1915, BL, Add. MS. 50562, fols. 92–93.

55. Bernard Shaw, *Cashel Byron's Profession*, vol. 4 of *Collected Works*, 94–95.

56. Karl Pearson, *The Chances of Death and Other Studies in Evolution* (London: Edward Arnold, 1897), 1:113, and *National Life from the Standpoint of Science*, 2d ed. (London: A. and C. Black, 1905), 55.

57. Milner to Beatrice Webb, 19 Oct. 1906, 22 May 1908, Passfield Papers, British Library of Political and Economic Science, II 4c fols. 193–95, II 4d fols. 31–34.

58. Shaw to George Samuel, 23–24 Dec. 1899, *Letters*, 2:123.

59. Synopsis of Shaw's remarks at Fabian Society meeting, 23 Feb. 1900, *Fabian News* 10 (Mar. 1900): 2–3.

60. Shaw to William Archer, 23 Apr. 1894, *Letters*, 1:427.

61. Bernard Shaw, *The Devil's Disciple*, vol. 2 of *Complete Plays with Their Prefaces* (New York, 1975), 130.

62. Olivier, *Writings*, 10–13.

63. Webb and Webb, *Local Government: Parish and County*, 360–68, and *Local Government: Manor and Borough*, 545–68.

64. Wells, *Anticipations*, 88, 146.

65. Matthew, *Liberal Imperialists*, 72–99.

66. Semmel, *Imperialism and Social Reform*, 48–73.

67. Wells, *Autobiography*, 650–55.

68. Searle, *Efficiency*, 150–54.

69. Ibid., 177–96. Peter Rowland, *David Lloyd George* (New York: Macmillan, 1976), 236–42.

70. John E. Kendle, *The Round Table Movement and Imperial Union* (Toronto: Univ. of Toronto Press, 1975), pp. 46, 74, 81–88, 109–10, 144, 151–54, chap. 6.

71. Rudyard Kipling, "The Miracle of Purun Bhagat," vol. 7 of *Writings in Prose and Verse* (New York, 1925).

72. Searle, *Efficiency*, 54–58. Winter, *Socialism and the Challenge of War*, 42–50.

73. Hynes, *Edwardian Turn of Mind*, chap. 2.

74. H. W. Nevinson, *Changes and Chances* (London: Nisbet, 1923), 72–75, 91–93. J. A. R. Pimlott, *Toynbee Hall* (London: J. M. Dent, 1935), 54, 78–79, 179–87. Werner Picht, *Toynbee Hall and the English Settlement Movement*, trans. Lilian A. Cowell, rev. ed. (London: G. Bell, 1914), appendix.

75. C. R. Ashbee, "Memoirs," 1938, Victoria and Albert Museum Library, 1:340–41, 389–91.

76. Semmel, *Imperialism and Social Reform*, 62, 222–25.

77. Wells, *Machiavelli*, 360. Interview with Neville Masterman. Jason[J. L. Hammond], *Past and Future* (London: Chatto and Windus, 1918), chap. 4.

78. G. L. Prestige, *The Life of Charles Gore* (London: Heinemann, 1935), 268.

79. W. P. Jolly, *Sir Oliver Lodge* (London: Constable, 1974), 161.

80. Galsworthy to Joseph Thorp, Feb. 1911, in John Galsworthy Papers, University of Birmingham Library, 1054.

81. G. R. Searle, *Eugenics and Politics in Britain 1900–1914* (Leyden: Noordhoff International, 1976), chap. 2.

82. Ibid., p. 2.

83. Bernard Shaw, *Man and Superman*, vol. 2 of *Complete Plays*, 777.

84. Semmel, *Imperialism and Social Reform*, 40–41.

85. Booth, *Life and Labour*, 1st ser., 1:37–44, 154–55, 162–67, 175–76.

86. John Brown, "Ideas Concerning Social Policy and Their Influence on Legislation in Britain, 1902–1911" (Ph.D. diss., University of London, 1964), 92–108, 296, 318–31. Michael Freeden, *The New Liberalism* (Oxford: Oxford Univ. Press, 1978), 184–85, 206–9.

87. In *The Heart of the Empire*, ed. C. F. G. Masterman (London: T. Fisher Unwin, 1901), 172, 264.

88. Searle, *Eugenics*, chaps. 8–9.

89. Bernard Shaw, *Major Barbara*, vol. 3 of *Complete Plays*, 28, 60–61.

90. Wells, *Anticipations*, 256–59.

91. Ibid., 272–74.

92. H. G. Wells, *A Modern Utopia*, vol. 9 of *Works*, 127–130.

93. Anne Oliver Bell, ed., *The Diary of Virginia Woolf* (New York: Harcourt Brace Jovanovich, 1977), 9 Jan. 1915.

94. *The Diary of Beatrice Webb*, 29 June 1898 (Teaneck, N.J.: Somerset House, 1978, microfiche). Beatrice Webb to Catherine Courtney, 2 July 1898, *Letters*, 2:72–73.

95. Wells, *Machiavelli*, bk. 3, chap. 4. Searle, *Eugenics*, 86–89. *Fabian News* 2 (Mar. 1892): 1–2; 19 (Dec. 1907): 95; 20 (Jan. 1909): 18; 20 (Apr. 1909): 40; 20 (July 1909): 64; 25 (May 1914): 42–43; 30 (Jan. 1919): 13.

96. Freeden, *New Liberalism*, 185–94.

97. C. F. G. Masterman, "In Dejection near Tooting," in *In Peril of Change* (New York: B. W. Huebsch, 1907).

98. J. L. Hammond, *Charles James Fox* (London: Methuen, 1903), 273–74.

99. Memorandum to Sir Henry Campbell-Bannerman, BL, Add. MS. 41240, fols. 138–41.

100. Masterman, ed., *Heart of the Empire*, 141–42, 168–69, 174–76, 239. Lucian Oldershaw, ed., *England: A Nation* (London: R. Brimley Johnson, 1904), 206–9.

101. B. Seebohm Rowntree, *Poverty: A Study of Town Life* (London: Macmillan, 1901), 133.

102. C. F. G. Masterman, *Heart of the Empire*, 48–49, and *From the Abyss* (London: R. Brimley Johnson, 1902), chaps. 1, 5.

103. H. W. Nevinson, *Essays in Rebellion* (London: Nisbet, 1913), 82.

104. J. A. Hobson, *Imperialism: A Study* (Ann Arbor: Univ. of Michigan Press, 1980), 154–65.

105. Ibid., 86–87.

106. Semmel, *Imperialism and Social Reform*, 195, 198.

107. Leonard Woolf, *Beginning Again* (New York: Harcourt Brace Jovanovich, 1972), 129–30.

108. Searle, *Eugenics*, chap. 5.

109. Halévy, *Rule of Democracy*, 172–74, 199–203.

110. Wells, *Anticipations*, 84–85, 150–155, and *Machiavelli*, 122–154.

111. Bernard Shaw, *John Bull's Other Island*, vol. 2 of *Complete Plays*, 914.

112. Christopher Caudwell, *Studies in a Dying Culture* (New York: Monthly Review Press, 1971), 84–92.

113. T. S. Simey and M. B. Simey, *Charles Booth* (London: Oxford Univ. Press, 1960), 32–33, 98–100.

114. Gilbert Murray, *An Unfinished Autobiography* (London: George Allen and Unwin, 1960), 18.

115. Kitty Muggeridge and Ruth Adam, *Beatrice Webb* (New York: Knopf, 1968), 166, 171.

116. Wells, *Anticipations*, 92, and *A Modern Utopia*, chap. 9.

117. Wells, *Autobiography*, 135.

118. Ibid., 330.

119. Shaw to R. Golding Bright, 2 Dec. 1894, and to H. G. Wells, 14 Sept. 1906, *Letters*, 1:465, 2:651–52.

120. Heindel, *American Impact*, 351.

121. Shaw, *Major Barbara*, 60.

122. L. T. Hobhouse, *Liberalism* (New York: Oxford Univ. Press, 1964), 99.

123. A. J. A. Morris, *C. P. Trevelyan* (Belfast: Blackstaff, 1977), 65–66, 75–76.

124. "The Great Law of Waste," Henry Arthur Jones Papers, British Theatre Museum Library.

125. *The Autobiography of Bertrand Russell* (London: Unwin, 1978), 167.

126. Sidney Webb to Jane Burdon-Sanderson, 25 Nov. 1887, *Letters*, 1:110–12.

127. *Diary of Beatrice Webb*, 17 Sept.–12 Oct. 1893.

128. Sidney Webb, "The Rate of Interest and the Laws of Distribution," *Quarterly Journal of Economics* 2 (1888): 188–208.

129. Charles Booth, "The Helplessness of Unorganized Labour," Charles and Mary Booth Papers, University of London Library, MS. 797, II/27/15.

130. S. G. Hobson, *National Guilds*, 3d ed. (London: G. Bell, 1919), 148–49, 182.

131. Sidney Webb, speech to Fabian Society, 27 Nov. 1896, synopsis in *Fabian News* (Jan. 1897): 43.

132. Wells, *Modern Utopia*, 82–87, 138–40.

133. Bernard Shaw, "The Simple Truth about Socialism," in *The Road to Equality*, ed. Louis Crompton (Boston: Beacon, 1971).

134. Bernard Shaw, *The Intelligent Woman's Guide to Socialism, Capitalism, Sovietism and Fascism* (Harmondsworth: Penguin, 1982), 477–79.

135. Shaw to Bridges, 4 Feb., 24 Mar. 1910, *Letters*, 2:896–99, 916.

136. Shaw, *John Bull's Other Island*, 842.

137. Wells, *Anticipations*, 196–99.

138. Richard Ellmann, "Two Faces of Edward," in *Edwardians and Late Victorians* (New York: Columbia Univ. Press, 1960), 191.

139. Royal A. Gettmann, *A Victorian Publisher: A Study of the Bentley Papers* (Cambridge: Cambridge Univ. Press, 1960), chap. 8.

140. Hugh Kenner, *The Pound Era* (Berkeley and Los Angeles: Univ. of California Press, 1971), 155. Wallace Martin, *The "New Age" under Orage* (Manchester: Manchester Univ. Press, 1967), 59, 256–64.

141. Richard Ellmann, *Yeats: The Man and the Masks* (New York: W. W. Norton, 1978), 214–15.

142. Leon Edel, *Henry James* (New York: Avon, 1978), 5:299–303.

143. James to Wells, 8 Nov. 1906, *Henry James and H. G. Wells*, ed. Leon Edel and Gordon N. Ray (Urbana: Univ. of Illinois Press, 1958), 113–14.

144. Wells to James, 20 Mar. 1907, ibid., 116.

145. James to Wells, 3 Mar. 1911, 21 Sept. 1913, ibid., 128, 173–76.

146. Wells to James, 19 Oct. 1912, 22 Sept. 1913, ibid., 169, 176–77.

147. H. G. Wells, *Boon*, vol. 13 of *Works*, chap. 4.

148. Richard Ellmann, *James Joyce*, rev. ed. (New York: Oxford Univ. Press, 1982), 607–8.

149. C. B. Purdom, *Harley Granville Barker* (London: Rockliff, 1955), 103, 107, 168, 211.

150. Ian Britain, *Fabianism and Culture* (Cambridge: Cambridge Univ. Press, 1982), pp. 10–12, chap. 8. Hobsbawm, "Fabians Reconsidered," 268–69. Eric Gill, "Socialism and the Arts and Crafts," address to Fabian Society, 31 May 1907, synopsis in *Fabian News* 17 (July 1907): 53–54. A. J. Penty, *The Restoration of the Gild System* (London: Swan Sonnenschein, 1906), 37–41.

151. Max Beerbohm, "Enoch Soames," in *Seven Men* (London: Heinemann, 1919).

152. Beatrice Webb to Lady Courtney, 18 Sept. 1911, *Letters*, 2:372.

153. P. N. Furbank, *E. M. Forster: A Life* (New York: Harcourt Brace Jovanovich, 1978), 1:160.

154. Leonard Woolf, *Sowing* (New York: Harcourt Brace Jovanovich, 1972), 91–92, 163–64, and *Growing* (New York: Harcourt Brace Jovanovich, 1975), 107–11, 178–200, 247.

155. Unsigned, "A Syndicalist on Scientific Management," *New Statesman*, 9 May 1914, 153.

156. Alastair Service, *Edwardian Architecture* (New York: Oxford Univ. Press, 1977), pp. 40, 68, chap. 9.

157. Sir Francis Galton, *Essays in Eugenics* (London: Eugenics Education Society, 1909), 42, 68–70, 99.

158. Semmel, *Imperialism and Social Reform*, 72.

159. Reader, *Professional Men*, 156–57. Jonathan Gathorne-Hardy, *The Old School Tie* (New York: Viking, 1978), 446–47.

160. Richard D. Altick, "The Sociology of Authorship: The Social Origins, Education, and Occupations of 1,100 British Writers, 1800–1935," *Bulletin of the New York Public Library* 66 (1962): 401.

161. C. F. G. Masterman, *The Condition of England* (London: Methuen, 1909), 82–85.

162. *Fabian News* 22 (July 1911): 58–59.

163. Harley Granville Barker, *Waste*, in *Three Plays* (London: Sidgwick and Jackson, 1909), 251, 267–70, 336.

164. Wells, *Autobiography*, 44–47, 125–31, 140.

165. Norman MacKenzie and Jeanne MacKenzie, *H. G. Wells* (New York: Simon and Schuster, 1973), 56–57, 122–23.

166. Wells, *Anticipations*, pp. 74–77, 81–82, 151–55, 243–48, chap. 8.

167. Wells, *Modern Utopia*, 246–52.

168. Wells, *Anticipations*, 254–56.

169. Barker, *Waste*, 271.

170. G. K. Chesterton, *Heretics* (London: John Lane, 1905), 16–19.

171. Joseph Conrad, "The Secret Sharer," in *'Twixt Land and Sea* (Garden City: Doubleday, 1924), 96.

172. Joseph Conrad, *The Secret Agent* (Garden City: Doubleday, 1924), 84–91, 100, 122, 140, 227.

173. Frederick R. Karl, *Joseph Conrad: The Three Lives* (New York: Farrar, Straus and Giroux, 1979), 440.

174. Joseph Conrad, "Heart of Darkness," in *Youth and Two Other Stories* (Garden City: Doubleday, 1924), 47–56. Hereafter cited in text as "Heart."

175. Benjamin Kidd, *Social Evolution* (New York: Macmillan, 1894), chap. 9.

176. Benjamin Kidd Papers, Cambridge University Library, Add. 8069: letters from Holland (undated, H63), Booth (17 June 1894, B165), Galton (11 Apr. 1894, G4), Garvin (15 letters, 1905–1912, G7–G21), Chamberlain (17 Dec. 1904, C40), and Milner (25 Mar. 1894, M333).

177. Rudyard Kipling, *Kim*, vol. 16 of *Writings*, chap. 8.

178. Pearson, *National Life*, 56.

179. Shaw, "On Going to Church," 380–81.

180. Shaw to Janet Achurch, 23 Mar. 1895, *Letters*, 1:504.

181. Sidney Webb to Beatrice Potter, 14 Mar. 1891, *Letters*, 1:265.

182. Shaw to Beatrice Webb, 30 July 1901, *Letters*, 2:235.

183. *Fabian News* 27 (Oct. 1916): 43–44; 28 (May 1917): 23–24; 28 (June 1917): 26–28; 29 (July 1918): 32.

184. Shaw, *John Bull's Other Island*, 1015–18.

185. Shaw, *Major Barbara*, 171–72.

186. Kipling, *Kim*, chap. 3.

187. Arthur Marwick, *The Deluge: British Society and the First World War* (New York: W. W. Norton, 1970), chap. 5. Armytage, *Engineering*, 251–53.

188. Rowland, *Lloyd George*, 284–327, 350–54, 379–81, 447–51.

189. Winter, *Socialism and the Challenge of War*, 194–96.

190. Robert Rhodes James, ed., *Winston S. Churchill: His Complete Speeches 1897–1963* (New York and London: R. R. Bowker and Chelsea House, 1974), 2502. Marwick, *Deluge*, chap. 5.

191. Oliver St. John Gogarty, *Blight*, in *Plays* (Newark, Dela.: Proscenium, 1972), 54–55.

192. MacKenzie and MacKenzie, *Wells*, 310.

193. Stanley Weintraub, *Journey to Heartbreak* (New York: Weybright and Talley, 1971), 197–99, 209–13. Bernard Shaw, *The Apple Cart*, vol. 6 of *Complete Plays*, 273–76.

194. Bernard Shaw, *Heartbreak House*, vol. 5, ibid., 37.

195. *Diaries of Beatrice Webb*, 5 Aug. 1917.

196. MacKenzie and MacKenzie, *Wells*, chap. 19.

197. Shaw, *Heartbreak House*, 31, 36–37, 164.

198. Paul Fussell, *The Great War and Modern Memory* (London: Oxford Univ. Press, 1979), 41.

199. Benjamin Kidd, *The Science of Power* (New York: Putnam's, 1918), chap. 3.

200. Marwick, *Deluge*, 213.

201. E. M. Forster diary, 22 Aug. 1914, E. M. Forster Papers, King's College Library, Cambridge University, F1/1.

202. D. H. Lawrence, *Women in Love* (New York: Viking, 1975), chap. 17.

203. John Maynard Keynes, *The Economic Consequences of the Peace* (London: Macmillan, 1971), 123.

204. Martin Green, *Children of the Sun* (New York: Basic, 1976), 140–41.

205. Lovat Dickson, *H. G. Wells* (Harmondsworth: Penguin, 1972), 344.

206. Martin J. Wiener, *English Culture and the Decline of the Industrial Spirit, 1850–1980* (Cambridge: Cambridge Univ. Press, 1981).

207. MacKenzie and MacKenzie, *Wells*, 420.

208. C. P. Snow, *The Two Cultures and a Second Look* (Cambridge: Cambridge Univ. Press, 1979), 40.

Chapter 5

1. Walter E. Houghton, *The Victorian Frame of Mind 1830–1870* (New Haven: Yale Univ. Press, 1973), 242.

2. J. L. and Barbara Hammond, *The Skilled Labourer* (New York: Harper and Row, 1970), 7, 212–13.

3. Peter Bailey, *Leisure and Class in Victorian England* (London: Routledge and Kegan Paul, 1978). James Walvin, *Leisure and Society 1830–1950* (London: Longmans, 1978), chap. 1.

4. Thomas Carlyle, *Past and Present*, vol. 10 of *Works* (London: n.d.), 210.

5. Ellen Moers, *The Dandy* (New York: Viking, 1960), pt. 4.

6. For instance, Fitzjames Stephen in the *Saturday Review*, 6 Mar. 1869, 318; Margaret Oliphant in *Blackwood's* 109 (Apr. 1871): 458–60; *Athenaeum*, 20 Feb. 1869, 272; and *Contemporary Review* 11 (May 1869): 150–51. See also caricatures of Arnold in *Vanity Fair*, 11 Nov. 1871, 154–55; and *Once a Week*, 12 Oct. 1872, 321.

7. Max Beerbohm, "A Cursory Conspectus of G. B. S.," in *Around Theatres* (New York: Taplinger, 1969), 173–75.

8. Henry James, *The Golden Bowl*, vol. 23 of *Novels and Tales* (New York, 1936–1937), xxii.

9. E. M. Forster, "Three Generations," lecture at University College, Nottingham, 28 Jan. 1939, E. M. Forster Papers, King's College Library, Cambridge University, E3, vol. 16, fols. 191–92.

10. Walvin, *Leisure and Society*, pt. 2. Simon Nowell-Smith, ed., *Edwardian England 1901–1914* (London: Oxford Univ. Press, 1965), pp. 376–77, 386–88, chap. 12. Raymond Williams, *The Long Revolution* (New York: Harper and Row, 1966), 263–64.

11. Walvin, *Leisure and Society*, 80–81, 90, 121–25. Helen Meller, *Leisure and the Changing City 1870–1914* (London: Routledge and Kegan Paul, 1976), chaps. 5–8.

12. Charles Booth, *Life and Labour of the People in London* (1902–1904; reprint, New York: AMS, 1970), final vol., pp. 47–59.

13. Williams, *Long Revolution*, 176, 198–206. R. C. K. Ensor, *England 1870–1914* (Oxford: Clarendon, 1936), 310–16, 532–36. W. J. Reader, *Professional Men* (New York: Basic, 1966), 208, 211.

14. David Cecil, *Max* (London: Constable, 1964), 57, 139–40.

15. Eleanor De Selms Langstaff, *Andrew Lang* (Boston: Twayne, 1978), 31–32, 115–20, 127, 137, 142.

16. Janet Dunbar, *J. M. Barrie: The Man behind the Image* (Boston: Houghton Mifflin, 1970), 56–60, 64–69, 79–81.

17. Shaw to H. G. Wells, 29 Sept. 1904, *Collected Letters*, ed. Dan H. Laurence (London: Max Reinhardt, 1965–1972), 2:454.

18. Shaw to Johnston Forbes-Robertson, 21–22 Dec. 1903, ibid., 383.

19. Bernard Shaw, *Sixteen Self-Sketches* (New York: Dodd, Mead, 1949), 65–69, 87.

20. Shaw to William P. Johnson, 13 Feb. 1893, *Letters*, 1:381.

21. Laurence Thompson, *Robert Blatchford: Portrait of an Englishman* (London: Gollancz, 1951), chaps. 5, 6, 8, pp. 116–18, 122–23, 130. Henry Pelling, *The Origins of the Labour Party*, 2d ed. (Oxford: Oxford Univ. Press, 1974), 96, 138, 161–62.

22. Norman MacKenzie and Jeanne MacKenzie, *H. G. Wells* (New York: Simon and Schuster, 1973), 78, 95–96, 105, 109. H. G. Wells, *Experiment in Autobiography* (New York: Macmillan, 1934), 251–60, 306–10.

23. Jerome Buckley, *William Ernest Henley* (Princeton: Princeton Univ. Press, 1945), pp. 150–51, 179, chap. 10. C. Lewis Hind, *Naphtali* (London: John Lane, 1926), chaps. 12, 26.

24. Amy Cruse, *After the Victorians* (London: George Allen and Unwin, 1938), 186–90, 206–15.

25. Paul Levy, *Moore: G. E. Moore and the Cambridge Apostles* (New York: Holt, Rinehart and Winston, 1979), 90–94.

26. *The Autobiography of Bertrand Russell* (London: Unwin, 1978), 65–66.

27. John Gross, *The Rise and Fall of the Man of Letters* (New York: Macmillan, 1969), 68.

28. Walter Raleigh, *Robert Louis Stevenson* (London: Edward Arnold, 1896), 14–16.

29. E. M. Forster, *Goldsworthy Lowes Dickinson* (London: Edward Arnold, 1962), 99.

30. Michael Holroyd, *Lytton Strachey: The Unknown Years 1880–1910* (New York: Holt, Rinehart and Winston, 1968), 79–82, 84, and *Lytton Strachey and the Bloomsbury Group* (Harmondsworth: Penguin, 1971), 35, 133, 149, 154.

31. Levy, *Moore*, 147–50.

32. Quentin Bell, *Virginia Woolf* (New York: Harcourt Brace Jovanovich, 1972), 1:157–61.

33. Virginia Woolf, *Night and Day* (New York: Harcourt Brace Jovanovich, 1967), 208.

34. Richard Ellmann, *James Joyce*, rev. ed. (New York: Oxford Univ. Press, 1982), 554, 693, 703.

35. G. K. Chesterton, "The Pun," in *Lunacy and Letters*, ed. Dorothy Collins (New York: Sheed and Ward, 1958).

36. James Joyce, *Ulysses* (New York: Modern Library, 1961), 20.

37. Gross, *Man of Letters*, 139–45.

38. George Saintsbury, *A History of Criticism* (Edinburgh: Blackwood, 1900–1904), 2:viii.

39. Walter Leuba, *George Saintsbury* (New York: Twayne, 1967), 42, 64–77.

40. Richard Ellmann, *Joyce*, 475, and *The Consciousness of Joyce* (Toronto and New York: Oxford Univ. Press, 1977), 126.

41. Joyce to Harriet Shaw Weaver, 17 Nov. 1922, *Letters of James Joyce*, ed. Stuart Gilbert, new ed. (New York: Viking, 1966), 1:194.

42. Ellmann, *Joyce*, 384, 390, 414, 607.

43. MacKenzie and MacKenzie, *Wells*, 154, 228–31, 306–7.

44. Dudley Barker, *G. K. Chesterton* (New York: Stein and Day, 1975), 12–13, 151–52, 212–13, 271.

45. Sydney Olivier, *Letters and Selected Writings*, ed. Margaret Olivier (London: George Allen and Unwin, 1948), 152–53.

46. Ian Britain, *Fabianism and Culture* (Cambridge: Cambridge Univ. Press, 1982), chap. 7.

47. Doris Langley Moore, *E. Nesbit*, rev. ed. (Philadelphia: Chilton, 1966), 76, 179.

48. Barker, *Chesterton*, 74, 117. Norman MacKenzie and Jeanne MacKenzie, *The Fabians* (New York: Simon and Schuster, 1977), 85.

49. Cruse, *After the Victorians*, chap. 10.

50. Brocard Sewell, *Cecil Chesterton* (Faversham, Eng.: St. Albert's, 1975), chap. 6.

51. C. R. Ashbee, *Craftsmanship in Competitive Industry* (London: Essex House, 1908), 60–68.

52. W. P. Jolly, *Sir Oliver Lodge* (London: Constable, 1974), 98–100.

53. Harley Granville Barker, "Agnes Colander," 1901, British Library, fol. 14.

54. Jason [J. L. Hammond], *Past and Future* (London: Chatto and Windus, 1918), chap. 13.

55. Bernard Shaw, *John Bull's Other Island*, vol. 2 of *Complete Plays with Their Prefaces* (New York, 1975), 1021.

56. Ellmann, *Joyce*, 703.

57. Leonard Woolf, *Beginning Again* (New York: Harcourt Brace Jovanovich, 1975), 33.

58. Bernard Shaw, *Our Theatres in the Nineties* (New York: Constable, 1931), 1:42–43.

59. Maisie Ward, *Gilbert Keith Chesterton* (London: Sheed and Ward, 1944), 96–99.

60. G. K. Chesterton, "Spiritualism," in *All Things Considered* (Philadelphia: Dufour, 1967), 148–49.

61. G. K. Chesterton, "January One," in *Lunacy and Letters.*

62. G. K. Chesterton, "The Architect of Spears," in *A Miscellany of Men* (1912; reprint, Freeport, N.Y.: Books for Libraries, 1969).

63. G. K. Chesterton, *The Napoleon of Notting Hill* (New York: Paulist, 1978), 193–97.

64. G. K. Chesterton, "Oxford from Without," in *All Things Considered*, 72.

65. Shaw to Janet Achurch, 23 Mar. 1895, *Letters*, 1:504–5.

66. Shaw to Charles Rowley, 11 Feb. 1907, ibid., 2:671–72.

67. Peter d'A. Jones, *The Christian Socialist Revival 1877–1914* (Princeton: Princeton Univ. Press, 1968), 69–71, 100–2, 118–22. Bailey, *Leisure and Class*, 158, 162. (Either Shuttleworth or Headlam may have been the model for the Reverend James Morell, the jolly socialist parson of Bernard Shaw's *Candida*.)

68. Booth, *Life and Labour*, 3d ser., 3:15–17.

69. Ibid., 2:118–39; 4:32–35, 147–49; 7:14–15.

70. Ibid., 3:49–57. T. S. Simey and M. B. Simey, *Charles Booth* (London: Oxford Univ. Press, 1960), 35.

71. Meller, *Leisure and the Changing City*, 145–49, 171.

72. Werner Picht, *Toynbee Hall and the English Settlement Movement*, trans. Lilian A. Cowell, rev. ed. (London: G. Bell, 1914), 73–85.

73. Walvin, *Leisure and Society*, 87.

74. Bernard Shaw, *Major Barbara*, vol. 3 in *Complete Plays*, 33.

75. C. F. G. Masterman, "The Religion of the City," in *In Peril of Change* (New York: B. W. Huebsch, 1907).

76. A. C. Benson, "Humour," in *At Large* (New York: Putnam's, 1908).

77. C. R. Ashbee to Laurence Hodson, 16 Dec. 1902, in "Memoirs," 1938, Victoria and Albert Museum Library, 1:138.

78. Sigmund Freud, *Jokes and Their Relation to the Unconscious*, trans. and ed. James Strachey (New York: W. W. Norton, 1963), 125–39.

79. Ward, *Chesterton*, 222–26. Cecil, *Max*, 41–42. Ashbee, "Memoirs," 2:307. Levy, *Moore*, 11–13, 293–94. Alun R. Jones, *The Life and Opinions of T. E. Hulme* (London: Gollancz, 1960), 121–22.

80. Shaw to Erica Cotterill, 27 Nov. 1907, *Letters*, 2:731.

81. Ivy Pinchbeck and Margaret Hewitt, *Children in English Society* (London:

Routledge and Kegan Paul, 1973), 384–86, 525–41, 622–37. Alec Ellis, *A History of Children's Reading and Literature* (Oxford: Pergamon, 1968), 127–31. Walvin, *Leisure and Society*, 121–23. Nowell-Smith, *Edwardian England*, 207–9.

82. A. J. A. Morris, *C. P. Trevelyan* (Belfast: Blackstaff, 1977), 26–27.

83. Jason [J. L. Hammond], *Past and Future*, chaps. 4, 5, 13, and "A Liberal View of Education," in Hilaire Belloc et al., *Essays in Liberalism* (London: Cassell, 1897). Sir John Brunner and J. L. Hammond, *Public Education in Cheshire in 1896* (London: John Heywood, 1896).

84. Lucy Masterman, *C. F. G. Masterman* (London: Frank Cass, 1968), 26–29.

85. Ibid., 168–69, 190–91. H. W. Nevinson diary, 21 Feb., 7 Mar. 1911, Bodleian Library, Oxford University, MS. Eng. misc. e. 616.

86. Pinchbeck and Hewitt, *Children in English Society*, 484–94.

87. J. B. Hobman, ed., *David Eder: Memoirs of a Modern Pioneer* (London: Gollancz, 1945), 74–77, 89–90, 95–99, 108. The colleague was Dr. Edward Glover.

88. C. F. G. Masterman, *From the Abyss* (London: R. Brimley Johnson, 1902), chap. 8. Interview with Neville Masterman.

89. Hammond, *Past and Future*, chap. 13.

90. C. F. G. Masterman, *The Heart of the Empire* (London: T. Fisher Unwin, 1901), 11–19, and *From the Abyss*, chap. 1.

91. Booth, *Life and Labour*, final vol., pp. 42–44.

92. Paul Thompson, *The Edwardians: The Remaking of British Society* (Bloomington: Indiana Univ. Press, 1975), chap. 4.

93. Jonathan Gathorne-Hardy, *The Old School Tie* (New York: Viking, 1977), chap. 12, pp. 317–26.

94. Ibid., 144–56, 210–22, 248–52. J. R. de S. Honey, *Tom Brown's Universe: The Development of the English Public School in the Nineteenth Century* (New York: Quadrangle, 1977), 104–17, 153–57, 371–72.

95. Bernard Shaw, *The Admirable Bashville*, vol. 2 of *Complete Plays*, 438.

96. Cornelia Meigs et al., *A Critical History of Children's Literature*, rev. ed. (New York: Macmillan, 1969), 288–301.

97. Frank Eyre, *British Children's Books in the Twentieth Century*, 2d ed. (New York: Dutton, 1973), 21–23.

98. Shaw to August Strindberg, 16 Mar. 1910, *Letters*, 2:907. Elmer W. Salenius, *Harley Granville Barker* (Boston: Twayne, 1982), 40.

99. *Publishers' Circular*, 5 Jan. 1895, 7.

100. Moore, *Nesbit*, 6, 42.

101. James A. Roy, *James Matthew Barrie* (London: Jarrolds, 1937), 180.

102. MacKenzie and MacKenzie, *Wells*, 141. H. G. Wells, *Seven Famous Novels* (New York: Knopf, 1934), preface.

103. Peter Green, *Kenneth Grahame* (London: John Murray, 1969), 86–88.

104. Rackham to Ernest Rhys, 1 Dec. 1924, BL, Egerton MS. 3247, fol. 1.

105. Roy, *Barrie*, 180–81.

106. Roger Lancelyn Green, *J. M. Barrie* (New York: Walck, 1961), 41–42.

107. Samuel Hynes, *The Edwardian Turn of Mind* (Princeton: Princeton Univ. Press, 1968), chap. 2.

108. Moore, *Nesbit*, 144. Jan Marsh, *Edward Thomas* (London: Elek, 1978), 14. Green, *Grahame*, 116–17, 150–54.

109. Green, *Grahame*, 166, 197, 249–52.

110. C. F. G. Masterman, *The Condition of England* (London: Methuen, 1909), 245–48.

111. Dunbar, *Barrie*, 95–97, 105, 115. Janet Adam Smith, ed., *Henry James and Robert Louis Stevenson* (London: Rupert Hart-Davis, 1948).

112. Brooke to Sir Edmund Gosse, 19 Nov. 1913, in Timothy Rogers, *Rupert Brooke: A Reappraisal and a Selection* (New York: Barnes and Noble, 1971), 56.

113. Green, *Grahame*, 113, 133. Buckley, *Henley*, chap. 10.

114. Henry James, *What Maisie Knew*, vol. 11 of *Novels and Tales* (New York, 1936–1937), xi.

115. Ibid., chap. 31.

116. Kenneth Grahame, *The Golden Age* (Chicago: Stone and Kimball, 1895), 105, 189.

117. H. de Vere Stacpoole, *The Blue Lagoon*, 21 st ed. (London: Ernest Benn, 1951), 70, 72.

118. Ibid., 265–67.

119. William Morris, *News from Nowhere*, vol. 16 of *Collected Works* (London, 1912), 37, 102, 134–36.

120. Holbrook Jackson, *The Eighteen Nineties* (New York: Putnam's, 1968), 253.

121. Isobel Spencer, *Walter Crane* (New York: Macmillan, 1975), 53, 60–63, 168–69.

122. Virginia Woolf, *Roger Fry: A Biography* (New York: Harcourt Brace Jovanovich, 1976), 153, 160–61, 164. Roger Fry, "Some Principles of Design," c. 1909–13, and "Children's Drawings," May 1917–1919, Roger Fry Papers, King's College Library, Cambridge University, II/10/D/1 fols. 10–12, II/4/1 fols. 5–6.

123. Ward, *Chesterton*, 222–26.

124. G. K. Chesterton, "The Toy Theatre," in *Tremendous Trifles* (Philadelphia: Dufour, 1968).

125. G. K. Chesterton, "Fairy Tales," in *All Things Considered*, and "The Library of the Nursery" and "A Fairy Tale," in *Lunacy and Letters*.

126. G. K. Chesterton, "Omar and the Sacred Vine," in *Heretics* (London: John Lane, 1905).

127. G. K. Chesterton, *Autobiography* (London: Hutchinson, 1969), 127. Interview with Neville Masterman.

128. William McDougall, "The Theory of Laughter," *Nature* 67 (1903): 318–19.

129. Saki [H. H. Munro], *The Unbearable Bassington* (New York: Penguin, 1947), 19, and "The Baker's Dozen," in *The Short Stories of Saki* (New York: Modern Library, 1958), 101.

130. H. H. Munro, "The Innocence of Reginald," in *Short Stories*, 40.

131. Munro, *Bassington*, 19–20.

132. Freud, *Jokes*, 108–9.

133. Emmanuel Le Roy Ladurie, *Carnival: A People's Uprising at Romans, 1579–1580*, trans. Mary Feeney (London: Scolar, 1980). For the Revolution of 1848, see Alexis de Tocqueville, *Recollections*, and Gustave Flaubert, *Sentimental Education*.

134. Barbara and John Ehrenreich, *Long March, Short Spring: The Student Uprising at Home and Abroad* (New York: Monthly Review Press, 1969), 98.

135. Joyce, *Ulysses*, 212.

136. Bernard Shaw, *Pygmalion*, vol. 4 of *Complete Plays*, 711.

137. Bernard Shaw, *John Bull's Other Island*, vol. 2, ibid., 1021.

138. Chesterton, *Notting Hill*, 193–97.

139. Shaw to Rev. H. Montagu Villiers, 3 Nov. 1905, *Letters*, 2:571–72.

140. Margaret Cole, *The Life of G. D. H. Cole* (London: Macmillan, 1971), 45–46, 53, 136–38, 158–60.

141. E. M. Forster, *A Room with a View* (New York: New Directions, n.d.), 180–81.

142. MacKenzie and MacKenzie, *Wells*, 28–29.

143. Barker, *Chesterton*, 141–42.

144. MacKenzie and MacKenzie, *Wells*, pp. 20–22, 395, chap. 13.

145. Wells, *Autobiography*, 74–76.

146. Masterman, *Masterman*, 184.

147. George Dangerfield, *The Strange Death of Liberal England 1910–1914* (New York: Putnam's, 1961), 89–92.

148. Ibid., 402–3.

149. H. H. Munro, "The Threat" and "The Gala Programme," in *Short Stories*.

150. H. W. Nevinson, *More Changes, More Chances* (London: Nisbet, 1925), 318.

151. Paul Fussell, *The Great War and Modern Memory* (London: Oxford Univ. Press, 1977), 9, 25–28. Gathorne-Hardy, *Old School Tie*, 144–45, 199–200. Ted Morgan, *Maugham: A Biography* (New York: Simon and Schuster, 1980), 187.

152. Walvin, *Leisure and Society*, 129. Victor Bailey, "Bibles and Dummy Rifles: The Boys' Brigade," *History Today* 33 (Oct. 1983): 5–9.

153. A. J. Langguth, *Saki: A Life of Hector Hugh Munro* (New York: Simon and Schuster, 1981), 258.

154. E. T. Cook, *Literary Recreations* (London: Macmillan, 1918), 150–51.

155. Fussell, *Great War*, 89, 194–96, 199–202, 205–20.

156. Walvin, *Leisure and Society*, 128–32.

157. Bernard Shaw, *Heartbreak House*, vol. 5 of *Complete Plays*, 146–48.

158. Ibid., 57–58.

159. Cecil, *Max*, 334–37.

160. Forster, "Three Generations," fols. 180–82.

161. Ellis, *Children's Reading*, chap. 17. Eyre, *British Children's Books*, 21–23. Marcus Crouch, *Treasure Seekers and Borrowers: Children's Books in Britain 1900–1960* (London: Library Assn., 1962), 38–39.

162. Martin Green, *Children of the Sun* (New York: Basic, 1976), 6–17.

163. Dunbar, *Barrie*, 170.

164. Max Beerbohm, "A Cloud of Pinafores," in *More* (1899; reprint, Freeport, N.Y.: Books for Libraries, 1967).

165. Andrew Birkin, *J. M. Barrie and the Lost Boys* (London: Constable, 1979).

166. Green, *Grahame*, chap. 16.

167. T. W. Mitchell, *Medical Psychology and Psychical Research* (New York: Dutton, 1922), 200–1.

168. Brooke to Katherine Cox, 5 Sept. 1910, *The Letters of Rupert Brooke*, ed. Geoffrey Keynes (London: Faber and Faber, 1968), 255.

169. H. G. Wells, "The Faults of the Fabian," in Hynes, *Edwardian Turn of Mind*, 398–99.

170. Shaw, *John Bull's Other Island*, 910–11.

171. Stanley Weintraub, *Journey to Heartbreak* (New York: Weybright and Talley, 1971), 16–18. Chesterton, *Autobiography*, 231–35.

Chapter 6

1. Alfred North Whitehead, *Science and the Modern World* (New York: Macmillan, 1957), 119–20.

2. Masao Miyoshi, *The Divided Self* (New York: New York Univ. Press, 1969).

3. Olwen Ward Campbell, "Memoir," in James Ward, *Essays in Philosophy*, ed. W. R. Sorley and G. F. Stout (Cambridge: Cambridge Univ. Press, 1927), 30–32, 38–39, 47.

4. Leonard Woolf, *Beginning Again* (New York: Harcourt Brace Jovanovich, 1975), 16–17.

5. Beatrice Webb, *My Apprenticeship* (London: Longmans, 1926), xiii–xiv.

6. Rudyard Kipling, *Kim*, vol. 16 of *Writings in Prose and Verse* (New York, 1925), chap. 15.

7. E. M. Forster, *Arctic Summer and Other Fiction* (New York: Holmes and Meier, 1980), 125, and *Goldsworthy Lowes Dickinson* (London: Edward Arnold, 1962), 47–48.

8. E. M. Forster, *Howards End* (New York: Vintage, 1954), chap. 22.

9. Havelock Ellis, *My Life* (Boston: Houghton Mifflin, 1939), 156, 163–68.

10. Peter Green, *Kenneth Grahame* (London: John Murray, 1959), 49–57, 61, 121–23, 150–54, 303. Kenneth Grahame, "The Lost Centaur," in *Pagan Papers* (London: John Lane, 1898).

11. Jason [J. L. Hammond], *Past and Future* (London: Chatto and Windus, 1918), chap. 13.

12. A. J. Penty, *The Restoration of the Gild System* (London: Swan Sonnenschein, 1906), 10–12.

13. W. H. Hudson, *Idle Days in Patagonia* (London: J. M. Dent, 1923), chap. 13.

14. Henry James, *The Ambassadors*, vol. 21 of *Novels and Tales* (New York, 1936–1937), 5. Hereafter cited in text as *Ambass.*

15. Joseph Conrad, "The Secret Sharer," in *'Twixt Land and Sea* (Garden City: Doubleday, 1924), 93, 99, 105–14, 142–43.

16. Samuel Butler, *The Way of All Flesh* (New York: Holt, Rinehart and Winston, 1948), chap. 31.

17. Ibid., chaps. 82–83, 85–86.

18. E. M. Forster, *A Room with a View* (New York: New Directions, n.d.), 317–18.

19. Richard Ellmann, *James Joyce*, rev. ed. (New York: Oxford Univ. Press, 1982), 85, 126, 340, 436–38, 546–49, 693.

20. James Joyce to Stanislaus Joyce, 13 Nov. 1906, *Letters of James Joyce,* ed. Richard Ellmann, new ed. (New York: Viking, 1966), 2:191.

21. Richard Ellmann, *The Consciousness of Joyce* (Toronto and New York: Oxford Univ. Press, 1977), 23–26, 53–57.

22. Philip Callow, *Son and Lover: The Young D. H. Lawrence* (New York: Stein and Day, 1973), 137, 215, 228, 244–46. D. H. Lawrence, *The White Peacock* (Cambridge: Cambridge Univ. Press, 1983), 383.

23. Lawrence to Edward Garnett, 19 Nov. 1912, *The Letters of D. H. Lawrence,* ed. James T. Boulton (Cambridge: Cambridge Univ. Press, 1979), 1:476–77.

24. D. H. Lawrence, *Women in Love* (New York: Viking, 1975), 179–80. Hereafter cited in text as *Women.*

25. Bernard Shaw, *Saint Joan*, vol. 6 of *Complete Plays with Their Prefaces* (New York, 1975), 42–44.

26. Alan Gauld, *The Founders of Psychical Research* (London: Routledge and Kegan Paul, 1968), 91–100, 293–95.

27. Paul Levy, *Moore: G. E. Moore and the Cambridge Apostles* (New York: Holt, Rinehart and Winston, 1979), 85.

28. *Journal of the Society for Psychical Research* 7 (Jan. 1895): 6–7.

29. T. W. Mitchell, *Medical Psychology and Psychical Research* (New York: Dutton, 1922), 137, 182–88.

30. *Journal of the Society for Psychical Research* 18 (Oct. 1917–Mar. 1918): 104, 127, 148–49.

31. *Proceedings of the Society for Psychical Research* 30 (July 1918): 1–32.

32. George Moore, *The Lake* (New York: Appleton, 1906), 255, 259.

33. Edward Carpenter, *My Days and Dreams* (New York: Scribner's, 1916), 143–45.

34. Oscar Wilde, "The Decay of Lying," in *The Soul of Man under Socialism and Other Essays* (New York: Harper and Row, 1970), 46–50.

35. Richard Ellmann, *Yeats: The Man and the Masks* (New York: W. W. Norton, 1978), chaps. 6–9, pp. 198–205.

36. "Ego Dominus Tuus," in *The Collected Poems of W. B. Yeats* (New York: Macmillan, 1974), 159.

37. Ellmann, *Yeats*, 216–20, 230–43.

38. Dudley Barker, *G. K. Chesterton* (New York: Stein and Day, 1975), chap. 5.

39. G. K. Chesterton, *The Man Who Was Thursday* (New York: Putnam's, 1960), 6, 132–33, 156.

40. Miyoshi, *Divided Self*, 330.

41. "Who I Am, and What I Think," in *Selected Non-Dramatic Writings of Bernard Shaw*, ed. Dan H. Laurence (Boston: Houghton Mifflin, 1965), 454.

42. Paul Fussell, *The Great War and Modern Memory* (London: Oxford Univ. Press, 1975), pp. 105–6, chap. 6.

43. Butler, *Way of All Flesh*, 198–99, 296.

44. Winston Churchill, *My Early Life* (New York: Scribner's, 1972), chap. 9.

45. John Galsworthy, *The Inn of Tranquillity* (New York: Scribner's, 1913), 12.

46. Shaw to E. C. Chapman, 29 July 1891, *Collected Letters*, ed. Dan H. Laurence (London: Max Reinhardt, 1965–1972), 1:302.

47. Arthur O. Lovejoy, *The Great Chain of Being* (New York: Harper and Row, 1960), 7.

Further Reading and Research

For full bibliographical information, the reader is referred to the endnotes, which list all the sources used in this book. This section makes a special note of some particularly valuable introductory works and manuscript archives.

Three older surveys of the period are still well worth reading: volumes 5 and 6 of Elie Halévy, *A History of English People in the Nineteenth Century* (1926, 1932), R. C. K. Ensor, *England 1870–1914* (1936), and Simon Nowell-Smith, ed., *Edwardian England 1901–1914* (1964). More up-to-date scholarship is compiled in Alan O'Day, ed., *The Edwardian Age: Conflict and Stability 1900–1914* (1979), and Donald Read, ed., *Edwardian England* (1982). Samuel Hynes, *The Edwardian Turn of Mind* (1968), is an elegant, perceptive intellectual history; see also his *Edwardian Occasions* (1972). Another good starting point is C. B. Cox and A. E. Dyson, eds., *The Twentieth Century Mind—1900–1918* (1972), a collection of essays exploring every important discipline. Among literary histories, the most thought-provoking are Richard Ellmann, ed., *Edwardians and Late Victorians* (1960), John A. Lester, Jr., *Journey through Despair 1880–1914* (1968), John Batchelor, *The Edwardian Novelists* (1982), and Jefferson Hunter, *Edwardian Fiction* (1982). The student of popular literature might begin with Amy Cruse, *After the Victorians* (1938). Paul Thompson, *The Edwardians: The Remaking of British Society* (1975), is the best social history, based on the oral history project "Family Life and Work before 1918." For political history, one should read George Dangerfield, *The Strange Death of Liberal England 1910–1914* (1935), but K. W. W. Aikin, *The Last Years of Liberal England 1900–1914* (1977), is more concise, thorough, and level-headed. Paul Fussell, *The Great War and Modern Memory* (1975), is a controversial literary history of the conflict. For an account of the home front, consult Arthur Marwick, *The Deluge: British Society and the First World War* (1965).

For the researcher in Edwardian intellectual history, a number of manuscript collections are worth investigating. The British Library has the papers of Bernard Shaw; his diaries are at the British Library of

Political and Economic Science, which also houses the Passfield Papers (Sidney and Beatrice Webb). The H. G. Wells Archive is at the University of Illinois at Champaign-Urbana. Nuffield College, Oxford, has the papers of the Fabian Society and G. D. H. Cole. Goldsworthy Lowes Dickinson, E. M. Forster, Roger Fry, John Maynard Keynes, and John Sheppard all have collections at the library of King's College, Cambridge. The Monk House Papers (Leonard and Virginia Woolf) and some Rudyard Kipling materials are kept at the University of Sussex Library. The Charles and Mary Booth Papers are divided between the Univerity of London Library and the British Library of Political and Economic Science.

Often, a minor intellectual figure can leave an unusually rich cache of unpublished documents—a revealing diary, for instance, or correspondence from leading authors and philosophers. One indispensable source for the study of Edwardian spiritualism is the collection of letters received by Sir Oliver Lodge—most of them at the Society for Psychical Research in London, some others at the University College London Library. The Arts and Crafts movement and an assortment of literary personalities are chronicled in the typescript memoirs of C. R. Ashbee, at the Victoria and Albert Museum Library. Anyone doing research on Liberals, radicals, and suffragettes should consult several collections at the Bodleian Library, Oxford: the papers of Gilbert Murray, J. L. and Barbara Hammond, John Masefield, and Evelyn Sharp, and particularly the voluminous diaries of H. W. Nevinson. The Macmillan Papers at the British Library and the Benjamin Kidd Papers at the Cambridge University Library also contain interesting literary correspondence.

Index